Phantoms of the Opera:
The Face Behind the Mask
A Complete Guide to the Appearances of
Gaston Leroux's Opera Ghost

John L. Flynn, Ph.D.

Galactic Books
Owings Mills, Maryland

Galactic Books
Post Office Box 1442
Owings Mills, Maryland 21117-9998

Phantoms of the Opera:
The Face Behind the Mask
By John L. Flynn, Ph.D.

PRINTING HISTORY
Revised & Updated 3rd Edition / September 2019

All rights reserved.
Copyright © 2006 by John L. Flynn

First published in the United States

Acknowledgements: Most of the photographs used in this book were issued by the original production companies at the time of the release for publicity purposes, and we make no claim as to ownership or copyright. We are simply reproducing them for the purpose that they were originally intended. Some of the photos are copyright of Universal Pictures; some are courtesy of M-G-M, The Really Useful Group, 20th Century Fox, and Warner Brothers.

This book may not be reproduced or transmitted,
in any form or by any means, without permission
of the publishers. For information, please contact
Galactic Books, P. O. Box 1442, Owings Mills, MD 21117.

Editor: Nicholas Carraway
Design & Layout: Edmund Dantes

Library of Congress Cataloging in Publication Data
Flynn, John L. Phantoms of the Opera:
The Face Behind the Mask
1. Phantom of the Opera--History and criticism. I. Horror films--History and criticism. II. Gaston Leroux--Plots, themes, etc. III. Title.

ISBN: 0-9769400-4-3

PRINTED IN THE UNITED STATES OF AMERICA

Table of Contents

0 –	Introduction: The Man Behind the Mask	5
1 –	A Biography of Erik	15
2 –	Gaston Leroux's 1911 Novel	19
3 –	Lon Chaney at the Masked Ball	33
4 –	The Enchanted Violin of Erique Claudin	55
5 –	Scorpions, Grasshoppers, and Vampires	69
6 –	The Mysterious Englishman	79
7 –	"Faust" and the Paradise	95
8 –	Trap Doors on a Hollywood Back Lot	113
9 –	In the Cellars of the Budapest Opera House	125
10 –	The Torture Chamber	133
11 –	An Opera Ghost's Love Story	147
12 –	Apollo's Lyre and the Song of Orpheus	161
13 –	Interesting Vicissitudes	187
	Appendix One: Novels and Other Written Media	207
	Appendix Two: Chronological Listing	211
	Selected Bibliography	221
	About the Author	223

*With apologies to M. Leroux, the chapter titles were inspired by those in his original novel.

Dedication:

For Natalia, my own
"Angel of Music"

Introduction

The Opera ghost really existed. He was not, as was long believed, a creature of the imagination of the artists, the superstition of the managers, or a product of the absurd and impressionable brains of the young ladies of the ballet, their mothers, the box-keepers, the cloak-room attendants or the concierge. Yes, he existed in flesh and blood, although he assumed the complete appearance of a real phantom; that is to say, of a spectral shade.
   —Gaston Leroux, Le Fantôme de l'Opera (1911)

Mention *The Phantom of the Opera* at a dinner party or other social gathering, and each guest will have his or her own vivid, almost visceral recollection of the tale of a disfigured musical genius and his unrequited love for a beautiful, young singer. Someone will undoubtedly pantomime the famous scene from the silent era film in which Mary Philbin (as Christine Daae) sneaks up behind the Phantom, while he is playing the organ in his subterranean lair, and unmasks the great Lon Chaney, revealing his horribly disfigured face to the audience and her. Another guest is likely to burst into song, recalling "The Music of the Night" from the Andrew Lloyd Webber musical. Still another guest will strike the pose of Erik as the Masque of the Red Death at the masked ball, while yet another may describe the scene in which the Phantom cuts the cables free and sends the magnificent chandelier crashing down upon the patrons of the Paris Opera House. The original story contains so many richly textured scenes that each of us, at one time or another, has been seduced by the Phantom, and embraced the dark, labyrinthine world of author

Gaston Leroux.

For many, the love affair with Erik—that masked "phantom" of the Paris Opera House—began in 1925, with the first of many imaginative thrillers Carl Laemmle produced for Universal Studios; for others, it was more than a decade ago when a youthful Michael Crawford emerged from behind the mirror, swept Sarah Brightman (as Christine Daae) off her feet, and carried her down into his lair below the playhouse; for recent filmgoers, it was the moment Gerard Butler took Emmy Rossum into his arms in Joel Schumacher's Hollywood spectacular. Few others have actually encountered the Phantom in print, and yet *Le Fantôme de l'Opera* has inspired more than a dozen films, two television movies, one miniseries, several stage productions, and a Tony award-winning musical--45 productions in all. However, the question of the ninety-five year-old novel's popularity provides many elusive answers. Why would the tragic tale of a disfigured composer and his love for a young opera singer—a story clearly rooted in the annals of Victorian melodrama—continue to remain such a favorite subject for adaptation?

Perhaps the reason for its longevity and prolificacy has to do with a message that is universal: the beauty or darkness of the human soul should not be measured by outward appearances or deformities. Or perhaps it has something to do with myth and our collective unconscious. Though the original classic by Frenchman Monsieur Gaston Leroux is a fairly recent entry (published in 1911), the origins of the Phantom's story may be traced directly back to much earlier forms in legend and folklore. Or perhaps it has more to do with our love of creative individualists who, though they are often portrayed as villains, reflect our inner desire to rebel against conformity. Whichever the case, we have embraced the Phantom of the Opera and allowed his deeply rooted, mythic tale to be a ubiquitous part of our popular culture. The purpose of this book is to expose the various guises of the Phantom and to discover why its nearly one-hundred year-old story continues to entertain us.

Part horror story, part historical romance, and part detective thriller, the story of the masked musical genius who lives beneath the Paris Opera House is certainly a familiar one to millions of readers and moviegoers. But in all fairness to Gaston Leroux's classic tale, the terms "horror" story or "monster" story are largely inappropriate. "Horror," by definition, suggests an intense, painful feeling of revulsion or loathing, and "monster" conjures images of an offensive grotesque who commits perverse acts of random violence. These terms might more amply describe the bestselling potboilers of Stephen King or Dean Koontz, or the splatter films of Herschel Gordon Lewis or Tobe Hooper, but certain not the work of Monsieur Leroux or his greatest creation, the Opera Ghost.

Alone, misunderstood, shunned by those who see him, Erik the Phantom is certainly no monster; his acts of violence are committed solely for the woman he loves and to protect his world of anonymity. In fact, this much more contemporary version of the "Beauty and the Beast" fable rightly belongs in a class by itself or, at the very least, with the select group of imaginative, Victorian masterpieces that include *Dracula*, *The Strange Case of Dr. Jekyll and Mr. Hyde*, and *The Adventures of Sherlock Holmes*.

Because *The Phantom of the Opera* draws from such a rich literary heritage, questions about the nature of beauty and ugliness, good and evil, creativity and conformity elevate most of our recollections of the book or its many other incarnations above the commonplace. Joseph Campbell, in his treatise on the power of myth in literature [*The Hero With a Thousand Faces*], recognized that man chose certain archetypes and symbols to deal with those questions. Clearly, several archetypal or symbolic characters from the last two hundred years have provided the mythopoetic basis (and are forerunners) of Leroux's doomed, musical genius. Aylmer, the alchemist in Hawthorne's "The Birthmark," is the archetype for the first mad scientist and a symbol for those misguided individuals who equate beauty with goodness and ugliness with evil. Shocked by his wife's "visible mark of earthly imperfection"—a symbol in his mind of mankind's fallen nature—he takes drastic steps to remove the ugliness. Tragically, he fails to recognize that her beauty extends beyond the physical plane, and his experiments contribute only to her death. The Beast, in the classic children's fable, is visually repulsive; he is described as a creature "so frightful to look upon that men would faint in fear." But inwardly, his soul reflects kindness, gentility, and unselfish devotion to his beloved. By sharp contrast, Beauty's two sisters who are very pretty have cold hearts and cruel dispositions. In fact, when Beauty agrees to live with the Beast in order to spare her father's life, they berate and torment her with the knowledge that they have married handsome, clever husbands. Befittingly, Beauty's love breaks the old curse and transforms the Beast into a handsome prince, reminding all of us "a true heart is better than either good looks or clever brains."

Erik the Phantom believes that old French fable and goes to great lengths to insure that he will live "happily ever after" with the woman of his dreams. Unfortunately, his idealistic, fairy-tale vision of love is out of place in the real world. No matter how kind, gentle, and well intentioned the great composer and musical tutor may be, he fails to consider Christine's feelings. Later, distraught over her decision to love another man, the Phantom abandons all traditional avenues of courtship to pursue his own maniacal desires for her. Erik is, after all, a product of his own environment; his "birthmark" represents an outward manifestation of evil to all those who behold him, and he becomes the monster that they all believe him to be. Abducting the young opera singer, he demands that she remain in his labyrinthine world below the Paris Opera House as his wife in exchange for her lover's life. Christine accepts his unholy bargain and, in doing so, transforms Erik. Although he does not change into a "handsome prince," he begins to understand the real meaning of love. Still outwardly hideous, Erik reveals the true beauty of his soul by allowing the woman he loves to go off with his rival.

Thematically, the Phantom story also concerns the struggle of the individual to express creativity in a world that rejects his passion for life. Those roots of nonconformity lie not only in the "Beauty and the Beast" fable and the classic novel by Gaston Leroux, but also in older, literary conventions and attitudes from Greco-Roman mythology and medieval folklore. Both the legend of Orpheus and the story of Phineus are parables of human presumption—about artists who struggle against the will of god for the love of a woman—that pre-

date the Phantom story by some five thousand years. Orpheus, the Thracian poet whose music moved even inanimate objects, descends into the subterranean regions of Hades (and crosses the Stygian river) to parlay with the devil for the release of his wife at the cost of great suffering and eternal damnation. When he returns without her, infuriated Thracian citizens tear him to pieces. Phineus (Caliban in some traditions) loses his betrothed Andromeda to the handsome Perseus because he cannot invoke the muse of lyric poetry (Euterpe) to save her from the sea monster. Both acts challenge the natural order of things, and both individuals suffer similar punishment from the gods for their arrogance. Similarly, the medieval story of Dr. Faustus (or "Faust")—which is often fused (or confused) with Leroux's novel in cinematic traditions—portrays a man who is willing to sell his soul to the devil in exchange for the answers to the mysteries of the universe. "Faust", like Orpheus and Phineus, defies the gods (or, in this case, a Judeo-Christian god), and only the love of Helen (the woman "whose face launched a thousand ships") can save him from eternal damnation. These familiar stories of struggling, passionate artists and their demonic pacts contribute much to our understanding of the circumstances behind Erik's tragic tale.

Like its mythological, legendary, or literary precursors, the theatrical translations of the last ninety years have relied heavily upon many of the same traditions and themes for inspiration. This continued use of common elements, familiar archetypes, and set symbols has certainly not diminished the audience's enduring affection for Leroux's story; but, rather, it has enriched the material with a variety of ingenious and imaginative narrative approaches. After all, how many times can the same story be told if the focal point remains unchanged? Much can be learned about the Phantom, his personality traits, and origins by considering each adaptation as a separate facet or interpretation.

For example, in the 1925 version starring the great Lon Chaney, the Phantom is an escapee from Devil's Island who has been tortured in the dungeons below the playhouse. His motives for revenge and notoriety overshadow all other *rationale de compri*. Both the 1943 and the 1962 versions portray the Phantom as a wholly sympathetic character whose face has been scarred by acid thrown by a rival composer. While he secretly desires to have his musical talents recognized by the owners of the theatre, he works selflessly (behind the scenes) so that the young diva can ascend to greater glory. In 1974's "Phantom of the Paradise," Brian DePalma's satiric rock opera that fuses the legends of "Faust" and the Phantom, Winslow Leach (as the titular character) must contend not only with exploitative record promoters but also demonic pacts. The Phantom in Andrew Lloyd Webber's Tony award-winning musical and subsequent film is part Valentino and part mad, mu-

sical genius. Charming, confident, and seductive, Erik proves more than a match for the lovesick Raoul and nearly succeeds in winning Christine with his "music of the night." His incarnation in the 1989 version (with Robert Englund as the Phantom) is a cold-blooded assassin who dispatches street ruffians, like a Victorian "caped crusader." When Erik fails to win Christine's hand in his own era, he time travels into the present in order to try again. Other Phantoms have included a bloodsucking vampire (in a 1963 film), a disfigured actor haunting a movie studio (in 1974), a classically trained conductor (in 1983), an impresario whose terrible secret is guarded by his father (in 1990), and a young man raised and protected by intelligent rats (in 1998).

And even though the Phantom has worn the same guise (with subtle variations) for eighty years, the face behind the mask has provided audiences with a diversity of characterizations. Lon Chaney, the legendary "man of a thousand faces," evokes pity and fear with a repulsive, macabre, and entirely believable makeover (which the actor alone devised). In fact, the unmasking of Chaney's Phantom by Mary Philbin—considered one of the great moments of the silent cinema—caused many moviegoers in 1925 to faint at the horrible sight. Claude Rains, a soft-spoken and distinguished British actor, brought much pathos to the role as a shy, middle-aged Phantom. A

fellow countryman of Rains, Herbert Lom gave the Phantom a distinctly British flavor with his Shakespearean training and gentlemanly reserve. More recently, however, Michael Crawford's youthful exuberance and romantic charms have added much to his interpretation, while Robert Englund's Erik walks the psychological tightrope between manic-depression and ultra violence. Gerard Butler, Maximilian Schell, Charles

Dance, Jack Cassidy, Julian Sands, and others have also contributed their own special acting talents to create other interesting portraits of the Opera Ghost.

However, with the exception of the 1925 version and the Andrew Lloyd Webber musical, most adaptations have strayed far from the original story as authored by Gaston Leroux. Erik was born with a physical deformity, much like the Elephant Man, and developed a highly intelligent, resourceful, and creative personality in order to compete with "normal" men. Filmmakers have chosen instead to portray the Phantom as a normal man who has suffered an unjust yet accidental disfigurement. Thus, his obsession with Christine and his desire for anonymity could be simplified into a single motive—revenge. The Phantom of the novel was also a master mason and architect who contracted for work on the Paris Opera House and built his world of mazes, trap doors, and secret chambers. Most cinematic and theatrical adaptations, which have focused on the more horrific aspects, have completely failed to explain how Erik became custodian of such a wondrous lair. Leroux's Phantom was also a master of disguise and did travel beyond his sanctuary into the streets of Paris. Only one version (made in 1989) has permitted him to venture out beyond the cellars of the playhouse. Other attempts in the last few years to return the romance and mystery of the original story have proven to be less than successful. Regrettably, the definitive version of *The Phantom of the Opera* has yet to be made; perhaps, it never will be. Perhaps the definitive version is the one that we create in our own minds each time we read Gaston Leroux's words and imagine, just for a moment, that we are the Phantom or Christine alone in the darkest recesses of the Paris Opera House.

Although many critics and student of popular culture often dismiss the various adaptations of Leroux's work as largely interchangeable, the motion pictures and theatrical productions are distinguished from one another through differences in characterization, visual style and approach, and translation. This book will examine each of those productions on the basis of that criteria in an effort to expose the various Phantoms of the Opera and to discover why the story continues to be an integral part of our cultural identity.

Author's Notation about Filmography

The film and theatrical entries found throughout the book are meant to provide a complete listing of all the motion pictures inspired by Gaston Leroux's classic novel. Only films about or related to or inspired by *The Phantom of the Opera* are included, although there may be some crossover to other horror subjects. The entries have been arranged chronologically (whenever possible) to accompany the text. Titles of foreign films have been translated into English, with careful precision, the English-language title appearing in parenthesis. Certain films, most notably those from independent producers, which were re-released under different titles, are noted by their alternate titles whenever possible. Each listing gives the year under which the film appeared, and for the purposes of this book, the date of a film represents the year of its general release rather than its production. Although the credits have been exhaustively researched and compiled, some are missing, particularly in the early period. Since some records, identifying the director, producer, writer, and stars, were poorly kept, the filmography lists all the known information. Producer credits for films from countries where the film industry is a national asset are meaningless and have been omitted. And in many other countries, where directors are true auteurs, only a single entry of their work is listed. Credits for theatrical and/or other related projects have also been thoroughly researched and provided throughout the book.

~ 1 ~
A Biography of Erik

> **Phantom:** *Fear can turn to love - you'll learn to see, to find the man behind the monster: this repulsive carcass, who seems a beast, but secretly dreams of beauty...*
> —*The Andrew Lloyd Webber Musical (1986)*

In *The Phantom of the Opera*, Gaston Leroux chose to protect the identity of the "Opera Ghost" by referring to him simply as Erik or "the Phantom." Not once does Leroux identify his family name. Though we are given a few details about his background, most of his personal history remains forever cloaked in secrecy. Recent historians and biographers have debated whether his last name was "Destler" or "Claudin" or "Carrier" or "Petrie" based upon obscure records unearthed during a recent excavation of the original site of the Paris Opera House. They have also argued about his birthdate in 1830 or 1831 and whether he came from a working class or aristocratic family. Years of exhaustive research have produced precious little information beyond the material the journalist and news correspondent left us...

Erik was born in September 1830 or 1831 (??) in a small village not far from Rouen, France. His father was a master mason and builder, and his mother was the town's washerwoman. His earliest memory had been of a mask being placed over his head in the cradle to hide his horrific features. As a young boy, his fellow schoolmates tormented Erik because of his facial disfigurement. He ran away from home at the age of thirteen, when the horror and embarrassment of his deformity threatened the very livelihood of his parents. For several years, he appeared in fairs and carnivals as the "living corpse," and traversed the whole of Europe, moving from fair to fair, befriending the other sideshow "freaks." When a greedy showman at the fair of Nijini-Novgorod refused to pay his standard fee, Erik strangled him in his sleep and became a fugitive from justice.

In 1849, he found refuge among the Gypsies, and completed his strange education as an artist, magician, ventriloquist, stage performer, mind reader, and musician. He already sang as nobody on this earth had ever sung before, and soon became one of the Gypsies top performers. In order to protect his identity, Erik assumed a number of elaborate disguises but later relied solely on a mask he fashioned from leather and canvas to hide the look of his "death's head." Word of his astounding acts of ventriloquism and prestidigitation traveled with the caravans returning to Asia, and Erik's reputation quickly reached the attention of the little sultana—the favorite of the Shah-in-Shah of Persia—at the stately palace of Mazenderan.

The daroga of Mazenderan brought Erik to Persia in 1853 to entertain the little sultana, and for several months the Shah extended him every courtesy and luxury imaginable. Unfortunately, Erik had never known such pleasure, and was soon guilty of excesses beyond measure, for he did not know the difference between good and evil. His Majesty recognized his weakness for the good life, and exploited his talents by involving him in a number of political assassinations. Erik was, at first, appalled by the murder of the Emir of Afghanistan and other enemies of the Persian Empire, but in no time at all his diabolical inventiveness proved to be the scourge of the Shah's secret police. Similarly, he had very original ideas about architecture—no doubt learned from his father and the years he spent as a magician—and offered to create a palace for the sovereign so ingenious that "His Majesty would be able to move about in it unseen and to disappear" without detection at will. The Shah ordered him to begin construction on a new palace, but shortly before its completion in the winter of 1856, he decided that Erik and all his laborers should be put to death in order to protect the secrets of his new home. The execution of this abominable decree fell upon the shoulders of the daroga of Mazenderan, who had originally brought Erik to Persia. The daroga felt responsible for him and engineered a way in which he might escape. He then produced a corpse, half-eaten by birds that was found on the shore of the Caspian Sea, to prove that the French architect was indeed dead.

Just as before, Erik was forced to run for his life and sought refuge in Asia Minor, then finally Constantinople where he entered the service of the Sultan. Because of his propensity for disguise, he was employed first as a double for the Sultan. He would appear, dressed like the Commander of the Faithful and resembling him in all respects, at various locations around the country, while the Sultan conducted his affairs or slept. Later, he utilized his talents as a master builder to construct a mighty fortress with trap doors, secret passageways, and hidden chambers for the Sultan. But again, Erik had to flee Constantinople for the same reasons that he had left Persia; he knew far too much about the fortress and was now a liability.

Tired of his adventurous, formidable and monstrous life, Erik returned to France and sought the simple life of a builder/architect. Like any other contractor, he built "ordinary houses with ordinary bricks." When planning began on the famous Paris Opera House in December of 1860, his construction company tendered a bid for part of the foundation. His estimate was accepted, and he started work on the cellars of the enormous playhouse in the summer of 1861. One day, while reviewing the architectural plans of Charles Garnier (the 35-year old designer), his "artistic, fantastic, wizard nature" took over. Erik dreamed of creating a "dwelling unknown to the rest of the world, where he could hide from men's eyes for all time." It was at that moment he decided to make his dream a reality. Calling upon the talents he had used in the service of the Shah and the Sultan, Erik produced a dark, labyrinthine world of his own below the Paris Opera House—a honeycomb of passages and chambers which linked the mysterious subterranean lake to the theatre above. At night, while dreaming of his new home, he began composing an opera, entitled *Don Juan Triumphant*.

The Ministry of Fine Arts dedicated the state-funded building on January 5, 1875, with an elaborate masked ball, and M. Debienne and M. Poligny took over as the first managers of the Opera House. Not long after, Erik began his career as "creative consultant" (as well as "opera ghost"), demanding an allowance of 20,000 francs a month and a permanent box (Box Five) at his disposal for every performance. Fearful of the consequences, Debienne and Poligny reluctantly agreed to his terms.

Five years later, M. Richard and M. Moncharmin replaced the original managers of the playhouse, but refused to honor the terms of Erik's arrangement, dismissing it as superstitious hokum. Several unexplained deaths and the shattering of the Opera House's famous chandelier quickly persuaded them that the Phantom was real. Although authorities attributed the tragedies to the madness of the "opera ghost," the Vicomte de Chagny knew the awful truth. Jealous of Erik's affection for his fiancée Christine Daae, Raoul enlisted the aid of his brother and a Persian (the former daroga of Mazenderan) to hunt down and destroy "the phantom of the Paris Opera House."

Several months passed while Erik continued to tutor the young opera singer and completed work on his opera *Don Juan Triumphant*. Unfortunately, his hopes of having it produced were dashed by the intrusion of Raoul and the Persian into his secret lair. Erik was driven away (to his death?) before he could enjoy his final triumph. Thirty years later, excavators uncovered the remains of "The Phantom of the Opera." His skeleton was found lying near the little well, where Erik had first held Christine fainting into his trembling arms, on the night when he carried her down to the cellars far below the famous playhouse.

Whether you've read or seen *The Phantom of the Opera* once or a hundred times, or are encountering the story for the first time, be ready to be seduced by the darkly romantic tale of a disfigured musical genius and his unrequited love for a beautiful, young singer. Those richly textured scenes that portray Erik's secret lair, Christine's unmasking of the Phantom, the luscious music of the night, the masked ball, and the crashing chandelier are all here within these pages, and so much more. Just turn the page, and prepare to fall in love with Erik and Christine, Raoul, the Persian, and all of the other characters that inhabit Gaston Leroux's classic story...

~ 2 ~
Gaston Leroux's 1911 Novel

> *When I began to ransack the archives of the National Academy of Music, I was once struck by the surprising coincidences between the phenomena ascribed to "the ghost" and the most extraordinary and fantastic tragedy that ever excited the minds of the Paris upper classes; and I was soon led to think that this tragedy might reasonably be explained by the phenomena in question. The events do not date more than thirty years back...connecting the more or less legendary figure of the Opera ghost with that terrible story.*
> —Gaston Leroux, Le Fantôme de l'Opera (1911)

Gaston Leroux's famous novel *Le Fantôme de l'Opera* opens thirty years after the death of the Phantom when workmen, digging in the cellars below the Paris Opera House, unearth a skeleton. Leroux, a noted drama critic and journalist of the time, had learned about a real-life discovery excavators had made of a skeleton below the famous playhouse, and speculated in his introduction to the novel that the discovery was the final piece of evidence to prove the existence of the "phantom." For several years, he had studied documents and letters and diaries, which had attested to the existence of a "ghost." He had searched through the archives of the National Academy of Music for evidence, and he had interviewed people who had seen something that were out of the ordinary. But the skeleton was positive proof. For Monsieur Leroux, "the Opera Ghost really did exist!" Little did the author realize that his reputation as a storyteller would be forever assured by these famous lines (and the ones that followed). Certainly, growing up in the last decades of the 19th century, he could never have dreamed that audiences one hundred years later would continue to read and enjoy his most famous work.

Gaston Louis Alfred was born in Paris, France, on May 6, 1868, to Julien Leroux, a public works contractor, and Marie-Alphonsine, the daughter of a shipbuilder. He was raised in St. Valery-en Caux, a small coastal village in Normandy, near his grandparent's shipbuilding company. As a boy, he developed a love for sailing, swimming and deep-sea fishing. Educated at the College of Eu, Gaston excelled in all disciplines. He was especially proficient in literature, embracing the works of Alexandre Dumas and Victor Hugo, and began writing pastiches of their work while in school. His dream was to become a writer, but in order to please his father, he studied law in Paris instead, acquiring a law degree in 1889. When his father died later that same year, he was left a sizeable fortune. Unfortunately, young Leroux squandered his money on wine, women, and song in less than six months time.

Still disinterested in the law, he began work as a freelance author writing verse for several newspapers. His breakthrough came when L'Echo de Paris published a sonnet he had written about a local actress. Other publications eventually followed that led to a position as a drama critic for the paper. By 1890, he had become a courtroom reporter, then a full-time journalist, and from 1894 to 1906, he traveled around the world as a correspondent, sending features back about various world events (including the Russian Revolution of 1905). In the early 1900s, he began writing novels, his first success being *The Seeking of the Morning Treasures* (in 1903).

Leroux then wrote a series of mystery novels about an amateur detective, starting with *The Mystery of the Yellow Room* (in 1907). In this novel, he created the character of Joseph Rouletabille, a French detective who appeared with a head "like a billiard ball" the antithesis of Sherlock Holmes. Said Leroux, "When I sat down to pen that story, I decided to go 'one better' than Conan Doyle, and make my 'mystery' more complete than even Edgar Allan Poe had ever done in his *Stories of Mystery and Imagination*. The problem which I set myself was exactly the same as theirs—that is, I assumed that a crime had been committed in a room which, as far as exits and entrances were concerned, was hermetically closed. That room opened; all the evidence of the murder is there, but the murderer has mysteriously disappeared." In addition to the detective novels, he published several horror novels, including *The Queen of the Sabbath* (in 1909), and produced a handful of theatrical plays, but never achieved wide fame, except among mystery aficionados.

In 1910, he began work on the novel that would guarantee his fame for years and generations to come—*The Phantom of the Opera*. At first, the manuscript was nothing more than a collection of notes gathered together over the years by the journalist and news correspondent Leroux had become. For example, he had written a complete account of the 1896 disaster at the Paris Opera House in which one of the chandelier's heavy counterweights had fallen from the ceiling and killed a patron of the playhouse. He possessed the architectural plans of Charles Garnier's 1860 playhouse, and knew about the secret passageways and mysterious subterranean lake. But it wasn't until the discovery of the skeleton that the novel fell into place. By making use of diaries, journal entries, and alternating first-person narratives, Leroux was able to execute a chilling tale that cleverly walks the fine line between truth and fiction. A less experienced author might have produced a modest thriller, which would have been quickly dismissed as fantasy, but Monsieur Leroux's vivid, journalistic style provides the reader with a kind of verisimilitude that makes the characters and settings seem borrowed from the headlines of the daily post. Indeed, as Gaston Leroux contends in the introduction, many of the events of the novel are real.

The Phantom of the Opera was published in book form in 1911, and somewhat surprisingly did very little business in the first weeks. Reviews of the book had been lukewarm, and readers who had enjoyed his mystery stories dismissed the material outright. However, when newspapers in Great Britain and the United States began to carry a serialized version of the story (with graphic images of the Phantom), popularity of the tale increased. The silent film version in 1925 with Lon Chaney generated renewed enthusiasm, and soon not a bookstore in Paris could keep up with the demand for the novel. Today, Leroux's name is forever linked with the tragic tale of the disfigured composer and his love for a young opera singer.

Gaston Leroux went on to write a dozen other novels, and even saw several of them made into short films, but not one would capture the imagination of future generations like *The Phantom of the Opera*. Shortly before his death, the portly author confessed a special affinity for his reworking of the *Beauty and the Beast* fable, and hoped that cinema would do his story justice. Because of health problems, related to his obesity, Leroux never had the opportunity to see the silent film version. He died unrepentantly from a urinary infection on April 15, 1927, at the age of fifty-nine, and was buried in Nice, France. Even to his deathbed, Leroux maintained that his "Opera Ghost really did exist!" Today, Gaston Leroux's name is forever linked with the tragic tale of a disfigured composer and his love for a young opera singer.

His introduction to *Le Fantôme de l'Opera* suggests that the following narrative was based on painstaking research into an actual case. "The Opera Ghost really existed," he asserts in the first line of his book. "He was not, as was long believed, the creature of the imagination of the artists, brains of the young ladies of the ballet, their mothers, the boxkeepers, the cloakroom attendants, or the concierge. No, he existed in flesh and blood, though he assumed all the outward characteristics of a real phantom, that is to say, of a shade."

In 1881, during the retirement gala of M. Debienne and M. Poligny, the departing managers of the Paris Opera House, several young, ballet dancers gather backstage to discuss the mysterious appearances of a ghostly figure in fine dress clothes. For many months, the Opera House had been filled with plenty of gossip related to the "phantom," but no one could quite agree on what he looked like. Joseph Buquet, the chief scene-shifter, claims to have actually seen the ghost and describes him as a living corpse: "He is extraordinarily thin and his dress-coat hangs on a skeleton frame. His eyes are so deep that you can hardly see the fixed pupils. You just see two big black holes, as in a dead man's skull. His skin is ...a nasty yellow, and all the hair he has is three or four long dark locks. ..." Meg Giry, the daughter of the woman who attends the Phantom in Box Five, admonishes Buquet, warning him to hold his tongue, fearing that his words will anger the ghost. Sometime later, Madame Giry reports that Buquet has been found hanged beneath the stage -the first victim of the Phantom's wrath, even though his death is dismissed as an accident.

That same evening, a young singer named Christine Daae triumphs by first singing passages from "Romeo and Juliet," then assuming the part of Margarita in "Faust" after the Spanish diva La Carlotta has taken ill. The audience is quite taken by her performances and wonder why she has languished so long in the shadow of the other diva. Philippe Georges Marie, the Comte de Chagny, and his younger brother Raoul, the Vicomte, are among the audience members who acclaim her and rush backstage to congratulate Christine. (Raoul met Christine many years before as a "little boy who went into the sea to rescue" her scarf and has been secretly in love with her ever since.) The young singer is overwhelmed by the attention and faints, only to be revived in the arms of her childhood lover. She is happy to see him, but cuts their meeting short for no apparent reason. Suspicious, Raoul listens at her dressing-room door and overhears a man's voice talking to her about the performance. Later, when Christine leaves for the night, he inspects the unlocked room to discover no one at all.

The Phantom appears at the farewell party M. Richard and M. Moncharmin, the two new owners of the Opera House, are throwing for Debienne and Poligny. No one takes note of him simply because they think he's with the other guests of the party. When he finally speaks, telling of Buquet's death, everyone turns to listen. He warns the new managers to abide by his original agreement, then departs, leaving everyone quite aghast. Monsieurs Richard and Moncharmin retire from the party to inquire about the stranger's threats, and the old managers give them a copy of the Opera Ghost's contract (written in red ink with ninety-eight clauses and four conditions). According to the age-old document, the Phantom demands an allowance of 20,000 francs a month and a permanent box (Box Five) to be at his disposal for every performance. It is also the reason that the former managers were forced to sell their interests in the theatre. They simply could not keep up with the ghost's unreasonable demands and maintain a profit. Richard and Moncharmin think that it's all part of an elaborate practical joke, probably perpetrated by their predecessors, and decide to ignore his demands.

A few days later, the new managers receive the first of many notes from the Phantom (signed simply O.G., for Opera Ghost). Christine Daae is to be given the lead in their new production, and his box is to remain open; otherwise, they face the wrath of the Phantom. Annoyed, they defy his requests and sell box five for all the remaining performances. Their rash actions unfortunately lead to a disruption of the night's activities. Madame Giry is called upon, and she relates how the Opera Ghost disturbed patrons to box five during a performance of "Faust." Richard and Moncharmin think she is mad and decide to dismiss her from the theatre.

Meanwhile, Christine Daae has second thoughts about how she treated Raoul and sends him a note, telling the young Vicomte that she plans to visit the grave of her father in Perros-Guirrec in Brittany on the anniversary of his death. Raoul accompanies her, and learns how Christine came to Paris. (Her father was the greatest violinist in Scandinavia, and Valerius, a world-renowned musical professor, offered to tutor him and his talented daughter. One summer, while vacationing in Brittany, Raoul took violin lessons from her father, and rescued "little Lotte's" scarf from the sea. When her  father died, she came to Paris to learn from Valerius. Her father had promised to send her an "angel of music" on his death-bed, and when she started singing at the Paris Opera House, Christine began learning from a new tutor.) Raoul confesses his love for her, but she rejects him again, saying she has no time for love.

At the grave of her father in Perros, Christine is visited by the "Angel of Music." He begins playing "The Resurrection of Lazarus" (a favorite tune of her father's) on a violin, and she is lulled into a trance by the notes of the music. Raoul interrupts their tranquility, confronting Christine with his knowledge of a man in her dressing-room. She becomes pale and frightened, and rushes away into a nearby church. Raoul follows after her and is suddenly attacked by a specter with a death's head. Hours later, his unconscious body is returned to the inn by the Phantom.

Determined to get to the bottom of the mystery, M. Richard and M. Moncharmin go to Box Five and can find nothing unusual. Bravely, they decide to watch that Saturday's performance of "Faust" from

the box themselves, but the Phantom has other plans. "So, it is to be war between us!" he declares. The Opera Ghost sends another note, demanding that 1.) His box be returned to him, 2.) Christine Daae be cast as a replacement for La Carlotta, 3.) Madame Giry be restored to service, and 4.) His back wages be paid. If his demands are not met, and in a timely fashion, the theatre will suffer a catastrophe beyond measure. Monsieurs Richard and Moncharmin again choose to ignore him.

"Faust" opens with little to no problems. M. Richard sits in Box Five, and La Carlotta is brilliant in the role of Margarita. During the performance, the aging diva receives a note, insisting that she withdraw, so that Christine Daae can continue in her place. La Carlotta defies the instruction, suspecting a plot contrived by her rival and the Vicomte, and continues with the performance. Suddenly, she loses her voice and begins to "cro-ack" like a toad. The audience responds with laughter, and the two managers collapse in their chairs in humiliation. "She is singing tonight to bring the chandelier down!" the Phantom announces, then releases the chandelier, killing the woman who had been hired to replace Mme. Giry.

Following the great tragedy, which all but ruins the reputations of Richard and Moncharmin, Christine vanishes as well. Raoul is distraught by her disappearance, and seeks out Madame Valerius, the widow of the famous music professor, thinking Christine may be lodging with her. But instead he learns that Miss Daae is with her new tutor, the Angel of Music, who lives in heaven. Mme. Valerius reveals that the young singer has been receiving music lessons from him for nearly three months now. Raoul believes that she is with his rival, and leaves the house in despair. Moments later, she passes him in a carriage on the road. Then days later, he receives a note from

Christine asking him to meet her secretly at the masked ball.

Every year, the Paris Opera House throws an elaborate masked ball to bless the theatre's annual good fortune. Unfortunately, Monsieurs Richard and Moncharmin have little to celebrate this year. Several unexplained deaths have occurred in their playhouse, and they have had to replace the expensive chandelier. Both managers wish they could forget all this nonsense about the Phantom, fearing that he will strike again.

At five minutes to midnight, Raoul arrives for his rendezvous with Christine, who is dressed as a red domino. Narrowly escaping the sinister clutches of a scarlet-garbed figure with a death's head, purported to be Edgar Allan Poe's "Red Death" but recognized by Raoul as the Phantom, the young lovers hide in Christine's dressing-room where they can talk. Miss Daae urges the Vicomte to release his love for her, because she can no one, except the Phantom. Raoul admonishes Christine for protecting him and decides the only way to be rid of his rival is to expose "the Angel of Music" for the fraud that he is. Suddenly, the room is filled with a strange voice - a voice Raoul has heard before - and Christine, lost in a trance, steps into the mirror and vanishes. The young Vicomte is shocked by what he sees.

The next day Raoul pays a visit to Madame Valerius and finds Christine with her. She is wearing a ring that the Phantom has given her. The Vicomte de Chagny demands to know his rival's name, but then reveals that he already knows his name because he was eavesdropping again. The "Phantom" is Erik. Christine cries out in terror, warning him to forget all he remembers, or her "Angel of Music" will turn his wrath on the Vicomte. Disconsolate, Raoul leaves the two women, and signs aboard a polar expedition that leaves France in less than one month.

Christine returns to the playhouse in triumph, since La Carlotta refuses to return until the Opera Ghost has been properly exorcised. All Paris heralds her performance, and she has finally achieved the success that the young singer so richly deserves. Prior to his departure, Raoul attends one final show. Miss Daae sees him in the audience, and arranges to meet the Vicomte on the roof of the theatre after the last act.

High above the Paris Opera House, the two lovers resolve their differences and enter into a secret engagement. Christine also begins to tell Raoul everything she knows about Erik: Three months ago, the Phantom kidnapped her through the mirror, put her on horseback, then rowed her down a mysterious, subterranean lake to his home. He warned her not to look behind the mask, then knelt at her feet in worship. He was no angel, or ghost, but simply Erik. When she demanded her freedom, he gave it to her, then broke into a harmonious melody which put her to sleep. One their first morning together, he gave her gifts, offered her breakfast, and showed her his composition-in-progress – "Don Juan Triumphant." He had been working on that one opera for nearly twenty years, and when it was complete, he knew that he would die. Christine offered to sing the piece with him, but instead the two sing "Othello." At which point, she torn the mask from his face, and discovered his hideous visage.

Impetuously, Raoul interrupts her story, proclaiming that he will kill Erik, but Christine simply tell him to "be silent" and continues with her story. The young singer was, at first, frightened by his horrible face, but then, seeing his sorrow, looked upon him without fear. Feeling sorry for him, she continued to lie to Erik by confessing her love, and even accepted an engagement ring from him. She soon gained her freedom, and returned to the surface world, with the promise that she would again return to him. Raoul is totally aghast by the story and vows to take her to safety in three days time. Unbeknownst to the two young lovers, the Phantom is perched on a statue of Apollo, high above their heads, and has been listening to every word of Christine's betrayal – a betrayal that wounds his heart.

Raoul and Christine exchange a final kiss, and as they do, Erik's ring slips from her hand. (As long as she wore the ring, she would be protected from his wrath.) The Phantom allows his presence to be known, and the young lovers leave the roof, fearing Erik is in pursuit. As they depart, the Persian is standing at the foot of the stairs and suggests that they take a different route. Later that night, Raoul awakes, thinking that the Phantom is watching him, and blindly fires several shots. One of the bullets finds its mark, physically wounding Erik.

Philippe arrives with a gossip paper, announcing Raoul and Christine's engagement, and tells his younger brother, in no uncertain terms, that titled aristocrats cannot marry opera singers. Furthermore, the Comte de Chagny is convinced that Miss Daae is mad, with her wild stories about ghosts. Raoul rebukes his older brother's charges, and leaves for the theatre. During the night's performance of "Faust," Christine suddenly vanishes on stage before the audience, and Raoul rushes madly to her dressing-room. He knows that Erik, the "Angel of Music," has taken her for his own dastardly purposes.

At about the same time Monsieurs Richard and Moncharmin discover that 20,000 francs, which they placed in an envelope for the Phantom, has been substituted with false bank notes. They accuse Madame Giry of the deception, but she is able to prove her innocence. Later, when additional funds disappear, even though they had been attached to Monsieur Moncharmin's coat by a safety pin, the police are summoned to resolve all the mysteries. Unfortunately, they are somewhat less than helpful, first suspecting Raoul, then Philippe of the theft and subsequent abduction of Christine Daae.

The Persian interrupts their wild speculations, by explaining that he recognizes the style and work of the Phantom. He reveals that he has been pursuing Erik for years and that he could provide valuable assistance in tracking the man through the labyrinthine world below the Opera House; but they are not interested in working with an amateur. Raoul, on the other hand, suspects the authorities will waste too much time pursuing dead ends, and allies himself with the mysterious visitor from the East. The two men arm themselves with pistols, and descend into the cellars through the mirror in Christine's dressing-room. All the while, they hold their arms up as if ready to fire their weapons, as a precaution against the deadly effects of the Punjab lasso, which has already been used to strangle Buquet. Descending into the darkness, they encounter many wild and strange happenings. The two men eventually reach what they think is Erik's lair, and lower themselves inadvertently into a torture chamber, which has no visible means of escape.

Meanwhile, the Phantom reveals his desires to live a normal life, like others, with Christine as his wife. He has created a lifemask to hide his deformity, and hopes that, in time, she will learn to love him. She tells him simply that she will never love him. Angered, Erik forces the young singer to choose between a wedding mass or a requiem, life with him or the death of her lover. He imprisons Christine in the rooms adjacent to the torture chamber, so that she can converse with Raoul through the walls, and gives her several hours to decide their fate. Before eleven in the evening, she must select one of two ornamental boxes -the scorpion-shaped box or the grasshopper. One of them will save the men's lives, and the other will destroy the Opera House.

Raoul and the Persian suffer through several tortures at the hand of the Phantom. First, they are roasted alive, and begin to hallucinate that they are in a jungle or a desert. Then, they are nearly drowned, as the room is suddenly flooded with water. Finally, seeing that Miss Daae has chosen the scorpion, Erik stops his insane tortures and brings them to his quarters. The two men are brought back to life by the loving hand of Christine, ministering to their wounds. Erik apologizes for his cruelties, and explains that he now understands the true meaning of love. (Christine has kissed him, without fear.) Later, after the men have been returned to the surface, Erik pays a visit on the Persian to tell him that he is dying. He regrets the unfortunate drowning of Philippe, but has reunited the young lovers and sent them away. Prior to his departure to the Opera House, the Phantom asks his old, Eastern friend to see that he is properly buried, with her ring, in the cellars below the theatre. Three weeks later, a simple, three-word obituary is published in the newspaper: "Erik is Dead."

In his epilogue to *Le Fantôme de l'Opera*, Leroux explains how the Persian was the only one to have known the entire story. The author had visited the foreigner weeks before his death, and was able to puzzle together the balance of Erik's sad tale. Born a monster, he fleed home at an early age and made his way across Europe, traveling as a freak in the circus. In Persia, he became a master builder-architect, constructing a unique palace for the Shah. In Paris, he tendered a bid for construction of the opera house, and hid himself away in the dark, labyrinthine world below. Following Erik's last visit, he blocked all the secret passages to his home, and buried the completed score for "Don Juan Triumphant." He then sat down and died, a poor, unhappy man.

Gaston Leroux concludes his narrative with a few, simple words: "The reader knows and guesses the rest. It is all in keeping with the incredible yet veracious story. Poor, unhappy Erik! Shall we pity him? Shall we curse him? He only asked to be 'someone,' like everybody else. But he was too ugly! And he had to hide his genius or use it to play tricks with, when, with an ordinary face, he would have been one of the most distinguished of mankind! He had a heart that could have held the empire of the world; and in the end he had to content himself with a cellar. Surely we may pity the Opera ghost!"

Le Fantôme de l'Opera is a daring, tour-de-force which grips the reader with the very first words of the Introduction and holds him spellbound until the end. It is both a mystery tale, with horror elements, and a tragic love story, with its Victorian characters caught helplessly in a romantic triangle. Although it is likely that the novel would have vanished into obscurity, like many of Leroux's other works, Universal's 1925 film with Lon Chaney assured its place in popular culture. Both the motion picture and Chaney's extraordinary performance generated considerable box office appeal for contemporary audiences worldwide. Interest reached a fever pitch as the public hungered to know more about the Phantom,

and many turned to the original novel. Hardly successful in its original release, the novel has continued to add readers with each subsequent production.

Gaston Leroux went on to write a dozen other novels and even saw several made into short films, but not one would capture the imagination of future generations like *Le Fantôme de l'Opera*. Shortly before his death, the portly Frenchman confessed a special affinity for his reworking of the *Beauty and the Beast* fable, and hoped that cinema would do his story justice. Monsieur Leroux's tragic tale of a disfigured composer and his love for a young opera singer remains today as the Frenchman's singular legacy to the world of literature and popular culture.

John L. Flynn

~ 3 ~
Lon Chaney at the Masked Ball

Christine: You... You are the Phantom!
Erik: If I am the Phantom, it is because man's hatred has made me so... If I shall be saved, it will be because your love redeems me.
—*The 1925 Silent Film Version*

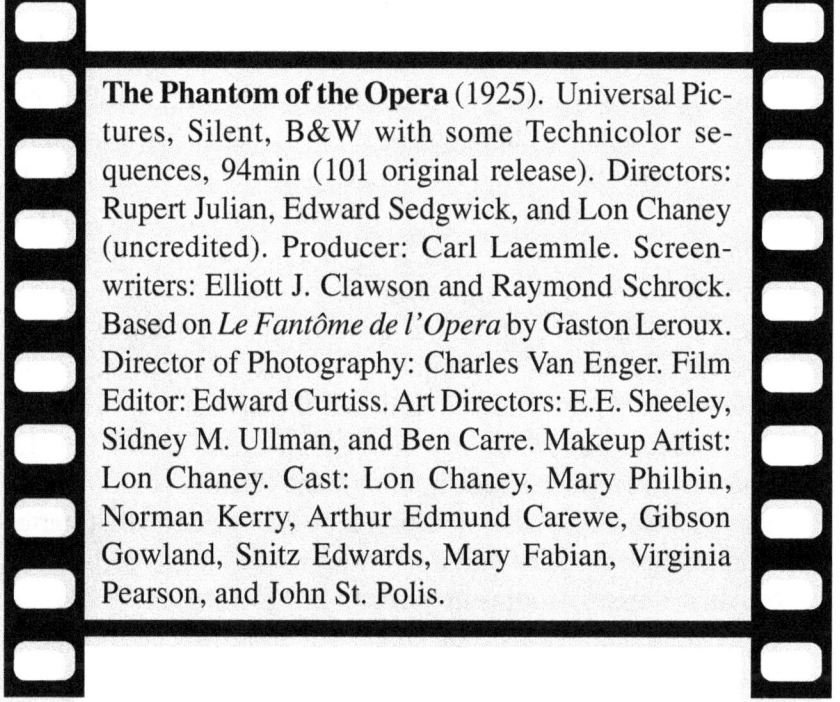

The Phantom of the Opera (1925). Universal Pictures, Silent, B&W with some Technicolor sequences, 94min (101 original release). Directors: Rupert Julian, Edward Sedgwick, and Lon Chaney (uncredited). Producer: Carl Laemmle. Screenwriters: Elliott J. Clawson and Raymond Schrock. Based on *Le Fantôme de l'Opera* by Gaston Leroux. Director of Photography: Charles Van Enger. Film Editor: Edward Curtiss. Art Directors: E.E. Sheeley, Sidney M. Ullman, and Ben Carre. Makeup Artist: Lon Chaney. Cast: Lon Chaney, Mary Philbin, Norman Kerry, Arthur Edmund Carewe, Gibson Gowland, Snitz Edwards, Mary Fabian, Virginia Pearson, and John St. Polis.

The 1925 version of "The Phantom of the Opera" was (and remains to this day) the best of the cinematic translations of Gaston Leroux's classic 1911 novel. Fraught with production delays, creative disputes, and infighting, the silent picture still managed to transcend its troubled origins to become the biggest box office feature of the year. The film also broke new thematic ground which would have a long-range influence on Universal's horror series. By making the villain a sympathetic character (who functions as both protagonist and antagonist), the adaptation demonstrates considerable insight: Erik the Phantom becomes a monster only after the society which views ugliness as evil has rejected him. But the real strength of the production lies with the incredible performance of Lon Chaney, "the man of a thousand faces." Even though the film may appear "dated," "hokey," "overly melodramatic," or "an antique for collector's only" as some contemporary critics have contended in their recent reviews, Chaney still thrills as the mysterious masked Phantom.

The Screen Story

In the opening reels of the silent film, the presence of an opera ghost is established by inexplicable shadows on the wall or mysterious silhouettes glimpsed for a second in stairwells. Everyone believes that a phantom haunts the playhouse, but Joseph Buquet (Gibson Gowland) is the only man who has actually seen him. He describes the Phantom to a dozen chorus girls, who twirl and shriek in excitement, then warns them not to look too closely behind his mask. "He has no nose!" the stagehand reveals. "His eyes are ghastly beads in which there is no light, like holes in a grinning skull. His face is like leprous parchment, yellow skin strung tight over protruding bones." The sudden appearance of an odd-looking man in evening clothes and an astrakhan cap causes Buquet to end his description abruptly. Suspected of being the Phantom himself, the mysterious stranger is actually a secret policeman named Ledoux-the "Persian" (Arthur Edmund Carewe). He has been hunting "The Phantom of the Opera" for more than ten years, but is no closer now than when he first started. As Ledoux slips gingerly into the shadows, the chorus girls scurry back to their dressing-rooms in terror.

The Paris Opera House, sanctuary for song lovers, rose nobly over medieval torture chambers and hidden dungeons. Melody floats through its long hallways and dark corridors, even to the executive offices where a strange deal is being closed. Once they have sealed the contract for the sale of the playhouse, Monsieurs Debienne and Poligny warn the new owners about the Phantom. They must abide by the original agreement with the Opera Ghost, or they will face terrors beyond their imagination. Monsieurs Richard and Moncharmin believe that the warning is part of an elaborate practical joke (probably perpetrated by their predecessors), and choose to ignore Debienne and Poligny. No sooner have the former managers departed, however, then Carlotta's mother (Virginia Pearson) appears with a letter from the Phantom. The letter demands that Christine sing the role of Marguerite in "Faust" on Wednesday night, or a major disaster will occur. Outraged, Carlotta's mother insists that her daughter will sing; but when Wednesday night arrives, Carlotta (Mary Fabian) is strangely ill, and Christine Daae (Mary Philbin) has taken her place.

Part of the audience, on Wednesday night, Philippe De Chagny (John Sainpolla) questions his younger brother Raoul (Norman Kerry) about Miss Daae. "I hear a lot of rumors, Raoul. Be careful," he warns him, but the Vicomte is so madly in love with Christine that he ignores his brother's warnings. He hurries backstage, at the conclusion of the performance, and takes the young singer into his arms. Their romantic scene is cut short, when Raoul's sweet words turn to talk of marriage and family. Christine reminds him that she will never leave the opera, and that he must forget about their love. Feeling rejected, Raoul de Chagny leaves her dressing room, and pauses momentarily in the corridor outside.

Meanwhile, from hidden places beyond the walls a melodious voice, like the voice of an angel, reminds Christine that he alone has placed the world at her feet. (Raoul listens from the other side of the door with suspicion.) The Phantom promises that all Paris will one day worship her, but the young singer must first forget all worldly pleasures and concentrate on her music. Christine agrees, then insists that "the angel of music" should come to her soon in human form.

A few days later, the new managers receive the first of many notes from the "Phantom" (signed simply O.G., for Opera Ghost). His instructions are very clear: Christine Daae is to be given the lead in their new production, and his box seat is to remain open; otherwise, they face the wrath of the Phantom. Annoyed, they defy his requests and sell box five for all the remaining performances. They then attempt to calm Carlotta and her mother who believe that Christine's friends (notably Philippe and Raoul) are plotting against the diva. Richard and Moncharmin assure them that the new production will feature Carlotta, not Christine. However, when the directors of the Paris Opera House disobey his orders to let the young singer appear on stage, the Phantom becomes angry. Watching from the catwalks high above the stage, he realizes that they must all be taught a lesson in terror. "Behold! She is singing to bring down the chandelier," the Phantom shouts aloud, then sends the giant crystalline chandelier crashing into the audience.

Following the great tragedy, which injures a dozen audience members, the Phantom emerges from the mirror in Christine's dressing room. Dressed in a black cloak and white mask, he quickly hypnotizes the young singer, then directs her through the labyrinth of catacombs and across an underground lake to his hidden lair. Once there, he confesses his love for Christine (which has been aroused by her purity), and warns that she must never attempt to look behind the mask. The Phantom then sits at an organ and plays "Don Juan Triumphant," his own composition, requesting that she accompany him. She refuses, recognizing him as the dreaded opera ghost. He professes to be neither an angel, nor a demon, but simply Erik. "Man's hatred made me the Phantom," he tells her, "but your love redeems me." Overwhelmed by his passion, and finally unable to resist the temptation to see her tutor's face, Christine tears the mask away to reveal the Phantom of the Opera's unholy visage.

"Feast your eyes, glut your soul, on my accursed ugliness!" the Phantom exclaims madly, forcing her to look at him squarely in the face. The young singer fights his grasp and begs for her freedom in the name of love. He reluctantly agrees to let her return to the playhouse, but then reminds Christine that she is forever bound to him. She acknowledges his terms, and promises him that she will never see Raoul again.

One night each year all Paris mingled at the merry, mad Bal Masque de l'Opera. Party goers revel in all manner of costume, while Raoul searches the crowd for his beloved Christine. In the midst of the revelry strode a fearsome figure in crimson cloak and scarlet skull -Edgar Allan Poe's "Red Death" in primitive, two-tone Technicolor - the Phantom. Everyone stands aside in horror, as he attempts to walk among them and rebuke their merriment. But his grand entrance is foiled by the embrace of the two young lovers. When Erik does finally spot his rival -the Vicomte -and Christine at the top of the steps, he is much too late to prevent them from escaping safely into the darkness.

High above the Paris Opera House, the singer confesses her fear of the Phantom, proclaiming that "he's a monster" and begging Raoul to take her away. The two lovers resolve their petty differences and decide to flee to England after tomorrow night's performance. Unbeknownst to them, the Phantom is perched on a statue of Apollo, high above their heads, and has been listening to every word of the young woman's betrayal. Enraged by what he has heard, Erik curses them both, and tries to prevent the lovers from leaving the roof. When

Raoul and Christine attempt to circumvent his wishes, the mysterious Persian intervenes, directing them to an alternate escape route. Further enraged, the Phantom returns to the masked ball to proclaim his superiority over all he surveys, then disappears through a convenient trapdoor.

At nine o'clock the following evening, Raoul arrives with a carriage that will take his beloved to safety immediately after the performance. However, the Phantom has other plans for Christine. Subsequent to poisoning several backstage workers and strangling Joseph Buquet, Erik again abducts the young singer in the midst of her final curtain call. Powerless to stop him, Raoul watches the events unfold before his very eyes in horror, then races backstage moments too late. The Phantom has made a clean getaway with Christine! Ledoux, the mysterious Persian, emerges from the shadows and reveals to the Vicomte that he has been pursuing Erik for over ten years now. He knows how the man operates, and will take Raoul to the singer if he promises to follow his instructions. The young aristocrat agrees, and the two men quickly descend into the cellars below through the mirror in Miss Daae's dressing-room. All the while, they hold their arms up to the level of their eyes, as a precaution against the deadly Punjab lasso the Phantom uses to kill his victims.

Descending into the darkness, they encounter many wild and strange happenings. The two men eventually reach what they think is Erik's lair, and lower themselves inadvertently into a torture chamber, which has no visible means of escape. Meanwhile, in his subterranean lair, the Phantom curses Christine for having betrayed him. All he wanted was to live a normal life with her as his wife. But she wants no part of his nightmare! Angered, Erik forces the young singer to choose between a wedding mass or a requiem, life with him or the death of her lover. "If you turn the scorpion, you have said 'yes' and spared de Chagny," he instructs her to choose between one of two ornamental boxes. "Turn the grasshopper, and the Opera House is blown to a thousand bits!" The Phantom races off to deal with another intruder, leaving Christine alone to deal with her dilemma. (Philippe has not only stumbled into the dark, labyrinthine world below the playhouse, looking for his brother, but also become the madman's next victim. Little does Erik realize, when he is drowning the Comte de Chagny, that hundreds of townspeople have also followed the trail to his hidden lair.)

Raoul and the Persian suffer through endless tortures at the hand of the Phantom, until Christine turns the scorpion, flooding their room. Provided that he will save them from drowning, she promises to do anything Erik asks. The Phantom agrees to her bargain, and reluctantly pulls the two men to safety.

When a second series of alarms announce the arrival of more intruders, Erik wrests Christine from the arms of her lover and races off in Raoul's carriage. Pursued by the torch-bearing mob, the Phantom recklessly drives his coach through the Parisian streets. The vehicle finally overturns, and he is forced to flee on foot without his beloved Christine. Eventually, they surround him near the Cathedral of Notre Dame, and move in for the kill. Trapped, cornered, with nowhere left to run, Erik tries to hold them at bay with a magician's trick, but they are not amused. The crowd grabs the Phantom, beats him severely, then throws his limp, nearly-dead body into the Seine river to drown. Finis.

Production Notes

Delighted with the returns from "The Hunchback of Notre Dame" (1923), the first of Universal's new horror series Carl Laemmle looked around for another property to send before the cameras. He remembered that he had met Gaston Leroux the previous summer (while vacationing in Paris) and had enjoyed reading the copy of *Le Fantôme de l'Opera* he was given by the author. Although he found the 1911 novel to be overly melodramatic, the story of a masked, disfigured composer haunting the Paris Opera House was exactly the kind of high-concept drama that interested Laemmle. Several problems (to which the studio chief often referred to as "opportunities") immediately presented themselves: How could they film scenes in-and-around the Opera House setting? Who would direct the picture? And, more importantly, who would play the lead role of Erik the Phantom?

In those days, since most studios actually found it cheaper to construct replicas of existing places (rather than shoot on location), the film mogul decided to build a magnificent set of the playhouse (one that would rival the Notre Dame set). Construction of the mammoth structure was begun in April 1924 on Stage 28 at Universal Studios, and was completed a few days before actual filming began late that summer. Ben Carre was called in to design the sets, and although he had worked at the Paris Opera House, he had already been living in California for some time doing sets. Because the auditorium set would have five tiers of box seats and hold hundreds of extras, a steel framework (imbedded in the concrete foundations) was used in place of the customary wooden planking. The skeleton was later reinforced with corrugated iron. Carl Laemmle's decision to build the Opera House proved to be such a sound one that the huge indoor set has never been struck. In fact, the auditorium has appeared over the years in several other features, including the 1943 version of "The Phantom of the Opera," "A Double Life" (1948), "Torn Curtain" (1966), and "The Sting" (1973). Today, the only part of the set sill standing is Ben Carre's Opera House, though the only parts left completely untouched are the boxes and stage sides.

The Phantom's dark, labyrinthine world below the playhouse was actually built under the floor of Stage 28 in a huge water tank. Other sets, notably the Grand Foyer (with the double staircase) and the roof (with the huge statue of Apollo), were built in full scale just adajacent to the playhouse. Laemmle's first major concerns about the production were resolved by set designer Charles D. Hall and the uncredited Ben Carre, but the issue of a director and a star remained irresolute.

Carl Laemmle's first choice as a director was Wallace Worsley, the man responsible for the successful "Hunchback of Notre Dame." But Worsley was reluctant to work for the studio chief again (after all the problematic interference he had endured while filming the 1923 silent), and declined numerous monetary incentives. Laemmle's next selection was Rupert Julian, a former actor from New Zealand who had distinguished himself as a director by salvaging Erich Von

Stroheim's "The Merry-Go-Round" for Irving Thalberg. After turning two low-budget thrillers, "Love and Glory" (1923) and "Hell's Highroad" (1924), into moderate successes, the hot, young director was signed contractually in an exclusive agreement with Universal Pictures. Carl Laemmle was not bothered by Julian's reputation as an arrogant auteur, and eagerly handed him the studio's biggest project. He would soon regret that decision, but at the time the aging film mogul was concerned with only one problem: How could he acquire the services of the legendary "man of a thousand faces" from his arch-enemy at M-G-M?

Lon Chaney, a legend in the silent film era, was known as "the man of a thousand faces" for good reason. Having played a gallery of tortured grotesques, from Fagin in "Oliver Twist" (1922) to Quasimodo in "The Hunchback of Notre Dame" (1923) for a pittance at Universal, Chaney had been lured away by a better salary offer at Metro-Goldwyn-Mayer. Thus, when his former studio began preproduction on "The Phantom of the Opera," Hollywood's boy wonder was contractually bound to a rival company. Carl Laemmle

remained undaunted. The Universal studio chief was so convinced that Chaney was the only actor who could play the title role that he actually called Louis B. Mayer, the president of M-G-M, to discuss how he might arrange to have Lon "loaned" back to Universal for one final film. After several weeks of secret negotiations with Mayer and associate Irving Thalberg, Laemmle secured his former contract player for a role that would become legendary. Chaney was delighted to find himself back at his old studio with a much higher salary, and literally transformed himself into the character of Erik the Phantom.

Ten weeks into the shoot, however, Laemmle came to regret his decision to team Chaney with Julian. Friction between his perfectionist star and the arrogant auteur had brought the production to a standstill. Portions of the film shot in a primitive red-and-blue Technicolor process had been scrapped by Julian, restored by Chaney, then scrapped again and rescheduled for shooting by Julian. An entire sequence, with Lon Chaney as Erik drowning in his forgotten, underground lake, was filmed in eight different ways by Julian and then discarded. Mob scenes with several thousand extras storming the Phantom's lair were filmed by both Julian, then scrapped. The concept of a dark, romantic triangle between Erik, Christine, and Raoul was changed by Julian (in direct opposition to Chaney) in order to expand the role of Norman Kerry as the young aristocrat. To further complicate matters, Lon Chaney's father had become seriously ill and was dying during the production, but because of Julian's rigorous shooting schedule, the great actor was refused time off to attend the sickbed. (Between takes, Chaney spent time on the phone, checking on his father's condition.)

When Carl Laemmle learned of all these difficulties, he screened a rough cut of the film (late in 1924) and was disappointed by what he saw. He fired Julian, gave the company a few days leave, then hired Edward Sedgewick to replace the New Zealander as director. Sedgewick had directed mostly routine action films, from "Live Wires" (1921) and "The First Degree" (1923) to "Two-Fisted Jones" (1925), and was the ideal choice to shoot the chase scenes at the climax of the film. But his limited range as a director allowed perfectionist Chaney to take over, directing whole sequences of the silent film himself.

Several sequences were shot in various color processes for the top general release prints. Technicolor was used for scenes from "Faust" and the Bal Masque scene; Prizmacolor sequences were shot for the "Soldier's Night" introduction, and Handschiegel (a process that uses stamps to hand-color prints) for the Phantom's notes and red cape on the rooftop. Regrettably, only the Technicolor Bal Masque sequence is known to survive (and appears as an IB print in the 1929 re-release). Just prior to Christmas 1924, production on "The Phantom of the Opera" wrapped on Stage 28 at Universal Studios, Hollywood.

The Film's Release and Critical Reaction

Following the Los Angeles previews in January 1925, Sedgewick was asked to add a number of comedy sequences, featuring Chester Conklin as a superstitious stagehand, in order to lessen the tension of the film. Further editing with the addition of new title cards was hastily undertaken weeks before the premiere to make the storyline more coherent. Finally, nearly a year after the production had begun, "The Phantom of the Opera" debuted in San Francisco on April 26, 1925, and made box office history. Considering the production delays, the creative differences, the hirings and firings, and the massive re-editing involved in trying to save the picture, the film turned out reasonably well.

Surprisingly faithful to its 1911 source, "The Phantom of the Opera" embraces many of the elements which made the book so memorable, including the masked ball, the chandelier disaster, Christine's journey to the Phantom's subterranean hideaway, and the famous unmasking. Gounod's "Faust," which also figured in the original novel, has been retained to suggest Erik's pact with dark, preternatural forces, and the inclusion of the mysterious Persian (identified as "Ledoux") draws attention to the Phantom's bloody past. The only major sequence that has been omitted from the film is the young singer's visit to her father's grave. Otherwise, the events of the book, from the opening scene with the ballet girls to Christine's deadly choice (between a scorpion and a grasshopper), have been beautifully rendered on film. The two-strip Technicolor sequence, in which Erik appears as Edgar Allan Poe's "Red Death" at the Masked Ball, is matched only by the unmasking scene as the best in the silent picture. When the Phantom makes his majestic entry down the grand staircase of the Opera, the dancing revelers part in horror (like the Red Sea before Moses). Costumed all in red, he is the living embodiment of death, and any who remain in his way fall victim as his prey. Regrettably, Erik's demise - so poetically realized in Leroux's narrative - has been exchanged for a routine chase and summary execution by the French mob.

Most of the acting is consistent with the given limitations of the silent cinema. Mary Philbin, a twenty-one year-old beauty queen, tries her best to add complexity to the role of Christine Daae but is ultimately handcuffed by the melodramatic direction of Rupert Julian. Norman Kerry is stiff and useless as the hero, and Arthur Edmund Carew turns in an effective yet underscored performance as Ledoux. As for the Phantom, Lon Chaney is arrogant, self-assured, mad, passionate, and darkly sinister in a role that he was born to play.

Unlike Gaston Leroux's mad musical genius who chose to hide his birth-defect from polite, French society, however, Chaney's Phantom was an escapee from Devil's Island. Confined during the Commune in the dungeon and torture chambers below the playhouse, he chose to remain. When the film opens, ten years later, he is still living there, out of sight, haunting the Paris Opera House. Although numerous references link the Phantom to his Middle-Eastern origins, no explanation is ever offered as to how Erik managed to furnish such a wondrous lair. His motivation (for saving Raoul and Ledoux) offers similar confusion. After saving the two men from drowning, he again kidnaps Christine and races from the playhouse in a stolen carriage. If (all along) he had intended to spirit the young singer away, why rescue the very men who might later track him to the four corners of the world? His actions make little sense for a man who has spent years developing a superior intellect in order to compete with normal men. But these inconsistencies, after all, are minor when you consider the film as a whole and recognize the outstanding central performance of Chaney as the living embodiment of Leroux's Opera Ghost.

Contrary to popular opinion at the time, Chaney's makeover as Erik the Phantom was not based on a mask or layers of face putty, but his own skill as a makeup artist. "There are tricks in my peculiar trade that I don't care to divulge any more than a magician would give away his art," Lon confided in an interview conducted a few months before his death. "In 'The Phantom of the Opera' people exclaimed at my weird makeup. I achieved the death's head of that role without wearing a mask. It was use of paint in the right shades and the right places - not the obvious parts of the face - which gave the illusion of horror."

Lon Chaney used not only grease paint to create the suggestion of a living skull but also special devices which altered the appearance of his face. First, he attached a strip of fish skin (a thin, translucent material) to his nostrils with spirit gum, pulled it back until he got the tilt he wanted, then attached the other end of the fish skin under his bald cap. For some shots, he inserted a small wire into his nose, which would spread his nostrils wide and tilt the tip upward and back to give a skeletal effect. According to cameraman Charles Van Enger, the wire cut into his nose and caused a good deal of bleeding. Then, he used prongs attached to protruding false teeth to draw his mouth back at the corners to achieve the skull-like grin. He glued his ears back. Drops in his eyes produced the bloodshot, pop-eyed look. Next, he placed circular disks of cotton and collodion in his mouth to accentuate his cheekbones, and finally, on the top of his head, he secured a domed wig of skin, stranded with lank hair. The result - which typically took several hours to achieve - was one of the greatest contributions to the silent cinema and assured Chaney's place in film history. The sight was said to have caused some patrons at the premiere to have fainted.

Although Lon Chaney's makeup merely hints at the hideous description of the Phantom from Leroux's original novel, it is certainly very effective. Prior to the film's release, not one photograph of Chaney's Phantom was issued to the press. Thus, when Erik's face is eventually revealed, late in the film, it was a terrifying surprise for audience members. The classic sequence of shots - regarded, by many, as the best montage ever devised in the history of the cinema -reveals his horrible visage not once but twice. By careful placement of his camera and the two lead characters, Julian doubles the shock value. For the first shock, though she cannot see his face, Christine removes his mask for the audience. Then, for the second shock, the Phantom turns to face her, and we see the horror reflected in her eyes. "Feast your eyes, glut your soul, on my accursed ugliness!" he exclaims to the young singer, but his message is really meant for the audience in what remains the best unmasking sequence in horror movies.

Critic Roberta O'Toole admitted: "I shrieked right out loud in the theatre and buried my head unashamedly on my husband's chest when Mary Philbin slipped the mask off Chaney as he sat playing the organ." The revelation sent shudders through most audience members, and caused many women to faint and grown men to cry in terror. So awful was the sight, many theatre managers (upon the advice of studio publicists) purchased additional stocks of smelling salts in advance to revive their nervous patrons. O'Toole, who was one of the few critics to write favorably about the movie when it first debuted, proclaimed that "his outraged visage was horror incarnate: bulging, blooshot eyes fatigued with violet semicircles beneath them; the grotesquely exaggerated mounds of cheekbones; the looked-up, flaring, porcine nostrils; the rotted, jagged teeth, like the rim of an enameled tin can top opened with a ragged knife; the scraggly strands of dead gray hair hanging like soggy serpentine from the incredible pyramid of a head. Chaney's Phantom is truly the master of all he surveys!"

Lon Chaney – The Master of a Thousand Faces

Even though many of her contemporaries did not share Roberta O'Toole's enthusiasm for the motion picture, "The Phantom of the Opera" soon became an unqualified success. Audiences were compelled by Chaney's performance, and returned again and again to be frightened by his Phantom. Each decade would have its stock menace, an expert in contortion and make-up, who became the cinema's resident monster and mad psychotic. In the Thirties and Forties, it was Boris Karloff; in the Fifties Vincent Price; in the Sixties Christopher Lee, and in the Eighties Robert Englund; but Chaney dominated the Twenties with a series of brilliant characterizations of legless freaks, twisted hunchbacks, and demented composers. "Don't step on IT! It may be Lon Chaney" was the catch phrase and slogan which identified the actor at the height of his career. Chaney, in real life, was a rather ordinary-looking, slightly middle-aged man, with horn-rimmed glasses and a face that made him look more like a business manager than an actor. He spent more than ten years of his life altering that image (by twisting his body or distorting his face), and established the fashion for movie monsters to come. His roles became so legendary that everyone in the industry began calling him "the man of a thousand faces".

Alonzo Chaney was born April Fool's Day of 1883 in Colorado Springs. Because both of his parents were deaf mutes, he developed skillful mine in learning to communicate with them. He dropped out of school at age 12 to care for his sick mother, and worked many odd jobs before joining his brother's traveling theatrical troupe. Lon Chaney began his career as a stage actor (in 1901), by playing a variety of roles from the hero to the villain to the spear carrier. "It was purely by chance," he dismissed his inate ability to undergo fearsome physical deformation.

"All during that time, the thing that interested me most was makeup, but not merely grease-paint and putty noses but mental make-up as well. If I played the role of an old man, I tried to crawl into the old man's mind. .." His first screen appearance was twelve years later in "Poor Jake's Demise" (1913). Executives at Universal Pictures (notably Carl Laemmle) saw great potential in Chaney's work and signed him to an exclusive contract for $5 a day. "The False Faces" (1919) was one of his earlier make-up jobs and virtually launched his film career. He continued to playa variety of roles which required the use of grotesque makeup or physical transformation, including Fagin in "Oliver Twist" (1922), Quasimodo in "The Hunchback of Notre Dame" (1923), and Erik, the disfigured composer, in "The Phantom of the Opera" (1925).

Lon Chaney followed his role in that silent classic by playing a fictitious vampire in Tod Browning's "London After Midnight" (1927). Universal tried several times to convince rival Louis B. Mayer (at M-G-M) to loan Chaney again for a film titled "The Return of the Phantom" (of the Opera), but the aging mogul refused. Instead Lon made "The Bugle Sounds" (1927), "Laugh, Clown, Laugh" (1928), and "West of Zanzibar" (1928). Carl Laemmle Jr. did finally manage to acquire him for the role of Dracula at Universal, but Chaney became suddenly ill and died of throat cancer on August 26, 1930, having spoken only once on the sound screen. (In fact, he spoke in four different voices, as a sideshow ventriloquist, in the talkie remake of "The Unholy Three", 1930.) Although only a handful of his 150 movie roles have survived to this day, Chaney is considered one of the great stars of the silent screen. And with his passing, the silent era came to a close, heralding a new epoch of sound motion pictures.

The 1929 Re-Issue

Two years after "The Phantom of the Opera" was released, Warner Brothers introduced the first "talkie" with "The Jazz Singer" and revolutionized the motion picture industry. Carl Laemmle and his corporate executives at Universal recognized that the silent picture was doomed by the new technology of sound and examined their existing roster of films in an effort to determine which ones might benefit from a sound track. Not surprisingly, they selected one the studio's most successful and influential films, "The Phantom of the Opera."

Whole dialogue sequences, featuring opera singer Mary Fabian (singing the role of Carlotta) and Norman Kerry, were written by Frank McCormack and shot by Ernest Laemmle. In the re-edited version, Virginia Pearson, who had played Carlotta in the silent 1925 version, is credited and referred to as "Carlotta's Mother" instead. Several sections, notably those featuring Chester Conklin, were dropped, while singing voices were recorded to highlight the various scenes from "Faust." Music and other sound effects were added to the silent sections, and Lon Chaney's Phantom was dubbed by a contract player. For the sound edition, Lon Chaney was not available, and contractually, Universal Pictures was not allowed to have mouth synchronization of the Phantom. However, they cleverly wrote third-person lines to be dubbed over shots of the Phantom's shadow. The voice to these lines was unacredited, but probably belonged to that of Universal regular Phillips Smalley. Nearly, forty percent of the film was re-shot in synchronous sound, and the rest had music or sound effects added.

"The Phantom of the Opera" was re-released in sound in 1929 using Vitaphone/Western Electric sounds disks. While less than a third of the motion picture had actual dialogue and singing, the re-release advertised "Talking! Singing! Dancing! Sound Effects! Music! Color!" And the first translation of Leroux's work enjoyed another brief moment in the spotlight before "Dracula" (1931), "Frankenstein" (1931), and their progeny established a brand new tradition for horror movies.

Finis

Slightly more than fifteen years after the film's debut, on December 11, 1940, Lon Chaney Junior attended a ceremony which honored his late father. Having just completed work on his first horror movie entitled "Man Made Monster" for Universal, young Chaney was following in his father's footsteps. On the great set of the Paris Opera House, five survivors of the original crew acknowledged him as Lon's successor and unveiled a plaque to his father, which read: "Dedicated to the memory of Lon Chaney, for whose picture 'The Phantom of the Opera' this stage was erected in 1924." Even though Lon Chaney and his illustrious son are no longer with us, the legacy of the Phantom lives on. That plaque and the original sound stage still

exists today, a popular stop on the famous Universal Studios Tour. And, if tour-goers listen closely, they can still hear the familiar chords of Bach's "Tocatta & Fugue in D Minor" echoing from the dark cellars of that familiar playhouse.

The silent version of "The Phantom of the Opera" is available on DVD and videocassette from a variety of sources. The videodisc version differs slightly from the others in that it offers both the 1925 original and the 1929 partial-talkie as well as marvelous behind-the-scenes material. The print restored by the Kino company is a 1929 re-release version that was re-edited, eliminating some scenes and inserting new material shot after the 1925 version was finished. This version also contains an original score composed by Gabriel Thibaudoux, and includes an operatic solo by soprano Claudine Cote. Kenneth Brownilow finished a complete restoration of the 1925 original edit in 1996 with an original score by BBC composer Carl Davis, but this film has only been shown twice in live performances and is not available commercially or on video. Another full restoration was completed by Richard Lloyd in 1999, with the transfer from D1 supervised by Kevin Phelan (Digital Film at The Moving Picture Company). The film is also available as a computer colorized version.

Other Related Productions

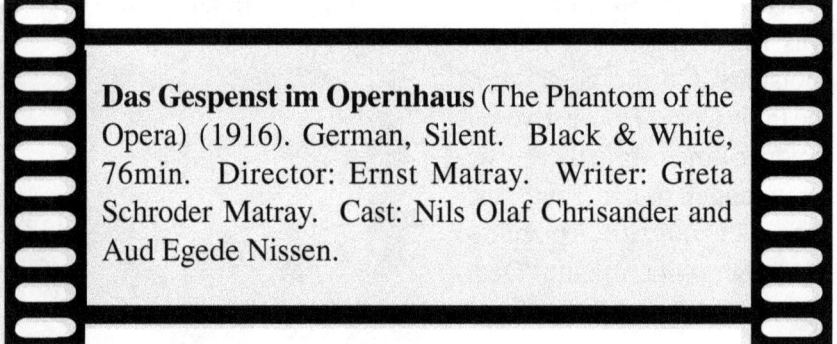

Das Gespenst im Opernhaus (The Phantom of the Opera) (1916). German, Silent. Black & White, 76min. Director: Ernst Matray. Writer: Greta Schroder Matray. Cast: Nils Olaf Chrisander and Aud Egede Nissen.

Five years after the publication of Gaston Leroux's famous novel, Ernst Matray's 1916 adaptation of "The Phantom of the Opera" debuted in Germany. It was the very first version of *Le Fantôme de l'Opera*, easily one of three or four most copied stories in the history of cinema. The tale of the disfigured musical genius and his unrequited love for a beautiful, young singer was a familiar one to most Europeans at the time, and featured Nils Olaf Chrisander and Aud

Egede Nissen in the roles of the Phantom and Christine. Shot by Matray, the Hungarian director who would later become a noted choreographer and dance teacher, the silent film relies on sexual undertones as well as shock-aspects that seem clearly dated now but were quite controversial in its day to advance the plot. Ironically, the titular character is only seen on screen for a bit less than twelve minutes in total throughout the whole film.

Frenchman Gaston Leroux had not given his permission for this German adaptation, and even though his country was at war with Germany, he sued the production company for copyright infringement in the world court. All known prints and negatives were destroyed under the terms of a settlement of the lawsuit. However, the film would subsequently surface in other countries, and incomplete copies of the 1916 motion picture still exist today.

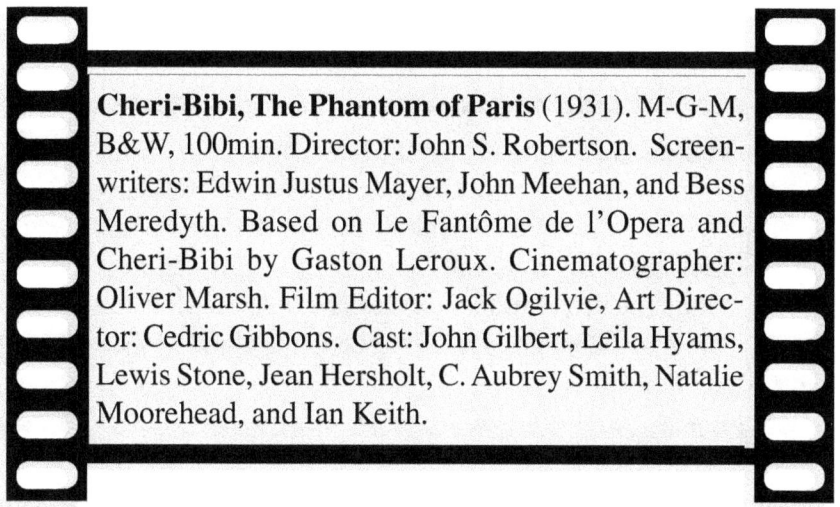

Cheri-Bibi, The Phantom of Paris (1931). M-G-M, B&W, 100min. Director: John S. Robertson. Screenwriters: Edwin Justus Mayer, John Meehan, and Bess Meredyth. Based on Le Fantôme de l'Opera and Cheri-Bibi by Gaston Leroux. Cinematographer: Oliver Marsh. Film Editor: Jack Ogilvie, Art Director: Cedric Gibbons. Cast: John Gilbert, Leila Hyams, Lewis Stone, Jean Hersholt, C. Aubrey Smith, Natalie Moorehead, and Ian Keith.

Very loosely based on two of Gaston Leroux's famous novels, *Le Fantôme de l'Opera* and *Cheri-Bibi*, this 1931 John Gilbert talkie featured the (then) highest paid star in Hollywood as Cheri-Bibi, the most celebrated magician & escape artist in France. Young & debonair, he enjoys the attentions of society and the love of one young woman, Cecile (Leila Hyams). But when her wealthy father Bourrelier (C. Aubrey Smith) is found murdered and all evidence points to Bibi, he must put all his considerable talents into evading the law long enough to clear his name - while being forced to live a life in the shadows as "The Phantom of Paris." Ultimately, he learns that

Maximillan, the Marquis Du Touchais (Ian Keith), his romantic rival, is responsible for the murder, and must take on Max's identity when he dies unexpectedly to clear his name and put the blame where it belongs.

Directed John S. Robertson, the movie was to have featured Lon Chaney in a role very similar to his Phantom of the Opera; in fact, studio boss Louis B. Mayer hoped to profit from the Universal silent as audiences were clamoring for a sequel. But Chaney died before he was to make it. Mayer cast John Gilbert, another box office draw, in the role instead. According to cinematic legend, Mayer bitterly hated Gilbert, but knew that he needed a star to sell the picture, and had an eight-picture contract with the actor. John Gilbert actually does a fine job throughout much of the film, and shines in sequences when he is forced into the shadows as the Phantom. One wonders what Lon Chaney might have done with the role.

Ye Ban Ge Sheng (Song at Midnight). (1937). Chinese, B&W, 113 min. Director and Writer: Weibang Mz-Xu. Producer: Shankun Zhang. Cinematographer: Boqing Xue and Xingsan Yu. Film Editor: Yinqing Chen. Production Designer: Yigan Mou and Yungqiao Zhang. Cast: Menghe Gu, Ping Hu, Shan Jin, and Chao Shi.

Directed by the great Weibang Ma-Xu, who fell out of favor with the Communists prior to World War 2, this unique version of Gaston Leroux's famous novel tells the story of a disfigured opera star and his plot for revenge on the local power cartel that destroyed his career. When a traveling opera company arrives at the run down provincial theatre, a mysterious hooded figure takes a keen interest in its young star. Their star is having problems but he is coached to triumph by the "phantom" (inexplicably referred to as "Dr. Song"), who reveals in flashback form to have been ruined when he romanced the daughter of an influential family. His young protege sings under the window of the Song's old love now deranged, who takes him for her former lover. When his old nemesis menaces the ingénue of the company, the Phantom attacks him and is burned in a tower building by an angry mob.

Even without the subtitles, "Ye Ban Ge Sheng" is easily followed. Viewers are helped by a familiarity with "The Phantom of the Opera." When the film debuted in 1937, Chinese intellectuals who had embraced Communism dismissed Weibang Ma-Xu's excellent adaptation. Ma-Xu remained undaunted, and made a semi-sequel with some of the original cast and crew, titled "Ye Ban Ge Sheng Xu Ji" ("Songs at Midnight, the Sequel") in 1941, but his new film had only very limited release in Hong Kong. Both productions were thought to have been lost during the war, but have recently surfaced on battered but watchable copies.

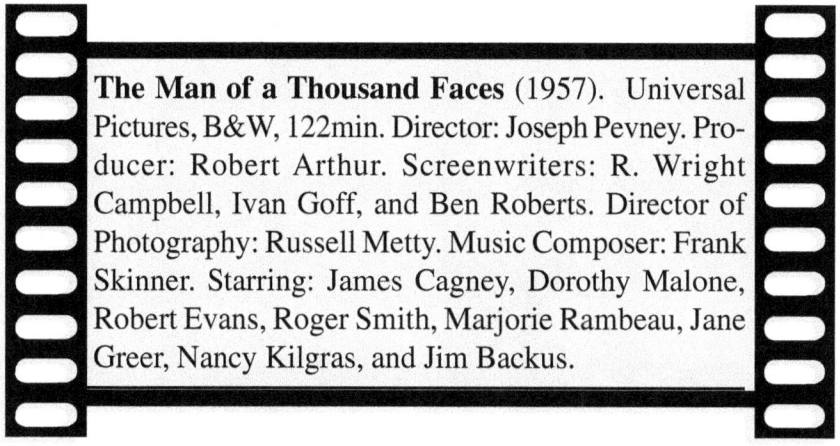

The Man of a Thousand Faces (1957). Universal Pictures, B&W, 122min. Director: Joseph Pevney. Producer: Robert Arthur. Screenwriters: R. Wright Campbell, Ivan Goff, and Ben Roberts. Director of Photography: Russell Metty. Music Composer: Frank Skinner. Starring: James Cagney, Dorothy Malone, Robert Evans, Roger Smith, Marjorie Rambeau, Jane Greer, Nancy Kilgras, and Jim Backus.

"The Man of a Thousand Faces" (1957) was a moderately successful biographical motion picture about the rise to fame of silent screen character actor Lon Chaney. The film recreates the famous unmasking from "The Phantom of the Opera," with Cagney wearing a less-than-believable mask, on the famous opera house set (Stage 28), opposite Nancy Kilgras as Mary Philbin. Other facsimiles of Chaney's disguises are used to recreate his famous gallery of tortured grotesques. Even though the script received an Academy Award-nomination, it is rather childlike in its simplicity, creating stereo-

types of the actor's deaf-mute parents (Nolan Leary and Celia Lovsky) and ungrateful wife (Dorothy Malone). The film does have a strong sense of period Hollywood, and provides a wonderful insight into the inner workings of the studio system. (Notation: the famous unmasking sequence with Lon Chaney was also spliced into Universal's 1951 mystery "Hollywood Story.")

~ 4 ~
The Enchanted Violin of Erique Claudin

[Christine covers her face and sobs]
Claudin: *They've poisoned your mind against me. That's why you're afraid. Look at your lake, Christine. You'll love it here when you get used to the dark. The music comes down and the darkness distills it, cleanses it of the suffering that made it. Then it's all beauty. And life here is like a resurrection.*
—The 1943 Version

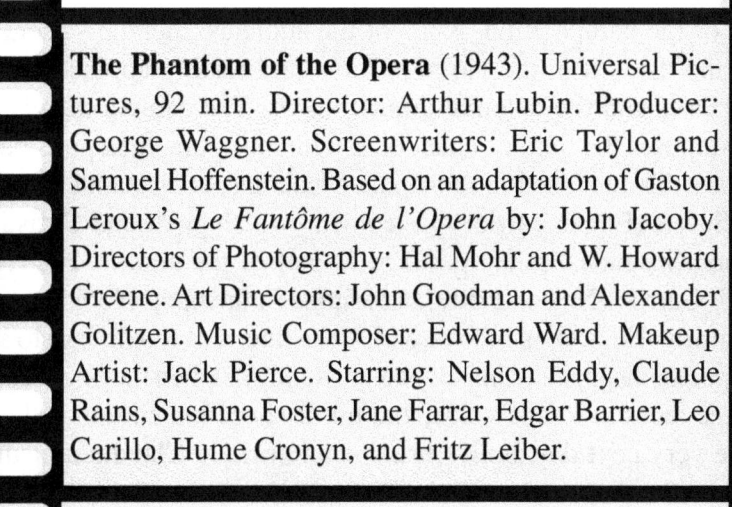

The Phantom of the Opera (1943). Universal Pictures, 92 min. Director: Arthur Lubin. Producer: George Waggner. Screenwriters: Eric Taylor and Samuel Hoffenstein. Based on an adaptation of Gaston Leroux's *Le Fantôme de l'Opera* by: John Jacoby. Directors of Photography: Hal Mohr and W. Howard Greene. Art Directors: John Goodman and Alexander Golitzen. Music Composer: Edward Ward. Makeup Artist: Jack Pierce. Starring: Nelson Eddy, Claude Rains, Susanna Foster, Jane Farrar, Edgar Barrier, Leo Carillo, Hume Cronyn, and Fritz Leiber.

The 1943 rendering of "The Phantom of the Opera," the most extravagant production of its time and the first sound version, is also the least satisfying in terms of cinema and cinematic adaptation. Produced at a cost of $ 1.75 million, the motion picture boasts lavish costumes, elaborate set designs, and operatic sequences recorded (for the first time) with pristine clarity. But the real menace, so chillingly portrayed by Lon Chaney in the 1925 silent and driving force of the film's action is conspicuously absent. In fact, when Universal Pictures revised most of the story's mythic elements and erotic horror in favor of a standard Forties musical, the central character of the Phantom was reduced to secondary importance. Whereas Gaston Leroux's story requires a strong figure to terrorize the Paris Opera House as well as compete for the attention of the young singer, the Phantom in this motion picture appears simply as an afterthought. Tragically, this flawed cinematic monstrosity, directed by Arthur Lubin, is more opera than opera ghost.

The Screen Story

The film opens predictably as the orchestra of the Paris Opera House begins playing the overture to Friedrich Von Flotow's "Martha." Erique Claudin (Claude Rains), one of the many violinists, appears very adept at his craft but continues to miss key transitions in the music. After twenty years of service to the orchestra, his fingers have grown weak, and he can no longer maintain pace with the hectic demands of the composition. None of the audience members seem to notice the discord in the violin section, and readily applaud as the curtain rises and the colonial drama begins. The camera travels up and juxtaposes the famous chandelier with the opera, then pulls back to reveal a distinguished-looking police man. Inspector Raoul Daubert of the Surete (Edgar Barrier) has come to watch girlfriend Christine Du Bois (Susanna Foster) perform as part of the chorus. His rival Anatole Garron (Nelson Eddy), a baritone in the opera, looks at him disdainfully. He, too, is in love with Christine, and would like to see the inspector disappear. Unfortunately (for him), when the opera ends, Christine races to Raoul's side, and misses her final curtain call.

The very next day, both Christine and Erique Claudin are summoned to the director's office. He reminds the young soprano that she must choose between two different lifestyles, one devoted to music, or one devoted to a husband and family. He does not want to see her years of singing wasted. As she exists, Erique is called. The two pass each other in the hall, and Claudin - enchanted by her beauty and talent - tells Christine that he is her eternal servant. Moments later, the middle-aged violinist is then discharged from the orchestra because the director realizes Claudin can no longer perform. Alone and discouraged, he returns to an empty household. Erique Claudin is broke and can no longer pay his landlady. For the last three years, he has been secretly paying Signor Ferretti (Leo Carrillo), a great music professor, to give her music lessons; but now the money has run out. Christine is totally unaware of Claudin's patronage or undying devotion, and he has nothing else to show for his twenty years of service except an unpublished concerto that he's written.

With the hopes of selling his manuscript, Erique Claudin sends it to Pleyel and Desjardins, then impatiently barges into the music publisher's office, demanding that he be given a few moments time. Pleyel (Miles Mander) is more interested in playing with his female assistant than looking at his work and tries to dismiss the distraught musician. At about the same time, Franz Litz (played by science fiction great Fritz Leiber's grandfather) sits down at a piano in the next room and plays a few notes (at the insistance of a junior patner). Hearing his composition played in the adjacent room and believing that it has been stolen, Claudin attacks and strangles Pleyel. He becomes hideously disfigured when a tray of acid is hurled in his face by the publisher's female assistant, and runs into the night, a broken man. The police are called, but Erique manages to elude them, escaping into a convenient sewer hole located beneath a stationary carriage. He follows the sewer tunnels into the dark, labyrinthine world below the Paris Opera House.

Several weeks later, the managers of the theatre notice that food, costumes, and other items are mysteriously vanishing.

Several backstage sightings of a masked figure in a dark cloak are reported, but no one seems to have gotten a very good look at him. They believe the mysterious figure is the Opera ghost.

"Amour Gloire," a fictitious opera utilizing themes from Chopin, opens the new season, and members of the rich, upper class crowd into the theatre. As Christine completes final preparation in her dressing room before going onstage, she is told by a disembodied voice that tonight all the world would know her voice. She tries to locate the source of the prophecy, but finds no one. During the performance, the Phantom gingerly slips poison into the resident diva's glass, and Christine is called to take her place when Laurence Biancaroll (Jane Farrar) can no longer continue. The young understudy triumphs in the lead role, and further enchants her two suitors with her angelic, charismatic voice. Below the opera house, Claudin listens to Christine's glorious performance and weeps with happiness.

The resident diva recovers from the poison, and accuses Christine and Anatole of attempted murder. Inspector Daubert dismisses the charges, claiming that someone else is responsible. He begins to piece together parts of the puzzle, and determines that Erique Claudin has been haunting the opera house on account of his dismissal from the orchestra. When a letter arrives demanding that the young singer be given the lead role in a concerto written by the deceased composer, Raoul arranges a trap to capture the murderer. He then places several of his men in the choral section of the new production. Dressed as one of the many costumed police officers, the Phantom easily infiltrates the troupe and starts searching for Christine. She has retired to her dressing room, at the insistance of Raoul, and does not plan to sing Claudin's concerto. Inspector Daubert and the managers have duped him, by assigning the lead role to Biancaroll. Angered, he cuts the chain that suspends the chandelier over the auditorium, and sends it crashing down. In the chaos following its lethal decent, Erique abducts Christine from backstage, taking her down through the long corridors to his underground lair. Once there, he begins playing his concerto. He insists that the young soprano sing along, and she does so unwillingly. Her voice echoes through the dark tunnels, and provides Raoul and Anatole with a direction to her whereabouts. The two men quickly follow in pursuit, the inspector from the Surete armed with his service revolver.

Meanwhile, Christine has managed to get closer and closer to Claudin. She finally snatches the Phantom's mask and reveals the disfigured face of the middle-aged violinist. At that very moment, her two suitors burst in and rescue her from his evil clutches. A shot is fired, and Erique Claudin is buried in a rockslide triggered by the sound. Raoul and Anatole rush the young singer to safety (in the nick of time). The final image of his mask and violin reminds the audience of the Phantom's unhappy demise. Later, in a needless postscript, both the baritone and the inspector arrive at Christine's dressing room door for dinner after her triumph on the stage. She dismisses them both in order to face her public, and the two bachelors decide to have dinner together.

Production Notes

The fact that "The Phantom of the Opera" (1943) is more of a musical spectacular than a bizarre thriller may reflect the cautious time in which the motion picture was made. The innovative richness of the Twenties and Thirties had been followed by a period of disintegration and decline wherein the horror film descended to its lowest level. The old Hollywood, which had produced such cinematic gems as Lon Chaney's "The Phantom of the Opera" (1925), Bela Lugosi's

"Dracula" (1931), and Boris Karloff's "Frankenstein" (1931), had passed away into legend, and what remained was an industry in which the values and foundations of the past had been muted and corrupted into something that was largely unrecognizable. Carl Laemmle Jr. was dead, and his eagerness to experiment with bold, original ideas and had been replaced by an attitude of conservatism as well as a general lack of vision. Wild-eyed auteurs, like Tod Browning and James Whale, were supplanted by business-suited executives with accounting ledgers and corporate mentalities. Productions became a matter of dollars and cents rather than imaginative creativity.

As a result, the new bosses of Universal Pictures, convinced that they knew what audiences really wanted, teamed the famous monsters of filmland with silly comics or simply turned to the safety of remaking past motion picture hits. They reasoned that members of the public, who had suffered through the ravages of the Depression and the climate of fear precipitated by the Second World War, would buy tickets to laugh at the likes of Abbott & Costello or be wowed by the latest advances in Technicolor and sound. The 1943 version of "The Phantom of the Opera" was conceived by that corporate mentality, rather than inspired by a creative director or producer who had a new vision of the Gaston Leroux classic.

Insult was added to injury when horror films came under attack for decency in the early Forties. During World War Two, horror films were banned in England, parts of Europe and North Africa because individual governments thought these motion pictures had a negative effect on morale. Soon after the war, stricter regulations dealing with theme and content were initiated throughout the world; in particular, the United Kingdom established the British Board of Film Censors. That organization became the watchdog of the Eastern Hemisphere, creating the first rating system for movies. A "U"-rating meant that a film was suitable for general audiences (today, the equivalent of a "G" rating.) An "A"-rating meant that the film was mature and suggested parental guidance (much like the "PG," or "PG-13" rating). The kiss of death for most movies, in that era of repression, was the "H"-rating, which meant that the film was graphic in its portrayal of horror (equivalent to an "R" or "X"-rating, today). The Motion Picture Association of America (MPAA) followed the lead of the United Kingdom.

Many horror films, except for the light, comic spoofs, were classified under that rating system and came under the attack of religious and civic groups. That threat translated to fewer markets and even less take at the box office. Studio executives became very cautious with the type of product they created, and may have insisted that a remake of "The Phantom of the Opera" focus more on opera than horror. Thus, the darker, expressionistic vision of the first motion picture was exchanged for a bright, Technicolor extravaganza. Featuring lavish costumes, elaborate set designs, and musical sequences that would be staged with a large cast of operatic singers, the production resembled a Busby Berkley spectacular, rather than a typical horror film. Universal Studios, which had distinguished itself in the past with low-budget horror films, Sherlock Holmes thrillers, and Abbott & Costello comedies, now looked at competing with the A-quality pictures of M-G-M, Paramount, and Warner Brothers.

Originally, the film had been intended as a vehicle for the popular singing actress Deana Durbin in the role of Christine, with Broderick Crawford cast as the Phantom. But the United States entry into World War Two in December 1941 meant that most leading men (Crawford included) would be drafted into military service. The celebrated but portly British actor Charles Laughton was the next choice of studio executives. A few years earlier, he had scored big with the remake of "The Hunchback of Notre Dame" (1940), and was renowned for his distinguished elocution. However, the project fell apart less than six weeks later due to production delays, salary negotiations, and numerous script revisions.

By 1943, Universal Pictures had again altered the focus of the motion picture. Deana Durbin and Charles Laughton were out, and the role of Anatole Garron was rewritten and enlarged to accommodate the baritone sensation Nelson Eddy (recently split from his "singing sweetheart" Jeanette MacDonald). He was to be paired with the newly discovered Susanna Foster, who had made her film debut in "The Great Victor Herbert" in 1940 at the age of fifteen. Producer George Waggner had hoped their teaming would create a new screen partnership, that Eddy and Foster would become "America's (new) singing sweethearts," but he failed to consider the vast discrepancy in their ages. Other production changes were likewise unexceptional and not fully thought out. Arthur Lubin, known primarily for his lackluster Abbott & Costello comedies, had replaced both Henry Koster and William Diertele as director, and contract player Claude Rains was cast in the secondary but pivotal role of the Phantom.

Claude Rains, a soft-spoken and distinguished British actor, was certainly no stranger to imaginative thrillers. Ten years before, he "appeared" in his first film as doomed scientist Jack Giffin, "The Invisible Man" (1933). Although audience members don't see him until the final seconds of the movie, Rains made a lasting impression in James Whale's brilliant adaptation of the H.G. Wells novel. He went onto play King John, opposite Errol Flynn and Basil Rathbone in "The Adventures of Robin Hood" (1938), and pivotal roles in "Mr. Smith Goes to Washington" (1939), "The Sea Hawk" (1940), and "Here Comes Mr. Jordan" (1941). Ironically, though he lost the role of the wolf man to Lon Chaney Jr., his portrayal of the sympathetic violinist in "The Phantom of the Opera" opened the door to numerous other opportunities. His breakthrough came as Inspector Louis Renault in what many consider to be the greatest motion picture ever made, "Casablanca" (1942). As the scheming, cynical director of police, Rains managed to upstage both Bogart and Bergman in a number of key scenes. That fine performance led to fifty other screen appearances in films as diverse as "Mr. Skeffington" (1944), "Notorious" (1946), "The Lost World" (1960), and "Lawrence of Arabia" (1962). His thirty-five year career ended with a small cameo in George Stevens' "The Greatest Story Ever Told" (1965); he died two years later. Though hardly one of the highpoints of his career, Rains essays a brief yet capable turn as the Phantom.

Unlike Gaston Leroux's mad musical genius, however, the second authorized version of *The Phantom of the Opera* (to reach the silver screen) is portrayed as a pathetic, old man whose musical abilities are fading. Whereas Lon Chaney's Erik was an escapee from Devil's Island who had been confined in the torture chamber below the theatre, Erique Claudin is an ordinary man whose life is suddenly changed by an unfortunate series of events. When he fears his musical concerto has been stolen and he wrongly strangles the unsympathetic publisher, a tray of acid is thrown into his face. Only then, does Claudin (as the Phantom) begin his journey toward madness, which climaxes with him dropping a chandelier on innocent bystanders. Soon after, he spirits the young singer away to his underground lair and declares his undying affection, like a lovesick teen, even though he is old enough to be her father. He even resembles Christine's father (from the book), more so than the Phantom. The original script revealed Claudin to be Christine's father, who abandoned her and her mother in order to pursue a musical career. When this was excised from the final film, it left Claudin's obsession with Christine unexplained and just a bit creepy.

The Frenchman's creation was born with his physical deformity, and developed his keen, highly resourceful personality in order to survive. His madness was the result of years of isolation and loneliness as well as the scorn of a society that viewed ugliness as evil. He tutors Christine because his soul is filled with music, and falls in love with her voice. Their two characters may appear to be superficially alike, but they are, in fact, two completely different, diametrically opposed individuals.

Besides the transmutation of the story's central figure, screenwriters Eric Taylor and Samuel Hoffenstein (working from an adaptation by John Jacoby) have greatly altered or discarded elements of Leroux's bizarre thriller to favor their musical monstrosity. Names have been inexplicably changed, and characters - not the least of whom is the Phantom - have been totally rewritten. Raoul, for example, is now a policeman, instead of an aristocrat; the Persian, Joseph Buquet, Madame Giry and her daughter have all been dropped, and baritone Anatole Garron has taken their place at center stage. While his appearance may provide a romantic tension (which should rightly belong to the Phantom) between Raoul and Christine, none of the other deletions make sense. Gounod's "Faust," utilized in the original novel to suggest a demonic pact, has been replaced with Flotow's "Martha" and two bogus operas comprised of themes from Chopin and

Tchaikowsky. While the music is very beautiful (including a new composition by Edward Ward), the pieces contribute very little thematically to the film. Because the war in Europe made it so difficult to track down who had who had the rights to most operas (coupled with the studios reluctance to pay the required royalties) all the operas performed in the film were either in the public domain or were based on classical music that was in the public domain. The film makers were able to slip in a reference to the opera Faust (which featured heavily in the original novel) by having Christine appear in the Marguerite costume as she comes off stage at the end of the film. Other elements, including the famous masked ball, Christine's nightly visit to her father's grave, and the lover's rendezvous on the roof of the Paris Opera House, and the torture chamber, are also curiously missing. Instead Taylor and Hoffenstein "treat" the audience to one fully-blown operatic sequence after another.

Director Arthur Lubin tries his best to make these disparate elements come together into a cohesive narrative; unfortunately, lacking the skill of an auteur like Browning or Whale, his cinematic approach to the material is rather a conventional one. He seems comfortable staging the large, lavish production numbers, but when it comes to creating an atmosphere of terror and menace, he is completely out of his depth. The Phantom's haunting of the Paris Opera House, which was filmed in the auditorium and stage set built for the 1925 version, is never fully explored by Lubin. Similarly, Christine's journey to Erique's underground lair lacks any tension or suspense. (She might as well be walking around a lake at night.) Even the revelation of the Phantom's face, which was one of the high points of the first film, is rather unspectacular.

Part of the blame for the failure of this important sequence belongs to the makeup supervisor. Jack Pierce, the artist who had made Boris Karloff into both the Mummy and the Frankenstein monster, had turned Bela Lugosi into the Transylvanian Count, and had transformed Lon Chaney Jr. into the wolf man, worked hard to achieve something special for Claude Rains other than the much celebrated death's head Chaney had created for the first film. Regrettably, when the mask is finally snatched from his face by Christine, there is nothing the least bit frightening about his face. He appears to have a simple birth mark or unpleasant skin ailment. Having served the industry for more than twenty-two years, Pierce had been responsible for a number of innovations in his particular field. But, with all the new advances in plastic and foam rubber, Pierce was unwilling to change and found his services no longer needed at Universal Pictures. He worked on his last monster film, "House of Dracula" (1945), two years later, and quietly retired in 1946. (Ironically, Pierce's designs for the Frankenstein monster would become the standard for the next thirty years.)

The Release and Aftermath

"The Phantom of the Opera," Universal's most expensive endeavor up to that time (costing a total of $1.75 million), was an enormous box office success when it was first released on August 27, 1943, and spawned a semi-sequel (entitled "The Climax") which premiered the following year. Although critics were quick to find fault with the production, particularly in light of the wonderful 1925 version, the film went onto win two Academy Awards from the Academy of Motion Picture Arts and Sciences for Best Art Direction (Alexander Golitzen and John Goodman) and Best Cinematography (W. Howard Greene and Hal Mohr) at the ceremony in 1944. Today, when viewed in retrospect on videocassette or DVD, the 1943 version clearly reveals its age. More opera than opera ghost, the film represents the weakest retelling of Gaston Leroux's familiar tale.

Other Related Productions

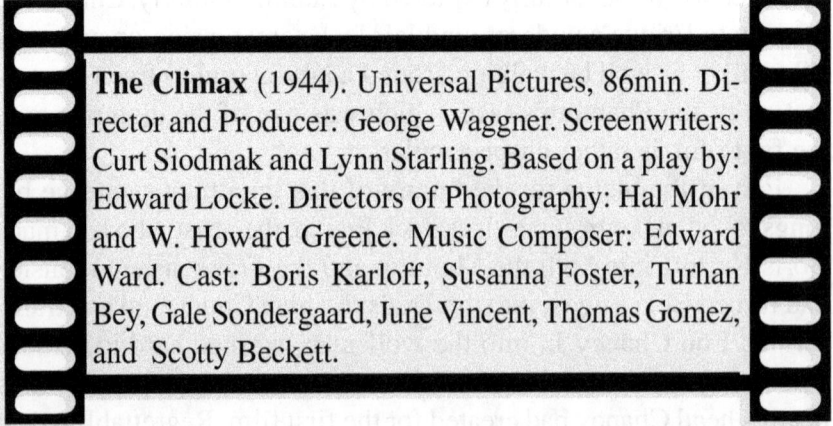

The Climax (1944). Universal Pictures, 86min. Director and Producer: George Waggner. Screenwriters: Curt Siodmak and Lynn Starling. Based on a play by: Edward Locke. Directors of Photography: Hal Mohr and W. Howard Greene. Music Composer: Edward Ward. Cast: Boris Karloff, Susanna Foster, Turhan Bey, Gale Sondergaard, June Vincent, Thomas Gomez, and Scotty Beckett.

The box-office success of "The Phantom of the Opera" (1943) generated this semi-sequel, which is really little more than a remake with Boris Karloff in the pivotal role of the "phantom" of the Paris

Opera House. Filmed on the same Academy Award-winning sets, utilizing the same lavish costumes and production team, and featuring the same leading lady, "The Climax" (1944) virtually repeats the condition of conflict in the earlier movie. Karloff (in his first color film) plays a mild-mannered, retiring physician Dr. Hohner of the Vienna Royal Theatre who, unbeknownst to anyone, had strangled his mistress ten years before and lives with her embalmed corpse in the dark, labyrinthine world below.  Apparently, she (June Vincent) was a famous opera singer, and when she refused to give up her career for a normal family life with him, he jealously murdered her. When he hears the voice of a young music student (Susanna Foster), the good doctor is convinced that his dead mistress

has been reincarnated, and he has the opportunity to win her love again. His plans, which include terrorizing the opera house, go awry, thanks to the intervention of a fellow student who loves her (Turhan Bey), and Karloff dies in a familiar conflagration that also consumes the body of his first love. Extremely predictable, particularly if you've just seen the 1943 version, the film is distinguished only by the presence of Karloff in one of his many roles as a sympathetic mad doctor.

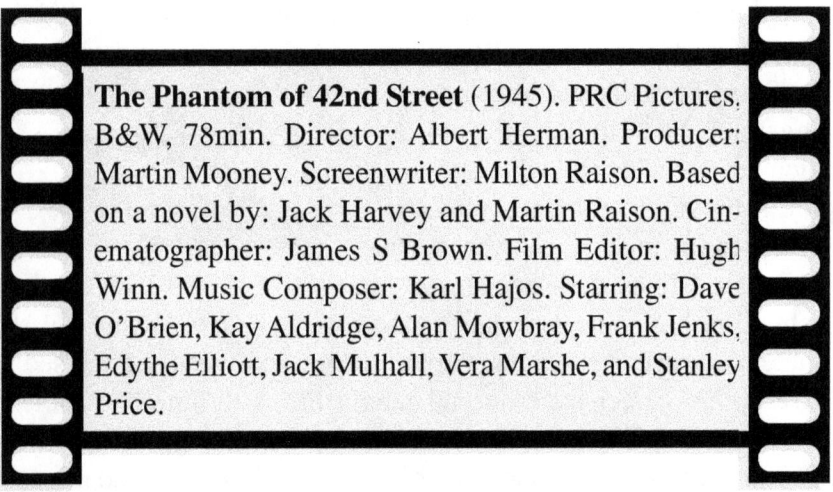

The Phantom of 42nd Street (1945). PRC Pictures. B&W, 78min. Director: Albert Herman. Producer: Martin Mooney. Screenwriter: Milton Raison. Based on a novel by: Jack Harvey and Martin Raison. Cinematographer: James S Brown. Film Editor: Hugh Winn. Music Composer: Karl Hajos. Starring: Dave O'Brien, Kay Aldridge, Alan Mowbray, Frank Jenks, Edythe Elliott, Jack Mulhall, Vera Marshe, and Stanley Price.

Low budget rip-off of the 1943 adaptation, "The Phantom of 42nd Street" finds a demented, disfigured actor haunting a Broadway theatre and seeking revenge for a past injustice. Newspaper critic Tony Woolrich (Dave O'Brien) and his wise-cracking cab driver Cecil Moore (Alan Mowbray) discover that the series of mysterious murders at the Acme Theatre have actually been committed by a "phantom." For the Charlie-Chan-like climax, he sets up an audition of Julius Caesar, hoping to lure the murderer into all-to-realistically participating in the assassination scene. In different hands, perhaps those of Ben Hecht or Edward Wood, this film could have been a breezy and biting satire about theatre critics and the theatre. Instead the film plots along with the dull direction of Albert Herman. All in all, not very original!

~ 5 ~
Scorpions, Grasshoppers and Vampires

He said, "I give you five minutes to spare your blushes! Here...In one of the caskets, you will find a scorpion, in the other, a grasshopper, both very cleverly imitated in Japanese bronze: they will say yes or no for you. If you turn the scorpion round, that will mean to me, when I return, that you have said yes. The grasshopper will mean no."

—Gaston Leroux, Le Fantôme de l'Opera

During the Science Fiction boom of the Fifties and early Sixties, when most of the major studios had stopped making horror films in order to poduce their own invasions from space, several foreign films based on Gaston Leroux's *Le Fantôme de l'Opera* appeared and disappeared with little notice or fanfare. "El Fantasma de la Opereta" ("The Phantom of the Opera," 1959), a stinging, comedic tale from a Mexican comic, "Ye Bang Ge Sheng" ("Mid-nightmare," 1961), a revenge fable from Hong Kong, and "Il Vampiro dell Opera" ("The Vampire of the Opera," 1964), a sexploitation film with vampires, each relegate the Phantom to supporting status. The tragic tale of a disfigured composer and his love for a young opera singer seems to take a backseat to slapstick comedy, ultraviolence, or soft core pornography, and the creators of those motion pictures do not appear concerned that they are strip mining a classic. At the same time, two other adaptations from Argentina treat the material with such reverence that the productions are literate but literally dead on arrival. Only one seemed truly inspired by Leroux.

Many films over the years have featured the word "phantom" in the title, but few have actually been about the famous "Phantom" of the Paris Opera House. Korkarlen is revealed to be "The Phantom Chariot" (1920) in the noted silent film, just as an old woman is identified as "The Phantom of Crestwood" (1932), a sinister monk in "The Phantom of the Convent" (1934), and Jack the Ripper in "The Phantom Is a Fiend" (1935). Other "phantoms" - in name only - have been the doomed brigantine Marie Celeste in "The Phantom Ship" (1937), insane inventor Bela Lugosi in "The Phantom Creeps" (1939), agent Nick Carter in "Phantom Raiders" (1940), a cart of death in "The Phantom Wagon" (1941), murderers on death row in "The Phantom Speaks" (1945), an extraterrestrial in "The Phantom from Space" (1953), a ghost in "Phantom of the Red House" (1954), a killer in "The Phantom of the Rue Morgue" (1954), an amphibious creature from some "black lagoon" in "The Phantom from 10,000 Leagues" (1955), more ghosts in "The Phantom Loves" (1961), more aliens in "The Phantom Planet" (1962), another masked fiend in "The Phantom of Soho" (1963), a tollbooth in "The Phantom Tollbooth" (1970), and a Sith Lord in "The Phantom Menace" (1999).

Not surprisingly then, when a motion picture appears that does feature a legitimate "Phantom," audiences, film historians and critics take note. Regrettably, these films, to which I refer with the chapter heading "scorpions, grasshoppers, and vampires," offer very little that is new to the mythos of Gaston Leroux's mad musical genius. With the exception of one classic horror film, they have been thankfully and mercifully forgotten.

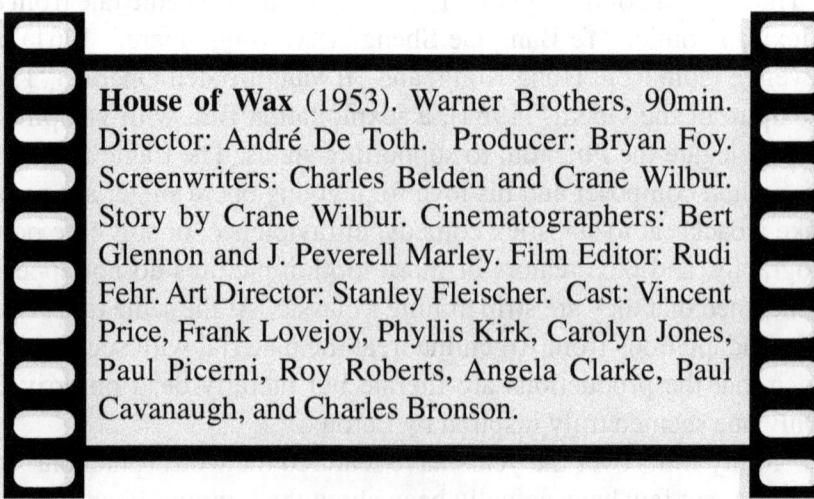

House of Wax (1953). Warner Brothers, 90min. Director: André De Toth. Producer: Bryan Foy. Screenwriters: Charles Belden and Crane Wilbur. Story by Crane Wilbur. Cinematographers: Bert Glennon and J. Peverell Marley. Film Editor: Rudi Fehr. Art Director: Stanley Fleischer. Cast: Vincent Price, Frank Lovejoy, Phyllis Kirk, Carolyn Jones, Paul Picerni, Roy Roberts, Angela Clarke, Paul Cavanaugh, and Charles Bronson.

While not strictly an adaptation of *Le Fantôme de l'Opera*, "House of Wax" (1953) seems to borrow key elements of the story to tell a most familiar tale. A horribly-disfigured sculptor (Vincent Price), burned in a fire set by his partner years earlier, opens the House of Wax in New York City, using the wax-covered bodies of corpses taken from the city morgue by Igor (Charles Bronson). His assistant begins to suspect his boss of foul play, especially after the sculptor sets his eyes on his assistant's lovely girlfriend (Phyllis Kirk) as Marie Antoinette. The sculptor's interest turns to obsession, and soon his desire to possess her as a wax figure clouds his judgment. During the suspense-filled climax, she pounds away at the sculptor's face to discover that he has hidden his gruesome features under a mask of wax. Price in his first horror film turns in a marvelous performance that seems inspired by Lon Chaney's Phantom. The unmasking scene is equally memorable, especially in NaturalVision 3-D (which is how Warner Brothers initially released the film). André De Toth relies on other familiar elements, some borrowed from the 1943 version of "The Phantom of the Opera," to keep our interest as he moves the ill-fated sculptor and two young lovers toward the final conflagration that destroys the wax museum.

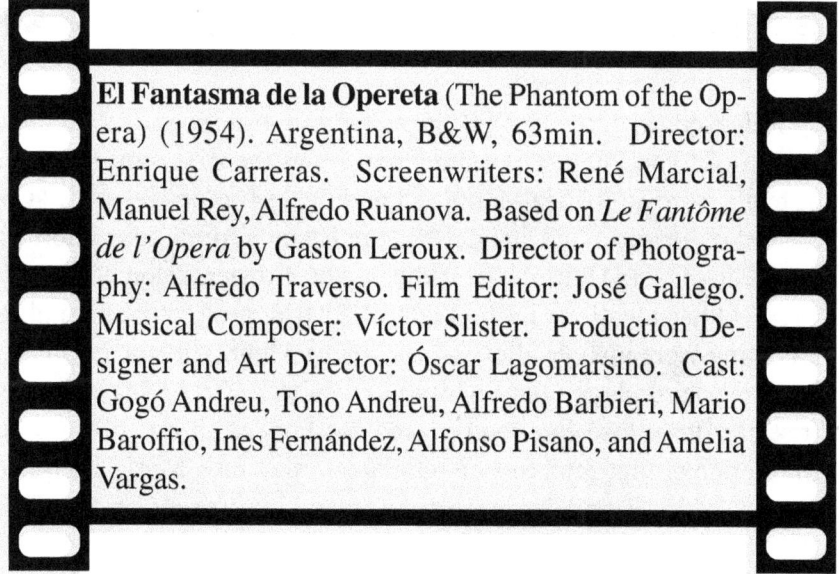

El Fantasma de la Opereta (The Phantom of the Opera) (1954). Argentina, B&W, 63min. Director: Enrique Carreras. Screenwriters: René Marcial, Manuel Rey, Alfredo Ruanova. Based on *Le Fantôme de l'Opera* by Gaston Leroux. Director of Photography: Alfredo Traverso. Film Editor: José Gallego. Musical Composer: Víctor Slister. Production Designer and Art Director: Óscar Lagomarsino. Cast: Gogó Andreu, Tono Andreu, Alfredo Barbieri, Mario Baroffio, Ines Fernández, Alfonso Pisano, and Amelia Vargas.

"El Fantasma de la Opereta" (1954) was the first of two adaptations of Gaston Leroux's *Le Fantôme de l'Opera* produced in Argentina. The film version was a fairly strict adaptation of the novel with much of the action compressed to fit its short running time. Gogó Andreu played the titular role of the Phantom, while his brother Tono Andreu doubled as the unscarred musical composer; Ines Fernández played Cristine, and Amelia Vargas was the diva Carlotta. The film was directed by Enrique Carreras; born Enrique Santes Morello in Lima, Peru, he became a hugely successful director of Spanish-language films. Together with his two brothers, Nicolás and Luis Carreras, he founded the company cinema producer General Belgrano, and produced some of the most popular films in Argentina.

El Fantasma de la opera (The Phantom of the Opera) (1960). Argentina, B&W, 60min. Director: Narciso Ibáñez Menta and Marta Reguera. Producer: Diana Alvarez. Screenwriter: Chicho Libanez-Serrador. Based on *Le Fantôme de l'Opera* by Gaston Leroux. Cast: Narciso Ibáñez Menta, Beatriz Día Quiroga, Juan José Edelman, José María Langlais, and Noemí Laserre.

Released on July 2, 1960, in Argentina, this Spanish-language version of "The Phantom of the Opera" was the first mini-series of the cycle Narciso Ibáñez Menta's "Obras Maestras del Terror" ("The Masters of Terror") on Channel Nine in Buenos Aires. The interiors of the Paris Opera House were filmed in the Theater Colón of Buenos Aires. Other locations in the Federal District around the capital of Argentina were also used. Narciso Ibáñez Menta, the most famous actor in Spain, played the Phantom opposite Beatriz Día Quiroga's Cristina. Juan José Edelman played the Persian in one of the rare film versions that featured his character, and José María Langlais was featured as Raoul de Chagny and Noemí Laserre as Carlota. This fairly literature version, which also features a subplot of smugglers using the Phantom's subterranean lair to hide their bounty, was hugely popular, and paved the way for other adaptations of famous horror stories.

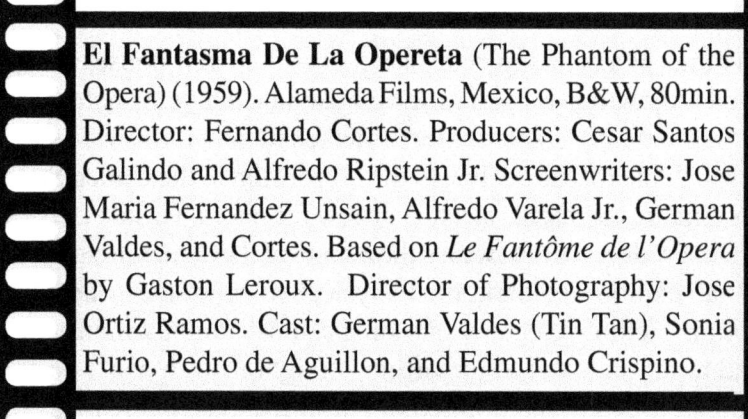

El Fantasma De La Opereta (The Phantom of the Opera) (1959). Alameda Films, Mexico, B&W, 80min. Director: Fernando Cortes. Producers: Cesar Santos Galindo and Alfredo Ripstein Jr. Screenwriters: Jose Maria Fernandez Unsain, Alfredo Varela Jr., German Valdes, and Cortes. Based on *Le Fantôme de l'Opera* by Gaston Leroux. Director of Photography: Jose Ortiz Ramos. Cast: German Valdes (Tin Tan), Sonia Furio, Pedro de Aguillon, and Edmundo Crispino.

Promoted as the first comedic version of the enduring classic, "El Fantasma de la Opereta" (1959) bears little resemblance to Leroux's story because it eliminates all vestiges of classic drama in favor of a relentless bombardment of vaudevillian humor and sexual innuendo which is neither funny nor the least bit interesting. Director Fernando Cortes, noted for "El Spectro de Televicentro" ("The Spectre of the Television," 1959) and "La Marca del Muetra" ("Creatures of the Walking Dead," 1960), meant for his film to be a comic, sexual romp about mistaken identities featuring the talents of local favorite Tin-Tan. Unfortunately, his direction is routine and pedestrian, and the acting is down right embarrassing.

After a brief, atmospheric pre-credit sequence in which the audience is given a glimpse of the brooding "Phantom," the plot (if one could call it that) follows the exploits of a "talented" young comic as he attempts to gain fame, fortune, and the love of a beautiful woman in the theatrical world of Mexico City. Fame and fortune are slow in coming, but Tin-Tan does manage to seduce every woman in sight, cannily playing the roles they expect from him, including that of the title role. When the "Phantom" learns that someone else has taken his identity, he emerges from his world of unending darkness to seek revenge, and then the real shenanigans begin. Of course, Tin-Tan always seems to be one step ahead of Erik, including a gang of Phantom wannabes when he opens his own theatre. But who is the true Phantom, and what does he want of the beautiful star? Tin-Tan easily defeats the mad musical genius, wins the hand of the beautiful young singer, saves the theatre from bankruptcy, and becomes the toast of the town.

"El Fantasma de la Opereta" is a routine haunted-house comedy, the type Hollywood stopped making over a dozen years before. But just as "Abbott and Costello Meet Frankenstein" (1948) was singularly responsible for the decline of the horror film in the United States, this foreign film represents an all-time low for fans of Gaston Leroux's tragic tale. Produced to showcase the talents of its vaudevillian comic, rather than explore the dark, metaphysical world of the "Phantom," the motion picture relegates one of the most famous monsters of filmland to the status of a supporting, straight man. It also assists in continuing the decay and dilution of one of the most interesting tales in cinema and literature. Not to be confused by the much superior "El Fantasma de la Opereta" (1954), this perverse travesty of Gaston Leroux's *Le Fantôme de l'Opera* has thankfully been forgotten. A US version was prepared by Jerry Warren with additional footage shot by Richard Wallace but never released. The original Spanish-language version with subtitles is the one that exists on home video.

Ye Bang Ge Sheng (Mid-Nightmare) (1961). Shaw Brothers International/Hong Kong, 97min. Director, Writer: Yuan Quifeng. Producer: Run Run Shaw. Based on *Le Fantôme de l'Opera* by Gaston Leroux. Starring: Le Di (Betty Loh Tih), Zhou Lai, Fang Li, Zhang Chong.

This Chinese remake of the 1937 Weibang Ma-Xu classic "Song at Midnight" is as far removed from Gaston Leroux's novel as any previous adaptation, but the influence of the Frenchman's tragic tale is clearly evident in each scene as written and directed by Yuan Quifeng. Produced at a time when Sir Run Run Shaw was first interested in competing in the international market, the film boasts elaborate sets, beautiful period costumes, and lush photography. But unfortunately these wonderful attributes fail to help raise the material above the commonplace. Quifeng's misreading of the original classic or his reliance on the Universal adaptation renders yet another revenge fable, with its inevitable bloody consequences.

The story begins by following the efforts of an actor in Republican China, named Song (Zhou Lai), to regain his freedom and his lost love Li (Le Di), the daughter of a warlord, after he has been arrested and imprisoned for revolutionary activities. While in prison, he learns that local officials know the charges against him are false, and that they have been filed falsely by Li's father, who doesn't want his only daughter involved with a communist. Song struggles to prove his innocence, only to have his face scarred beyond recognition in an acid attack by the angry official who must grant his release. Unable to return to the life he once knew or the woman he once loved, the actor hides himself in the desserted wing of an old theatre and circulates a rumor that he has died. Li is heartbroken with the news, unaware that he is really still alive and that her father was the sole person responsible for his imprisonment.

Years later, after the theatre has been restored to its former glory, Song learns to move through its secret passages and dark corridors without being seen. People think the place is haunted, and rumors about a deadly "phantom" reach a fever pitch. Predictably, the old disfigured man is befriended by a young actor (Zhang Chong), whom he helps and uses as a messenger to contact his lost love. Li is, at first, suspicious of the young actor, but finally accepts his words as truth. The former lovers are united, and Song reveals what he knows about her father. Together, they conspire to bring both the warlord and the angry official who burned him with acid to justice, but Song is drown as he attempts to avenge all his years of suffering and torment.

"Ye Bang Ge Sheng" has been saturated by Quifeng with images so simplified that they bear almost no resemblance to those in the original, and what remains is a pallid, lackluster slice of modernist entertainment. Shortly after completing this motion picture for Shaw, director Quifeng and noted Chinese actress Le Di formed the Gold Eagle Film Company, and produced a number of martial arts movies which were similarly pallid and lackluster. The company folded in 1967, and Le Di committed suicide at the age of 31 the following year. Since then, Yuan Quifeng has been inactive as a filmmaker. Even though Sir Run Run Shaw produced "Mid-Nightmare" (its English title) for international distribution, the production was lost in translation, and few copies of this film were seen beyond the Asian market. The film was remade in 1996 as "The Phantom Lover."

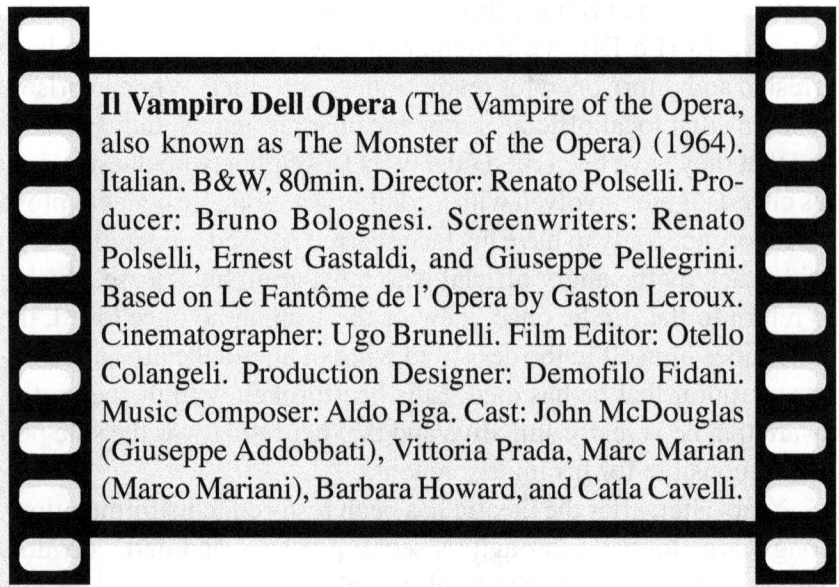

Il Vampiro Dell Opera (The Vampire of the Opera, also known as The Monster of the Opera) (1964). Italian. B&W, 80min. Director: Renato Polselli. Producer: Bruno Bolognesi. Screenwriters: Renato Polselli, Ernest Gastaldi, and Giuseppe Pellegrini. Based on Le Fantôme de l'Opera by Gaston Leroux. Cinematographer: Ugo Brunelli. Film Editor: Otello Colangeli. Production Designer: Demofilo Fidani. Music Composer: Aldo Piga. Cast: John McDouglas (Giuseppe Addobbati), Vittoria Prada, Marc Marian (Marco Mariani), Barbara Howard, and Catla Cavelli.

In many ways, "Il Vampiro Dell Opera" ("The Vampire of the Opera," 1964) can be seen as a companion piece to "Ye Bang Ge Sheng" (1961), each film presenting one side of the forces of obsession and revenge which determine the central character's motivation. "The Vampire of the Opera" is a meditation on the ravages of the flesh caused by uncontrolled sexuality, with one woman carrying the curse to her contemporaries, while "Mid-Nightmare"presents a violent discourse on the misuse of power in a sexually repressive state. In both worlds, love is either perverted or forbidden, and compassion has no place at all. Whereas the latter film seems content to be simply a revenge fable. the former is strictly concerned with obsessions of the flesh.

Drawing material from Gaston Leroux's famous *Le Fantôme de l'Opera*, Cocteau's "Beauty and the Beast" (1945), Terence Fisher's "Horror of Dracula" (1958), and a dozen other unlikely sources, Polselli's film chronicles the abduction, seduction, and conversion of a talented but unknown opera singer (Vittoria Prada) by a mysterious stranger (John McDouglas) into the joys of vampirism. When Christine (Prada) and members of her acting troupe enter a disused opera house to stage a new production, they are unaware that the theatre is haunted by a vampire. In the days that follow, as the troup begins rehearsal for an opera, they become increasingly edgy as they sense something is not quite right. Props disappear, then reappear somewhere else; elements of costumes are rearranged, and scenic backdrops are switched. Someone is deliberately causing them problems.

However, the "phantom" of this opera house is not a disfigured monster (as in the other versions of the story) but a hauntingly twisted vampire. When he takes Christine to his subterranean world, his need for blood overwhelms his interest in her musical abilities. She returns to the opera as a vampire and begins to suck her way through the chorus section. She first seduces and drains several of the women, then men in her troup. Lots of sexual orgies follow as the actors experience the joys of vampirism and unbridled passion, and McDouglas can't resist the temptation to enjoy each and every one of the new female vampires even though his heart beats for Christine. The movie ends with a predictable conflagration of the opera house.

Derivative, sexploitative, "Il Vampiro Dell Opera" ("The Vampire of the Opera," 1964) is a silly mix of classic tales that never quite rises above the mediocre. Polselli has a wonderful imagination but has trouble translating some of his fantasies onto the screen. He clearly demonstrates some skill as a writer, but he is a poor director. The acting appears awkward and amateurish, as one senses the director may have encouraged friends and financiers to take key roles. Although the film does have several good sequences, most of it is puerile, sadistic and exploitative, resembling a Hammer rip-off. However, it does anticipate the work of Jean Rollin's sexy vampire films, including "Le Viol de Vampire" (1967), and may have provided the impetus behind that Frenchman's series.

Polselli continued to make ruinous, perverse movies in which males seem to have an unending sexual potency and women - in various stages of bestial hunger – can't seem to get enough. Many of those soft-core pornographic films were made under the pseudonym Ralph Brown, including "Ritimagie Nerie e Segrete Orge del Trecento" ("The Ghasty Orgies of Count Dracula," 1973). Afer the splendid "Le Amante del Vampire" ("The Vampire and the Ballerina," 1960), in which two ballet dancers Luisa (Helene Remy) and

Francesca (Tina Gloriani) are terrorized in an old castle by an aristocratic vampiress (Maria Luisa Rolando), PolBelli's B work continued downhill with one disappointing film after another.

Renato Polselli started this motion picture as "Il Vampiro Dell Opera" ("The Vampire of the Opera," 1964), but when it was finally released in 1964, the title had changed to "Il Mostro Dell Opera" ("The Monster of the Opera"). The American version, atrociously dubbed and horribly edited by puritanical censors, played in a few art houses that year before disappearing forever.

John L. Flynn

~ 6 ~
The Mysterious Englishman

"Parts of London are a lost world! We can never know what caverns and dungeons and labyrinths rest beneath us! Or what madmen and monsters inhabit them!"
—*The 1962 Film Version*

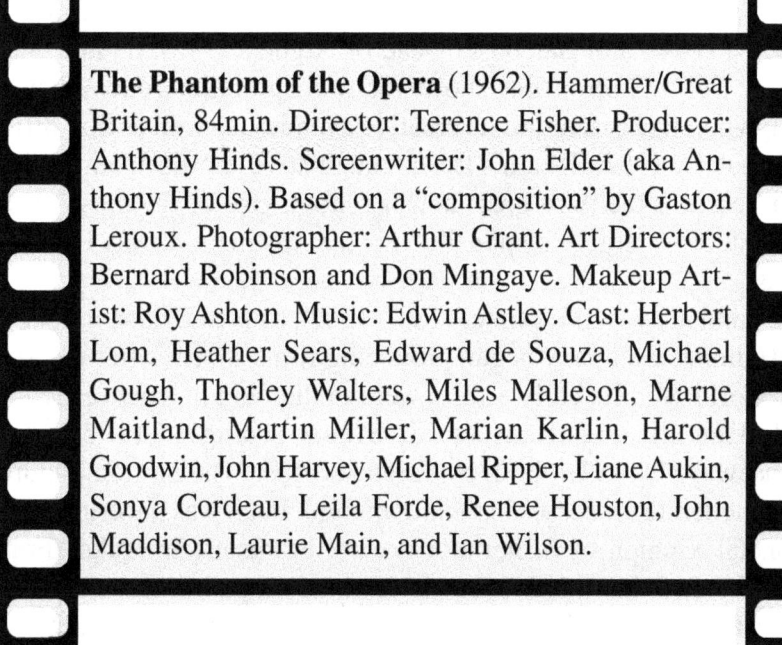

The Phantom of the Opera (1962). Hammer/Great Britain, 84min. Director: Terence Fisher. Producer: Anthony Hinds. Screenwriter: John Elder (aka Anthony Hinds). Based on a "composition" by Gaston Leroux. Photographer: Arthur Grant. Art Directors: Bernard Robinson and Don Mingaye. Makeup Artist: Roy Ashton. Music: Edwin Astley. Cast: Herbert Lom, Heather Sears, Edward de Souza, Michael Gough, Thorley Walters, Miles Malleson, Marne Maitland, Martin Miller, Marian Karlin, Harold Goodwin, John Harvey, Michael Ripper, Liane Aukin, Sonya Cordeau, Leila Forde, Renee Houston, John Maddison, Laurie Main, and Ian Wilson.

Terence Fisher's "The Phantom of the Opera" (1962), the third credited adaptation of Gaston Leroux's 1911 novel, elicits great pathos by placing emphasis (where it belongs) on the sensitive but tragic love of the disfigured composer for a young opera singer. Though some consider it flawed and faded today, the motion picture was the most expensive production mounted by Hammer Films (at the time). In fact, the small British studio had planned to release the film internationally, dubbed into all the major languages, with a huge advertising budget, but the inevitable comparisons to the 1925 and 1943 versions caused them to reconsider. Audiences who had become accustomed to the obligatory shock elements, the grue and gore of previous Hammer productions, viewed the film with major disappointment. Critics were also unusually harsh, and the motion picture disappeared shortly after its release in 1962. But when viewed in retrospect, Fisher's loving tribute to the genre may actually represent one of the high points in Hammer Films brief history.

Hammer Films

Although largely undistinguished until 1945, the British cinema had developed independently of its American counterpart, producing four notable fantasy classics - Menzies' "Things to Come" (1936), Korda's "Thief of Bagdad" (1940), Murphy's "Man in Half Moon Street" (1944), and Balcon's "Dead of Night" (1945). Its late entry into the field of horror films, however, was a propitious one. Whereas Hollywood had exhausted its creative avenues, as well as box office potential, by 1957, Britain's fresh, imaginative approach quickly established it as the third great horror school. One of the most prodigious studios, largely responsible for that distinction, was Hammer Films.

Founded by Will Hammer (1887-196?), a noted British producer, the Hammer Company began producing films shortly after the Second World War. Its early efforts were in the field of science fiction, including the excellent "Four-Sided Triangle" (1952) and "Spaceways" (1953) - both by Terence Fisher. The motion pictures were moderate successes in their own right; but it was the critical and financial triumph of Fisher's "Curse of Frankenstein" (aka "Frankenstein" in Britain, 1957) that determined the path which the studio would take. Like Carl Laemmle Jr. before him, Hammer was a shrewd movie mogul. He recognized the potential and popularity of certain American properties, and virtually any horror film produced by Universal in the Thirties and Forties was remade in a large screen format in the Fifties and Sixties. "Frankenstein" was followed by "The Horror of Dracula" (1958), and in subsequent years "The Hound of the Baskervilles" (1959), "The Mummy" (1959), "The Two Faces of Dr. Jekyll" (1960), "Curse of the Werewolf" (1961), and, of course, Terence Fisher's own "The Phantom of the Opera" (1962).

Hammer Films was distinguished by several key factors. The production values were generally of a high quality, extravagant by Hollywood standards, and the studio employed many of the finest talents of the British cinema. Combined with a fresh approach, which employed the new technologies of color and special effects, Hammer competed directly with the American market (as well as the open European one). And for nearly twenty years (between 1957 and 1975), the studio dominated the field with its imaginative thrillers. Although the films were not always successful at the box office, these motion pictures did represent excellance. They also gave the horror film a new lease on life, by restoring dignity to the famous monsters of filmland that, at the hands of Universal Pictures, had degenerated into stooges for Abbott and Costello. Clearly, Fisher's "Phantom" attempted to correct the errors of the 1943 version, while boldly challenging the orders of the studio that arranged for it to be made.

The Screen Story

The film opens in the fictitious London Opera House, then moves gracefully underground to focus on a man huddled over an antique pipe organ. The camera then follows his acid-scarred fingers as they move gingerly across the keyboard, and finally pans up to reveal the cyclopean visage of the Phantom (Herbert Lom). His canvas mask - dark, dirty and blood-stained -has been stretched across his entire face, leaving only a single portal for the right eye. His hair, which has been singed by fire, appears wind-blown. He resembles a dark, anonymous caricature of Ludwig Von Beethoven; yet beyond his outward appearance, there is a haunting pathos.

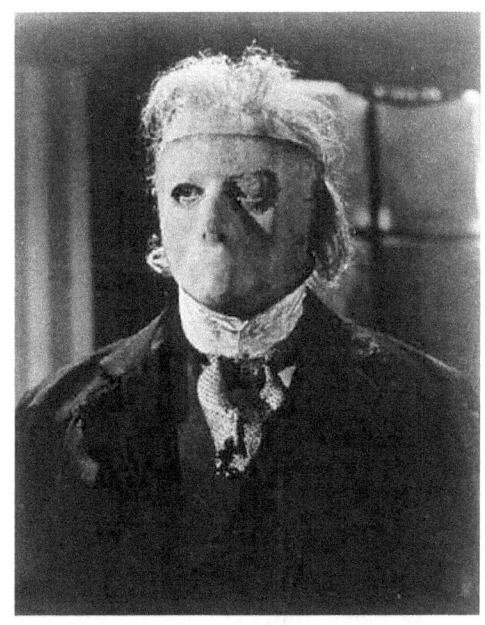

As the main titles close, the scene shifts back to the playhouse. People have gathered for the premiere of a new opera by Lord Ambrose D'Arcy (Michael Gough), entitled "The Tragedy of Joan of Arc." Impatiently, the composer counts the number of audience members, hoping for a sellout, then makes his way to a private box to watch the proceedings. Meanwhile, the Phantom has been working hard to see that the play doesn't open. First, he has destroyed several of the orchestra's instruments and defaced the show's poster which graces the entrance to the theatre; then, he has stolen the conductor's music, and finally crept into the resident diva's room to frighten her with his unholy visage. Unfortunately, his actions prove to be more a nuisance than a real menace, and the show opens with little delay.

Midway through the first act, as Maria (Liane Aukin) makes her debut as Joan of Ark, D'Arcy angrily dismisses Producer Harry Hunter (Edward De Souza) from his private box, then demands to know why the theatre manager has left box five vacant. Latimer (Thorley Walters) explains that people have complained about strange noises coming from the box. "Are you trying to tell me it's haunted?" the English lord asks irritably. Latimer reluctantly reveals what he knows about the legend of the Phantom, but D'Arcy is not impressed and orders the box sold for every performance. Sometime later, as the opera builds to an emotional climax, the body of a hanged man (possibly Joseph Buquet) plunges through scenery, bringing the proceedings to an immediate hault. Everyone believes that it is the work of the Phantom, but in reality, it is the wrongdoing of his servant, a misshapen dwarf (Ian Wilson).

"The Tragedy of Joan of Arc" closes on account of the mysterious death, and D'Arcy is enraged, thinking his work is forever condemned. Hunter is not as pessimistic, and even though Maria has left the production, he arranges to re-open in a few weeks with a new diva singing the lead.

Open auditions are held on the following day, and a young singer, named Christine Charles (Heather Sears, her singing voice dubbed by Pat Clark), comes to the attention of Hunter, D'Arcy, and the Phantom. Hunter likes her robust energy and enthuisiasm, and believes he can train her properly for the lead. Lord Ambrose D'Arcy is attracted to her youthful looks, and wants to use her sexually to satisfy his lust for young women. The Phantom, on the other hand, is moved to tears by her voice, and decides that she will be the one to carryon his musical legacy. She is offered the role of Joan of Arc, provided she will have dinner with the English lord. Dinner, of course, means that she will have to exchange her virginity for continued employment. In fact, when she retires to the ladies' dressing room, the Phantom warns her -from the shadows -that D'Arcy is not to be trusted. But Christine does not heed his warning. She arrives for dinner, and D'Arcy proposes they retire to his home for "private lessons." Luckily for Christine, Hunter also knows of Darcy's reputation and arrives just in time.

After an embarrassing exchange between the English lord and his producer, Hunter offers Christine the quiet dinner that she never received. The two exchange polite, pleasant conversation, until the subject turns to the problems at the London Opera House. Harry Hunter confesses that they have had more than their share of mysterious goings-on, from missing music, to torn costumes, to damaged scenery. He fears that something evil has begun haunting the theatre. Christine's story about a disembodied voice prompts Hunter to return to the theatre in order to investigate her dressing room. While he fumbles around in the dark, the Phantom enters and offers to tutor

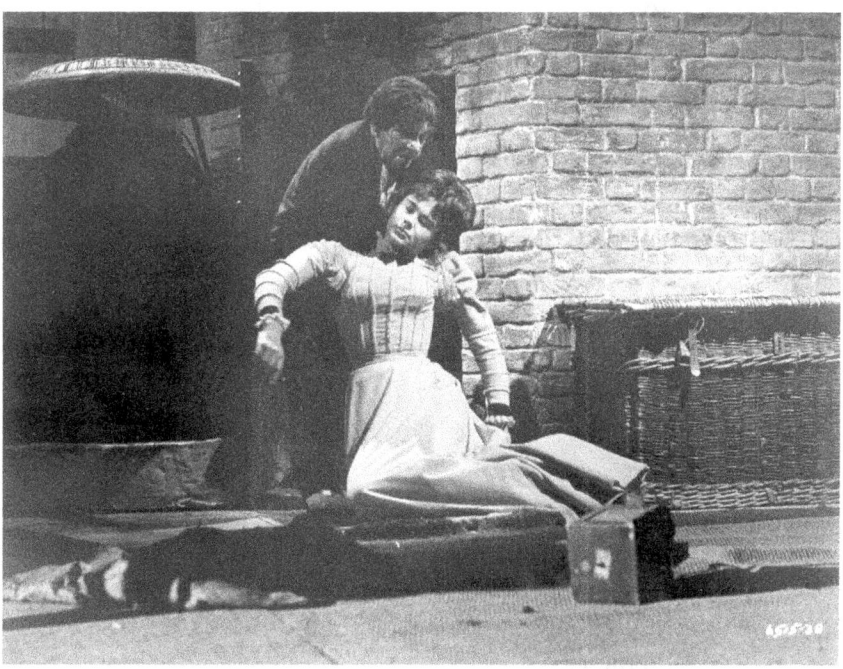

her. His unholy visage frightens the young singer, and causes her to scream in terror. At exactly the same moment, the local rat catcher is murdered (again) by the misshapen dwarf. The producer whisks Christine to safety, and calls upon the police to investigate.

Lord Ambrose D'Arcy, sexually frustrated by Christine's rejection of the previous evening, fires the young singer, and holds his own auditions. Hunter protests the lord's decision, and finds himself without a job. When the conductor and orchestra members try to appeal D'Arcy's rash actions, he dismisses them as well. He will produce and direct his own play, even though he has no one to play or sing the music.

Sometime later, Harry Hunter pays a conciliatory visit on Christine, and offers to take her to lunch. While he is waiting for her to change, Mrs. Tucker (Renee Houston), the house mother, tells him about an old music professor, named Petrie, who used to teach singing at the Academy. Hunter examines some of his old manuscripts and discovers that the music has a familiar quality. He inquires about the whereabouts of Petrie, and she tells him, "He was killed, burned to death in a fire, at Piggot's Printers near London Bridge." Hunter begins to suspect that Lord Ambrose may have stolen Petrie's music, and arranged to have the professor killed. But he must have proof.

For most of the morning and afternoon, Hunter and the young singer piece together clues, obtained at the police station and at the printer's, that suggest what really happened to Petrie. Meanwhile, the misshapen dwarf pays a visit on D'Arcy's latest protege/conquest and tries to stab her to death. She flees in terror, and the police begin to suspect the English lord is connected to all the strange happenings at the theatre.

Christine Charles returns home, after a lovely day with the dashing young producer, and discovers the dwarf waiting for her. She faints, and he carries her to the Phantom's dark, labyrinthine world below the playhouse. The lost lake, the many rows of candles, the mist-laden atmosphere, the antiquated pipe organ all tell her that she has entered another world. At first, she is terribly frightened, but the young singer slowly comes to realize that she is in no danger. The Phantom, who has a kind and loving demeanor, offers to give her a new voice in exchange for her valuable time and hard work. Christine agrees, and the two begin their many hours of rehearsal.

Following several unsuccessful attempts to produce and direct his own opera, D'Arcy is forced to take Latimer's advice and rehire Hunter. Harry believes that he knows the truth about D'Arcy's crime, but remains silent while he gathers additional evidence and resumes production of the show. Several weeks go by without incident. But because Christine has been disappearing every day to work with the Phantom, Hunter suspects that something might be terribly wrong with her. The producer goes to the river where Petrie supposedly drown, and follows the current to a sewer opening. The sewer opening leads him through a long maze of tunnels, which eventually opens into the dark world of the Phantom. (The misshapen dwarf tries to protect his master's secret by attempting to kill Hunter, but he is no match for the virile young producer.) Harry Hunter rises from the lost lake, relieves Christine of her fear, and demands an explanation from the Phantom.

Through an elaborate flashback, we learn that the Phantom is, in fact, the same Professor Petrie who was burned in a fire and thought drown. Many years before, he sought help from Lord Ambrose D'Arcy to publish and produce his work -a full symphony, two quartets, a piece for a violin, and a complete opera. D'Arcy offered him the paltry sum of fifty pounds for all the work, and Petrie, who was behind in his debts, was forced to accept his offer. Little did he know that D'Arcy planned to publish the work under his own name. When he accidentally discovers that his ten-year labor of musical composition is being printed with the lord's name, he breaks into the printing house to burn every manuscript. Petrie became trapped in the building, and was horribly burned by acid while trying to extinguish the fire. His features burned beyond recognition, he threw himself into the Thames river. But the misshapen dwarf rescued him from drowning, and he has lived in the tunnels below the playhouse ever since.

Both Hunter and Christine are moved by the Phantom's tragic tale, and agree to let him continue teaching the young singer in preparation for her debut. One week later, on the opening night of the opera, Petrie pays a final visit on D'Arcy. Ambrose demands that he remove the "ridiculous" mask, and tears it from his face to reveal the scarred features of the elderly professor. The English lord realizes that his secret has been discovered, and runs away in disgrace.

Moments later, the curtain rises, and Christine Charles appears on stage as Joan of Arc in Petrie's composition. Her triumphant performance moves the lonely Phantom to tears and the audience to a standing ovation. Above, in the catwalk over the stage, the misshapen dwarf changes positions to obtain a better view. His moments cause the chandelier to shift from side-to-side and the rope that holds it to unravel. From his vantage point in Box Five, only the Phantom recognizes the tremendous danger. Instinctively, he leaps onto the stage, pushing Christine to safety, and dies under the chandelier as its tremendous weight comes crashing down. The haunting image of his mask is all that remains of the Phantom as the closing credits roll.

Production Notes

Early on in the preproduction for "The Phantom of the Opera," Terence Fisher and writer-producer Anthony Hinds agreed to make their film much more like the 1925 silent adaptation with Lon Chaney than the all-musical version with Claude Rains. Fisher still liked the idea (from the 1943 film) that the Phantom was a tragic figure who had been wronged, and rewrote much of Leroux's character as a wholly sympathetic figure, with the dwarf committing the actual violence. Their approach attracted the attention and interest of Cary Grant who wanted to do a horror film, but not just any horror film. Originally, Grant expressed an interest in the character of the Phantom as a romantic lead, but as the writing progressed and the character became more watered down, he considered the role of Harry Hunter, Christine's lover and savior. Grant's interest in the project waned, and eventually the role of the Phantom went to Lom and the role of Hunter went to Edward de Souza.

Principal photography was completed at the Bray Studios, Down Place, Oakley Green in Berkshire, England and at the Wimbleton Theatre in Wimbledon. Director Terence Fisher does a good job of creating a dark and vaguely frightening environment, which adds much to the suspense. In fact, even though the setting has been moved to the mythical London Opera House, Fisher and Hinds have managed to capture the essence of Leroux's work. Certain sequences have been trimmed or eliminated for the sake of budgetary considerations or time constraints, but the tragic tale of a disfigured composer and his love for a young opera singer remains the focal point of the film.

Unlike the 1943 version, which seemed to downplay the story of the Phantom in favor of large, overblown operatic scenes, Fisher wisely concentrates on the Opera Ghost as well as his principle characters while drawing us slowly into his own hypnotic web. Indeed, one of the profoundly wonderful features about "The Phantom of the Opera" is that it takes us back to a cinematic era that was far less explicit, perhaps more poetic, and certainly more subtle in the way it depicts the sources of what scares us. Unlike the many contemporary horror films of his day - some of which he created for Hammer - the director relies less on the obligatory shock elements and more on building tension and suspense.

For most audiences, the world of Victorian England - with its gas-lit homes, damp foggy nights, and rain-swept cobblestone streets

- has long represented something dark and mysterious. Images of fictional characters like Sherlock Holmes, Count Dracula, Dr. Jekyll and Mr. Hyde, as well as the real life Jack the Ripper, come immediately to mind. Fisher expertly draws upon these associations to create a London that teems with boistrous coachmen, crabby washerwomen, rat catchers, police Bobbies; but all the of this production, also functions thematically on a multitude of levels. Photographed in such a way to make it seem beautiful, warm, and inviting, the lair teems with subterranean life. Though many of the characters suggest that it is a world of evil and ugliness, quite the contrary, it is a primeval place where men of vision can confront the unconscious drives over which civilization constructs its veneer. Thus, the mythical function of the Phantom - as the caretaker of this dark domain - is to release creativity, sexuality, and the primitive into the world. Some of the characters learn from his teaching, while others simply wish to steal his power. Christine, for example, though skilled as a singer, has never felt the music in her soul. She has lived a life of virginal piety, never daring to look at the dark side. When finally she does look upon him, the young opera singer understands the passion and sexuality that must be revealed through her music. On the other hand, D'Arcy who also lives in the repressed, Victorian society that denies those impulses feels the only way to restore his potency (as both a man and a composer) is to take it forcibly from Petrie. Ultimately, when he looks upon the Phantom, the image of unbridled passion and sensitivity frightens him. The English lord has never known these feelings and runs away in terror. Fisher cleverly realizes - as Leroux had before him - that the dark, subterranean world of the soul is much more revealing than

outward appearances.

"I have endeavoured, in the actor's performances and in the interpretation of the material scene by scene, to underline that conflict," Terence Fisher revealed in an interview conducted in 1974. "I think it is essential to bring to the audience's attention this conflict between the power of good and the power of evil." The strength of the film balances on the struggle between these two disparate forces, and the true resolution of the conflict occurs near the end of the picture in D'Arcy's chambers.

The Film's Release and Critical Commentary

"The Phantom of the Opera" was relased in the United Kingdom on June 25, 1963, and several weeks later in the United States on August 15, 1962. After the initial successes of Terence Fisher's other horror films for Hammer, including "The Curse of Frankenstein" (1957) and "The Horror of Dracula" (1958), his masterwork flopped on its first release. Fisher fell out of favor with Hammer Studios, for whom he was not given another film until 1964. Subsequent re-issues of the film on late-night television and on home video have helped to wipe away some of the critical reaction to "The Phantom of the Opera," but regrettably not all.

In 1962, audiences had come to expect beheadings, impalements, and bloody murders - the obligatory shock elements that had made Hammer Films famous - and when the motion picture failed to deliver these, word of mouth condemned the movie to an early demise. Also, many critics expressed their disapproval of Fisher's work. *Time* Magazine wrote: "The new Phantom is about as dangerous as dear old granddad dressed up for Halloween." *The New York Times* was even more critical: "The only shock is that the British, who could have had a field day with this antique, have simply wafted it back with a lick and a promise." *Newsweek* predicted a nice guy monster trend (as a result of Hammer's latest release), and suggested that a future production might be titled "Werewolf Come Home." All of them seemed to agree that there was little complexity to the Phantom's actions and that his character, lacking justifiable realism, was far too superficial to be taken seriously.

Regrettably, two of the novel's key sequences - the famous chandelier disaster and the ritual-like unmasking of the Phantom - are held until the final moments of the film; then they are used to further convince the audience (as if the audience needed further convincing) of the Phantom's altruistic nature. This may represent one of the only two blunders Fisher makes with his production. By having the chandelier fall accidentally - at exactly that moment - and the Phantom crushed as he sacrifices himself for the woman he loves, the director manipulates our emotions with a deus ex machina conclusion. Rather than allowing the action to flow naturally from what has already been established, he creates a false spectacle which is meant to bestow larger-than-life nobility upon the Phantom. The sequence betrays rather than enhances his vision of the Gaston Leroux's most famous work.

The director's other mistake is in making his central figure an ordinary man who has been hideously disfigured in a terrible accident. Unlike Gaston Leroux's mad musical genius or Lon Chaney's skull-faced demon, Fisher's Phantom is an elderly music professor whose life of unfulfilled fantasies and broken dreams has made him a recluse. Because his one chance to achieve fame and fortune was taken away from him by the unscrupulous impresario, he has spent ten years brooding in the damp cellars under the playhouse. Petrie's disfigurement has more to do with a broken spirit than an acid-scarred face, even though he remains hidden behind the pathetic, makeshift mask. Stripped of a vengeful nature, the Phantom is more of a minor nuisance than a threatening menace. In fact, the single-faceted, stereotypic character has little to occupy his time - other than play Bach on his pipe organ - until Christine arrives. Even his lackluster attempts to prevent the opening of "The Tragedy of Joan of Arc" sadly reveal his indecisiveness. Though he represents passion and creativity, he spends too much of his time as a rebellious monster without a cause. Therefore, when he is finally unmasked, it is somewhat of a letdown. We already know that the real monster is D'Arcy.

Herbert Lom contributes a wonderfully sympathetic portrait as the Phantom, but he is nearly upstaged - in scene after scene - by the work of Michael Gough as the wicked Lord Ambrose D'Arcy. Certainly no stranger to horror films, Gough has appeared in a dozen Hammer productions. Born in the British colony of Malaya in 1917, he made his London stage debut at the age of 19. Michael began his cinematic career in 1948 with a featured role in "Blanche Fury." He played the leading man in a series of low budget quickies during the

Forties and Fifties, but did not reach his stride until he was featured in Fisher's "Horror of Dracula" (1958). His inspired portrayal of Arthur Holmwood, the English aristocrat who must watch his fiancée suffer at the hands of Dracula, led to a long-term commitment to imaginative thrillers. Tall and gaunt, with an elegant presence, he specialized in haughty aristocrats or hammy mad scientists, appearing in more than a dozen horror films. Some of those include "Black Zoo" (1963), "Dr. Terror's House of Horrors" (1965), "The Skull" (1965), "Berzerk" (1967), "Circus of Blood" (1967), "The Legend of Hell House" (1973), and "The Boys from Brazil" (1978). Gough was recently featured as Alfred the Butler in Tim Burton's mega-hit "Batman" (1989).

Though best remembered as Peter Sellars' ill-fated boss in the Pink Panther films, Herbert Lom has made a career out of playing characters with great intellectual depth. Born Herbert Charles Angelo Kuchacevich ze Schluderpacheru in Czechoslovakia in 1917, he immigrated to England in 1939. His first role was as the beleaguered German leader in "Mein Kampf" (1940). Following World War Two, he played another important statesman (Napoleon) in two films, "The Young Mister Pitt" (1947) and "War and Peace" (1956). His memorable role as the Arab trader in "Spartacus" (in 1960) opened up a wide range of opportunities. Besides the title role in "Phantom," he

played Captain Nemo in "Jules Verne's Mysterious Island" (1961), a Southern plantation owner in "Uncle Tom's Cabin" (1965), Inspector Dupin in Edgar Allan Poe's "Murders in the Rue Morgue" (1971), and a psychiatrist in "The Dead Zone" (1983). "The Phanom of the Opera" was the only film he made for Hammer Films.

But the real star of "The Phantom of the Opera" is Terence Fisher. Born in 1904, Fisher left high school at 16 to join the Merchant Marine, and signed on for two additional tours of duty, traveling to some of the most remote parts of the world. At the age of twenty-eight, he went to work at Shepherd-Bush Studios as the "oldest" clapper boy. He graduated to assistant editor in 1934, and editor in 1936, working on a variety of low-budget films. His first directorial assignment came in 1947 with "Colonel Bogie," but his career really took off in 1952 when he directed three films for Hammer, including "The Last Page," "Wings of Danger," and "Stolen Face." During the next five years, he directed eight films for Hammer, including the critically-acclaimed "Four-Sided Triangle" (1953) and "Spaceways" (1953). He single-handedly launched the horror renaissance in 1957, with what many critics believe to be the best horror movie of the modern era, "The Curse of Frankenstein." He followed that triumph with another by re-interpreting the Dracula-myth with "The Horror of Dracula" (1958). Over the next two years, he brought back other mythical characters, starting with Sherlock Holmes in "The Hound of the Baskervilles" (1959), the mummy in "The Mummy" (1959), Dr. Jekyll and Mr. Hyde in "The Two Faces of Dr. Jekyll" (1960), and finally Robin Hood in "The Sword of Sherwood Forest" (1960).

After the commercial failure of Hammer's most expensive project, Terence lost much prestige at Hammer Studios, and was forced to seek employment elsewhere in the industry. He directed five other low budget features, including "The Horror of It All" (1963), "The Night of the Big Heat" (1964), and "Island of Terror" (1964), and was soon lured back to direct sequels to his two famous creations. Fisher continued directing both Dracula and Frankenstein films for Hammer until 1973 (when the studio developed financial problems). He died in 1980 at the age of seventy-six, having left a long, impressive legacy of some of the finest horror films.

Prior to his death, Terence Fisher described himself as a "humanist" who had had a life-long interest in the past, particularly the Victorian period. "I like those spacious days, when people had more time than they do now," he revealed in a 1974 interview. "I've certainly spent a career making films in that period frame."

Terence Fisher broke his twelve-year silence about the film and responded to critics in a 1974 interview. "You never have a 'perfect' structure before you start any film. I don't agree with the fact that the flashback structure destroyed the suspense of the second half of the film. The flashback gives the central figure complexity and realism," the seventy-year old director explained. "I may have underemphasized some things I wanted in 'The Phantom of the Opera' and overemphasized others. I emphasized the tragedy of the film which was an important thing to me. This man who has his music stolen, and his association with the girl."

Ironically, what may come to represent Fisher's best work cinematically was also the reason for his temporary fall from grace. Following the film's untimely demise at the box office, Terence lost a number of other important assignments to younger directors, like Freddie Francis, Peter Sasdy, and Roy Ward Baker. For the man who had single-handedly launched the horror renaissance, his ability to mount large-scale productions was severely curtailed. Hammer lost confidence in him, and he spent the balance of his career remaking the same types of films over and over. He did not make another Hammer film until 1964. In retrospect, however, "The Phantom of the Opera" emerges somewhat as a legendary production. Though it is certainly not a perfect motion picture, the film has come to represent one of the finer translations of Gaston Leroux's classic. Only the passage of time will come to vindicate

Fisher, and clearly time has nicely aged the 1962 version like a fine wine.

The motion picture is available on videocassette and DVD, and plays regularly on many of the cable channels. A longer version (at 108 minutes in length) was produced several years later for release on television. Featuring John Maddison and Ian Redmond as two Scotland Yard detectives on the trail of the Phantom, these several new scenes add little to the production as a whole, and actually reduce the impact of the sequences set at the Opera House. These additional scenes were shot especially for the release of "The Phantom of the Opera" on American television.

The Phantom of the Horse Opera (1961). Walter Lantz Productions, Animated, 5min. Director: Paul J. Smith. Producer: Walter Lantz. Music Composer: Clarence Wheeler. Cast: Grace Stafford.

From Walter Lantz, the creative force behind Woody Woodpecker, "The Phantom of the Horse Opera" was yet another take on the famous story. This short, animated family feature combined themes from the Wild West and Gaston Leroux's *Le Fantôme de l'Opera* to tell a hilarious tale of a cowboy, a horse, and the "phantom." This cartoon played as the lead-in to the Hammer Horror film in some theatrical venues.

John L. Flynn

~ 7 ~
Faust and the Paradise

The Phantom: *I will not allow my music to be mutilated by those greaseballs!*
Arnold Philbin: *Hey, take it easy -*
The Phantom: *I'M THE ONLY ONE WHO CAN SING "FAUST!"*
—*"Phantom of the Paradise" (1974)*

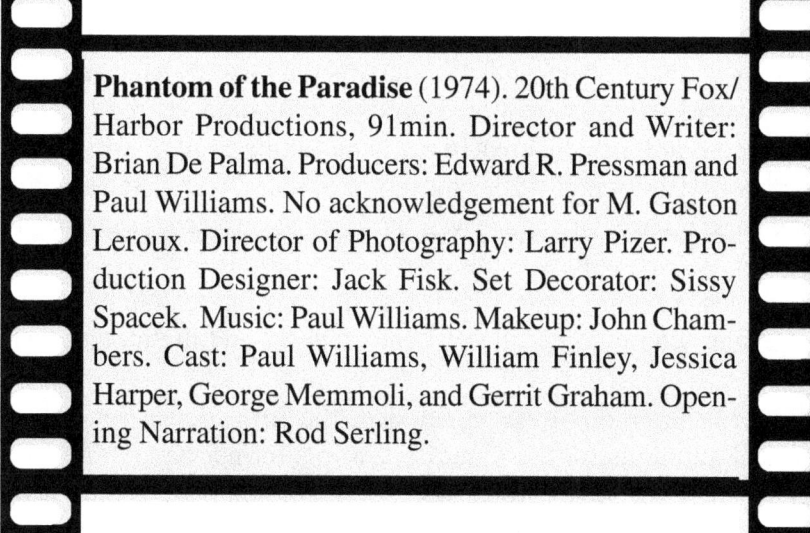

Phantom of the Paradise (1974). 20th Century Fox/Harbor Productions, 91min. Director and Writer: Brian De Palma. Producers: Edward R. Pressman and Paul Williams. No acknowledgement for M. Gaston Leroux. Director of Photography: Larry Pizer. Production Designer: Jack Fisk. Set Decorator: Sissy Spacek. Music: Paul Williams. Makeup: John Chambers. Cast: Paul Williams, William Finley, Jessica Harper, George Memmoli, and Gerrit Graham. Opening Narration: Rod Serling.

In marked contrast to the dark romanticism of Lon Chaney's silent classic (1925), Arthur Lubin's operatic monstrosity (1943), or Terence Fisher's flawed but beautiful adaptation (1962), Brian De Palma's "Phantom of the Paradise" is a poetic, subtly ironic, bitingly satiric, and occasionally brilliant re-interpretation of the famous story. The title of the film itself, an obvious reference to Gaston Leroux's novel as well as Goethe's "Faust" and John Milton's *Paradise Lost*, provides the first clue that all the pretensions of earlier adaptations have been dispensed with in order to return to the contextual essence structure. and theme of the original. Aware that Le Fantôme de l'Opera not only tells the tragic tale of a disfigured composer and his love for a young opera singer but also examines universal questions about the nature of beauty and ugliness, good and evil, illusion and reality, De Palma revises the Frenchman's work in terms that a hip, contemporary audience would understand. Thus, within the limits of cinema and cinematic adaptation, his film comes the closest (in contrast to the previous attempts) to producing a truly authentic modern rendering of Leroux's classic.

The Screen Story

Brian DePalma's modern, satiric remake of *Le Fantôme de l'Opera* opens with the darkened image of a dead bird (symbol of "Death Records") and the familiar, disembodied voice that once took television audiences on flights of the imagination in "The Twilight Zone" and "Night Galley." The pre-credits narration by Rod Serling informs us that Swan (Paul Williams) is the most popular musician in the world, having won more awards than anyone. He produced his first record at fourteen, created the band "Juicy Fruits," which itself inaugurated a wave of Fifties nostalgia, and built the first truly great rock palace - the Paradise. Swan, now creatively dead, searches for the "sound" that will make his own Xanadu come alive. The narrator concludes, saying: "This film is the story of the search...the sound ...the man who made it, the girl who sang it, and the monster who stole it. .."

Once the credits have concluded, the film focuses on several musical auditions for the Paradise. Swan's former band "The Juicy Fruits," a retro-punk parody of Sha Na Na complete a rock'n'roll song which asks "Do you remember. . .the sacrifices we've made for love." The lyrics help to underscore motivations for our three central characters, and provide a subtly ironic tone for the rest of the proceedings. As they exit the stage, Winslow Leach (William Finley) sits down at the piano to play a ballad from his rock opera. The naive, young composer has written a two-hundred page cantata which tells the story of "Faust," the legendary German magician who sold his soul to the Devil for worldly experience and power. When he begins to sing "I'd sell my soul for one love who would stand by me,"

Swan stops discussing business matters with flunky Arnold Philbin (George Memmoli) to listen. The all-powerful impresario is suddenly captivated by the lyrics of Leach's song, and confesses that his year-long search has ended. He has now heard the perfect song to open the Paradise. Dispatching his muscle-bound talent scout to purchase the rights to the song at any cost, he sits back to contemplate the success of his new acquisition.

One month later, Winslow Leach arrives at the corporate offices of Swan's record company ("Death Records"), believing that they have purchased his material on good faith. He discovers, much to his dismay, that Swan has actually stolen his song and plans to market the work under his own name. Ejected by security guards from the building, Leach goes to Swan's home -a large, fortress castle resembling Citizen Kane's Xanadu. Upon arrival' he meets dozen of women who are practicing his song in preparation for a personal audition with the all-powerful impresario. Leach pauses to offer one of the singers, a woman named Phoenix (Jessica Harper), special insight into the music, but is grabbed by Swan's bodyguards and thrown into the waiting arms of two crooked policemen.

Winslow is framed on drug charges and sent to Sing Sing Prison. There, he spends six months as a guinea pig in a scientific experiment that strips him of his singing voice. When a local news station broadcasts information about the opening of the Paradise Rock Palace, Leach freaks out and assaults one of the prison guards. He then escapes bent on vengeance, and heads for Swan's record factory in order to destroy the press that is producing copies of his song. Instead of committing sabotage, his head accidentally gets caught in the disc-pressing machine, and he is

permanently disfigured. Escaping into the night, half of his face torn away, he jumps into the East River and is presumed dead by the authorities.

Headlines from *Variety* announce the opening date of the Paradise, while a small news clipping reveals that the twisted composer who escaped from Sing Sing Prison has drown in the East River. During a rehearsal of his rock opera, Winslow Leach creeps in through the backstage door of the Paradise and makes his way to the wardrobe department. He adopts a bird-like mask to hide his deformity, and together with a black-leather jumpsuit and long cape begins to haunt the rock palace. His first attacks on Swan are harmless pranks, but his vengeance soon turns serious, using dynamite to destroy the hideously grotesque sets that are meant to illustrate his opera.

Swan quickly grows tired of the Phantom's interference and persuades Leach to join forces and rewrite his work for the grand opening. Winslow agrees, provided that Phoenix, the girl with whom he is infatuated, has the lead. The all-powerful impresario agrees, and offers a 1000-page contract - which is, in fact, a Mephistophelian pact with the devil - to the naive composer to sign. Leach signs it unwittingly with his own blood, and Swan announces: "Now we're in business together -forever!" [Swan then produces a modern alchemist's device for reconstituting damaged vocal cords and creates a synthetic voice for Leach. The voice is cracked, artificial, and scarcely recognizable as human, but does allow him to communicate. Unfortunately, he will never be able to sing again. and takes heart in the simple knowledge that Phoenix will provide the voice for his music.]

While Winslow Leach begins rewriting his work. chained in the dungeon of the Paradise, Swan executes a plan that will double-cross his captive. He demotes Phoenix to the status of a chorus girl and hires a gay. Muscle-bound, Elvis impersonator (Gerrit Graham) to sing the female lead. In fact, Swan introduces "Beef" to reporters at the airport, claiming to have discovered the punk-vampire singer in Transylvania. The all-powerful impresario also starts serving Leach a diet of amphetamines, in order to keep the naive composer in a drug-induced stupor. Once he receives the final revisions from Winslow, Swan's bodyguards seal him in a brick wall, in a scene that recalls Edgar Allan Poe's "Cask of Amontillado."

As thousands of music fans hurry to take their seats in the Paradise, the Phantom learns that he has been duped by Swan. Leach breaks out of his basement prison, and pays an impromptu visit on the cocaine-snuffing Beef. In a marvelous send-up of the famous shower scene from "Psycho," Winslow surprises Beef in the shower; but instead of threatening him with a knife, he gags the gay singer with a toilet plunger. He explains that no one will sing his music expect Phoenix, then disappears. Frightened, Beef tries to leave the Paradise, but is convinced by Philbin that "the show must go on!"

Curtains open on a set inspired by the silent German film "The Cabinet of Dr. Caligari," and several zombie-like singers appear, ripping body parts from audience members in order to create and resurrect the lead singer Beef, like Frankenstein's monster. The audience rock'n'roll with the sound and go wild in anticipation of an incredible concert. Meanwhile, the Phantom moves behind the scenes, climbing up ladders, walking across scaffolding. When Beef begins singing the first lines of his cantata, Winslow becomes enraged and hurls a lightning bolt that electrocutes the gay singer on stage. The audience members think that its part of the show, but Swan, alone, knows who is responsible. Thinking quickly, in order to avoid a panic, he instructs Phoenix to take center stage. She begins to sing and capti-

vates the audience with her voice, turning disaster into triumph.

After the concert, Winslow Leach tries to warn Phoenix of Swan's evil. but she doesn't believe him. She travels to the impresario's haunted castle. and signs her own pact with the Devil. Leach is so heartbroken that he tries to take his own life, but Swan reminds him that they are both under contract to a much lower source. "We all sell our soul to the Devil in one way or another," he tells the naive composer, then demands that Winslow write a whole new batch of long songs for Phoenix.

Rolling Stone magazine announces that the big finale at the Paradise will feature Swan, as "Faust", marry his new leading lady Phoenix. But, in reality, the all-powerful impresario intends to have the young singer murdered on stage. "An assassination live. coast-to-coast –that's entertainment!" Swan boasts. He is not interested in the young singer; he's had the love and affection of hundreds of young singers before. He wants to steal her voice, and he arranges the details of his assassination plans with Arnold Philbin. Once she is dead, Swan can legally take her voice, according to contract.

Winslow Leach learns of his dastardly plan and breaks into Swan's control room, hoping to find some evidence that will prove to Phoenix he's not insane. He finds instead the video taped contract Swan made with the Devil; as long as the tape is properly cared for, the recorded image of Swan will age in his place. Leach discovers that Swan, like Dorian Gray, has made a pact that will allow him to remain eternally young. The Phantom burns all of Swan's videos, then races off to save Phoenix.

Hungering for more blood, thousands of fans crowd into the Paradise. Winslow thwarts the would-be assassination, then swoops down onto the stage to tear the "Faust"-mask from Swan's face. The impresario's boyish features are deteriorating from the fire in the video room. The two men struggle for control of Phoenix, as mass chaos breaks out among the audience members. Finally, the violent climax is reached when Winslow produces a knife and stabs Swan to death. The mortal wounds cause Leach to start bleeding as well. He stumbles to the edge of the stage, writhing in agony, trying to reach Phoenix with his last, dying strength, then falls over dead. As Swan's body is carried away by crazed fans, Phoenix kneels over the Phantom's body and caresses his face.

Production Notes

Following the critical and popular success of "Sisters" (1973), Brian DePalma had many opportunities available to him to make any film he wanted, and chose to make a comical version of Gaston Leroux's classic novel from his own original script. He was simply not interested in making yet another straight version. The writer-director was also keenly aware of how popular rock operas had become, noteably the Who's "Tommy" and "The Rocky Horror Show," and felt that a Rock-n-Roll approach would be a fairly topical one for his new film.

"1 never had any intention of simply remaking *The Phantom of the Opera*. That had already been done about a half dozen times," Brian De Palma explained in an interview shortly after his film opened in 1974. "I took its idea of a composer having his music ripped off, endeavoring to kill the people who are massacring his music and putting on the girl he loves to sing it the way he wants it to be sung. That was the basic concept. I like the idea of a phantom haunting a rock palace as opposed to an opera house, but it isn't simply a matter of updating the classic horror story."

Brian De Palma is certainly no stranger to the genre of imaginative thrillers. From his humble beginnings in the satirical underground school of filmmaking, he has made nearly a career out of re-interpreting the work of masters, like Hitchcock and Eisenstein, for contemporary audiences. His first few motion pictures, "Murder a La Mod" (1968), "Greetings" (1968), and "The Wedding Party" (1969), were small, intimate pictures that demonstrate a superb understanding of cinematic technique. Filmed with college roommates on a budget that would barely cover the average wardrobe costs of movies today, they also reveal how much De Palma learned about drama from the theatre arts director at Sarah Lawrence College, Wilford Leach (his inspiration for Winslow Leach in "Phantom of the Paradise"). Brian went onto make a film version of the popular stage show "Dionysus in '69" (1970), then graduated to glossy, psychological horror films with "Sisters" (1973). He made "Carrie" (1976) and "The Fury" (1978) from two popular bestselling books, then directed a handful of movies based on original stories he had written. His clever imagination and fondness for Alfred Hitchcock helped underscore "Obsession" (1976) with references to "Vertigo," "Dressed to

Kill" (1980) with homages to "Psycho," "Blowout" (1981) with references to "North by Northwest," and "Body Double" (1984) with homages to "Rear Window." He turned to mainstream pictures with "Scarface" (1983), "The Untouchables" (1987), and "Bonfire of the Vanities" (1988) but De Palma still maintains a connection to his imaginative roots, studying characters that always seem to function on the fringes of society.

With a working title of "Phantom" (later changed to "Phantom of the Fillmore" and finally "Phantom of the Paradise"), DePalma assembled his cast of fringe-like characters from among the brightest and most creative talents in Hollywood at that time. He had written the role of Winslow Leach for William Finley, with whom he had previously worked, but briefly considered Paul Williams and Jon Voight before settling on Finley. During the early phases of casting, Williams turned down the role of Winslow not only because he didn't feel physically fit or menacing for the part, but also because he didn't want to use the role to send a message to the recording industry. Instead Williams embraced the role of Swan, the crooked record promoter. DePalma was asked by the studio to cast Peter Boyle as Beef, but Boyle was already committed to Mel Brooks for "Young Frankenstein" (1974). With Boyle unavailable, he sought Gerrit Graham who had been promised the role of Swan. The infamous "musical chairs" of casting, which Graham later remarked, meant that DePalma had not fleshed out their characters as fully as he would have liked in the early drafts of the script or pre-production. Like his previous pictures, he was counting on his actors, in particular Finley and Williams, to help bring his characters came into focus.

William George Finley, a long time compatriot of the director, was born in New York City, in 1942, and in his forty-year career as an actor has played a variety of twisted souls and sideshow grotesques, from Roy in "Eaten Alive" (1977) to Marco the Magnificent in "The Funhouse" (1981). Finely is ideally cast as the naive, disfigured composer, while Paul Williams turns in the best performance of his career as the all-powerful impresario who has sold his soul to the devil. Finley had been Brian De Palma's college roommate (along with actor Jared Martin), and learned his craft as a theatrical performer at Sarah Lawrence College from Wilford Leach. He was featured in supporting roles in "Murder a La Mod," "The Wedding Party," "Dionysus in '69," and "Sisters," then was offered the title role in "Phantom" when Paul Williams changed his mind to play the impresario. Bill later played psychic Raymond Dunwoodie who tracks Amy Irving in DePalma's "The Fury." During the early stages of production, Finley came up with the bird motif for the Phantom's costume, a collaboration with costume designer Rosanna Norton..

Paul Williams, the diminutive folk singer and composer, began acting in 1965, opposite Marlon Brando and Robert Redford, in "The Chase." He continued singing and playing bit roles, like Virgil in "Battle for the Planet of the Apes" (1973) until his breakthrough in 1974. Originally slated for the lead in "Phantom" (later changed to "Phantom of the Paradise" in order to avoid confusion with the King Features comic strip), Williams found the character of Swan much more interesting. The Motion Picture Academy of Arts and Sciences nominated him for an Academy Award in 1975 for his musical work in "Phantom of the Paradise." In fact, Williams performs many of the songs that we here. When Swan, for example, is adjusting Winslow's voice, the singer is not William Finley but Williams himself. This makes it for a little in-joke when Swan announces that the voice is "perfect." Williams continued playing rich, obsessed sociopaths in "Smokey and the Bandit" (1977), "The Muppet Movie" (1979), and "The Wild Wild West Revisited" (1979). Today, Paul Williams' reputation as a singer and actor has diminished considerably, but there can be little doubt of his enormous contribution to the success of De Palma's film.

The third part of the acting triumvirate in "Phantom of the Paradise" was actor and writer Gerrit Graham. Graham was also born in New York City (in 1949), and graduated from the Groton School in Groton Massachusetts in 1966. Like Finley, he has had a colorful career that has spanned nearly four decades. He has played recurring characters on "Star Trek: Deep Space Nine" (1993), "Babylon Five" (1994), and "Gargoyles" (1995), and been a featured performer in films as diverse as "Demon Seed" (1977), "Police Academy 6: City Under Siege" (1989), and "One True Thing" (1998). Graham has written for Disney cartoons, including "The Little Mermaid" (1989) and "The Prince & The Pauper" (1990), and also written the lyrics for the Grateful Dead song "Victim or the Crime." Gerrit Graham's turn as the punk-rock Vampire Beef is over the top and hilariously funny. (For trivia buffs, Graham's singing voice was dubbed by an uncredited Ray Kennedy.)

One of the most important non-speaking characters in the piece was the rock palace known as the Paradise, and DePalma chose the Majestic Theatre, located at 1925 Elm Street in Dallas, Texas. The old, run-down movie house seemed like the perfect location for the film. Sissy Spacek, who would later head-line DePalma's "Carrie," worked as a set dresser on the film, helping to transform the Majestic Theatre into the Paradise. Spacek, already an established actress, took the job to assist her boyfriend Jack Fisk who was the film's production designer.

For the scenes in which Winslow's character is disfigured in the record press, DePalma shot at a real pressing plant – the injection-molding press at the Ideal Toy Company plant. Initially, William Finley was concerned about whether the machine would be safe, but the crew assured him that it was. The press was fitted with foam pads (which resemble the casting molds in the press), and there were chocks put in the center to stop it from closing completely. The machine never worked the way it was supposed to work, and proved powerful enough to crush the chocks that it gradually kept closing. It was

Finley's speed and timing that saved him from truly being hurt, as he got his head out just in time. Incidentally, his scream in the scene was real.

The Release and Critical Commentary

Released on October 31, 1974, "Phantom of the Paradise" was intended as a Halloween treat for filmgoers, but instead became a holiday trick that few people wanted to see. The film became a box office flop, and was one of Twentieth Century-Fox's biggest disappoints in 1974. The only place in North America where the film had lasting power was in Winnipeg, Manitoba, Canada where it played on the screens for six months to young Rock-n-Rollers who understood the parody. Most critics did not accept Williams as the all-powerful impresario, and were very hard on the motion picture as a whole. Richard Combs wrote that "'Phantom of the Paradise' is too broad in its effects and too bloated in style to cut very deeply as a parody... closer to the anything goes mode of a MAD magazine lampoon." Tom Hutchinson and Roy Pickard view the movie as "the most grotesque and, in its gaudy way, unnerving version of the tale."

John Stanley simply calls it "bizarre..." Of course, most of those same critics reacted to "The Rocky Horror Picture Show" (1975), which debuted one year later, in much the same way, and that eventually became a cult favorite.

"Phantom of the Paradise" is every bit as good as "The Rocky Horror Picture Show." The film works on a multitude of levels as a thriller, a parody of horror films, a send-up of the music business, but most importantly as an examination of the sadistic rock scene of the early seventies. In fact, this combination pastiche horror and rock opera anticipates the cult following of Jim Sharman & Richard O'Brien's "The Rocky Horror Picture Show" (1975, which actually began as a London stage show in 1973) and Ken Russell's "Tommy" (1975) as well as the bizarre activities of performance groups like KISS. Part of the extraordinary force of De Palma's film can be attributed to his unique understanding of the subculture, which itself revels in the destructive and horrific images of pop nihilism. The director recognizes the angst and alienation young people feel in a world they did not create, and accepts their self-disfigurement, their deviant behavior, their outlandish costumes, their pagan-like worship of rock'n'roll icons as an outgrowth of the horror cinema.

"I have always been a fan of the horror genre." Brian De Palma further revealed in a 1974 interview. "In 'Phantom of the Paradise' I was trying to find a new way to enter that world. I thought the rock world is so stylized and expressionistic to begin with, that it would be a perfect environment in which to tell old horror tales."

De Palma also provides a loving, witty tribute to the horror genre, which spawned the earlier adaptations, with numerous references to the black-and-white thrillers of the twenties and thirties. Besides the many obvious references to the 1943 and 1962 versions of "The Phantom of the Opera," he pays tribute to "The Cabinet of Dr. Caligari" (1919), with the expressionistic sets and somnambulistic singers in Swan's show; to the 1931 version of "Frankenstein," with the assemblage of body parts and the creation of Beef by lightning as he is lowered onto the stage' to "Dracula" (1931), with gay singer Beef stepping from a coffin and bearing his fangs when he is first introduced to reporters; to "The Picture of Dorian Gray"(1945), with Swan staying boyishly young as his "video-taped" duplicate ages, and a dozen other throwaway homages. as diverse as Lon Chaney's "London After Midnight" (1927) and Alfred Hitchcock's "Psycho" (1960). These references help to underscore, through both subtle irony and biting satire, the reasons why a talented yet disfigured individual would find it necessary to hide behind a mask. Our culture has been conditioned through classical literature, fundamentalist religion, and - more recently - cosmetic advertisements to view ugliness as evil. De Palma recognizes this as one of the many themes in Gaston Leroux's classic and attempts to bring the message clearly home.

Winslow Leach's deformity is no more or less horrific than the disfigurement of a burn victim or facial injuries suffered by a returning Vietnam vet. However, in a society that stresses the "body beautiful," Leach is not only an outcast but someone to be feared by society. Complicated by the damage to his vocal cords and his need to use a mechanical voice to speak, Leach appears as a monster. When he tries to convince Phoenix that Swan is evil, she not only doesn1t believe him but is repulsed by his face. The young singer runs into the arms of the diminutive impresario for safety. Ironically, Swan is the real monster, the satanic force behind the madness. Boyishly attractive, wealthy, talented, and successful, he seduces women with his charm and controls others with his power. Produced by the same society that creates and immortalizes the Ted Bundys of the world, Swan is the net result of late twentieth century breeding —a sociopath. He has no conscience or regard for those around him, and takes advantage of everyone. Winslow, naive and misguided, is regrettably one of his many victims.

Unlike Gaston Leroux's mad musical genius, who totally dominated and terrified the Paris Opera House with his powerful personality, the "Phantom" of the Paradise suffers many indignities for his art before he initiates a course of action. His weak-minded, introspective personality allows Swan to deceive him time after time; he is the ultimate fall-guy, comic buffoon, and straight man to the larger than life impresario. His first attempts to haunt the rock palace are perfunctory, and his enrichment of the young singer's career appears to be more as a manager than a tutor. Winslow Leach is a parody of Erik the Phantom, satirically inspired by De Palma to provide audiences with a sympathetic protagonist.

Other comic distractions, or confusions of expectation, help make this tragic tale more accessible to contemporary viewers. Before one central character disappears behind a mirror, we expect the "Phantom" of the Paradise to emerge from his labyrinthine lair; but the director inverts the scene, having Swan actually surprise, then frighten the already confused Winslow Leach. When the Phantom sneaks upon Beef (Gerrit Graham), who's taking a shower a la "Psycho," we expect Leach to threaten him with a knife; but instead De Palma turns the scene comic by having the Phantom clamp a toilet plunger over Beef's mouth. Similarly, when the gay singer upstages Phoenix during the opening night performance of "Faust," our normal expectations call for the Phantom to drop a chandelier on Beef's head; instead the improvised scene has Winslow seize a neon-shaped lightning bolt from the set design and hurl it at his girlfriend's rival. The motion picture abounds with comic touches that make us laugh, while at the same time consider what the auteur is trying to tell us.

"My view of the world is ironic, bitter, acid, but basically funny, too. I'm a real gallows humorist. I see something funny in most grim circumstances," he commented in a recent article. Although irony and satire contribute much to the enjoyment of "Phantom of the Paradise," the real strength of the motion picture lies in De Palma's uncanny sense of atmosphere, rhythm, color, poetic ellipses, and his knack for building sequences in parallel action which converge into a single shot. He is a wonderfully gifted tactician who understands the elements that go into a good horror film.

Brian De Palma did weather the storm of criticism, and has since become one of the most important filmmakers in Hollywood. His unique retelling of Gaston Leroux's classic novel remains a popular, late-night cult film on college campuses to this day, along side "The

Rocky Horror Picture Show." "Phantom of the Paradise" is also currently available on home video, and plays regularly on many of the cable stations.

Other Related Productions

KISS Meets the Phantom of the Park (1978). Hanna-Barbara Productions, 96 min. Director: Gordon Hessler. Producer: Terry Morse. Screenwriters: Jan Michael Sherman and Don Buday. Cinematographer: Robert Caramico. Film Editor: Peter Berger. Original Music by Hoyt S. Curtin. Cast: Anthony Zerbe, Peter Criss, Ace Frehley, Gene Simons, Paul Stanley, Carmine Caridi, John Dennis Johnston, John Lisbon Wood, Lisa Jane Persky, John Chappell, Terry Lester, Don Steele, and Deborah Ryan.

When the rock band KISS (Gene Simmons, Paul Stanley, Peter Criss, and Ace Frehley) comes to do a concert at a popular theme park, they run afoul of the Phantom (Anthony Zerbe as Abner Devereaux). Devereaux has found a way to clone humans into robots in his underground laboratory at the park, and he plots to use the KISS concert as a launching platform for revenge against the unscrupulous partner who has stolen the park from him. Debonair, charming, and utterly frustrated that Melissa (Deborah Ryan), the girl of his dreams, fails to notice his overtures, the Phantom becomes enraged, and turns her boyfriend into his electronic zombie. She, in turn, enlists the help of the rock group, and KISS must use their special powers to stop him.

Scripted by Jan Michael Sherman, one of the creative talents behind "The Rocky Horror Picture Show" (1975), "Kiss Meets the Phantom of the Park" attempts to parody the whole rock concert scene in much the same way that DePalma's "Phantom of the Paradise" did, but is far less imaginative. Zerbe is delightfully wicked as the Phantom, but his character is relegated to secondary status so that Gene Simmons and the boys in the band can morph into superheroes in their KISS personas and save the world. Each band member remains true to his stage persona, with some added special powers to boot. But they are simply not very interesting. The fight sequences, which seem borrowed from the "Batman" television series, are particularly embarrassing. Deborah Ryan does a splendid job in the role of Melissa. She remains true to her boyfriend, even after discovering he's been turned into an automaton by Devereaux. But the real star of the piece should have been the Phantom. Featured songs include "Rock and Roll All Night," "Shout It Out," and "Beth."

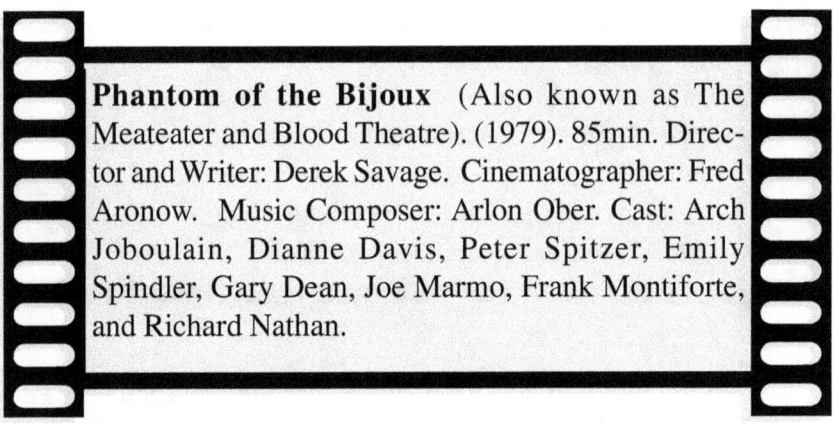

Phantom of the Bijoux (Also known as The Meateater and Blood Theatre). (1979). 85min. Director and Writer: Derek Savage. Cinematographer: Fred Aronow. Music Composer: Arlon Ober. Cast: Arch Joboulain, Dianne Davis, Peter Spitzer, Emily Spindler, Gary Dean, Joe Marmo, Frank Montiforte, and Richard Nathan.

Who would have guessed that Erik, the Phantom, was a cannibal? In "Phantom of the Bijoux" (1979), Arch Joboulian as the titular Phantom skulks around the abandoned Crest Theatre, screens old Jean Harlow silent films, and feeds on local teens that would dare trespass his hallowed halls. He even hangs one man so that others might stay away. But alas, no one has seen (or even heard of) "The Texas Chainsaw Massacre," and the teenage bodies (or rather what's left of them) continue to mount up, despite the feeble efforts of Lieutenant Wombat (Joe Marmo) of the local police department. Of course, when the new owner's daughter, Jeannie, shows up wearing her "Phantom of the Paradise" t-shirt, the Phantom thinks she resembles his idol Jean Harlow, and takes her to his shrine deep within the bowels of the theatre.

Released on home video alternately as "The Maneater" and "Blood Theatre," this low-budget slasher film bears very little resemblance to Gaston Leroux's classic novel, and has been thankfully relegated to the bargain bin at Walmart today.

Phantom of the Ritz (1992). Prism, 88min. Director: Allen Plone. Producer: Carol Marcus Plone. Screenwriters: Allen Plone and Tom Dempsey. Based on *Le Fantôme de l'Opera* by Gaston Leroux. Cinematographer: Ron Diamond. Music Composers: Wendy Frazier and John Madara. Cast: Peter Bergman, Russell Curry, Joshua Sussman, and Deborah Van Valkenburgh.

With equal parts of Gaston Leroux's *Le Fantôme de l'Opera* and Brian DePalma's "Phantom of the Paradise" (1974), this low-budget, direct-to-video quickie features yet another "phantom" stalking a theatre. In this case, the theatre is an abandoned movie palace once known as the "Ritz," and Ed Blake (Peter Bergman) has purchased the place to stage 50s-style Rock-n-Roll shows. The Phantom (Joshua Sussman), who narrates the film, explains that he has been living in the basement of the Ritz his entire life, and just wants a peaceful retirement. The lousy musical acts from the new owner's open auditions drive the Phantom crazy, and eventually he has to deal with the zany people (including a midget plumber) who now run his theatre. Then people start being killed in a rash of "accidents"... leading to the familiar conflagration. Deborah Van Valkenburgh, a familiar character actress from television and film, plays the nominal love interest. "Phantom of the Ritz" (1992) is aimed at the same audience that loved "Phantom of the Paradise" and "The Rocky Horror Picture Show" but totally misses its mark.

In 2000, the Phantom that once haunted the Bijou, then later the Ritz, has now moved to the suburbs to haunt a 26-screen megaplex on the night of the Hollywood premiere of "Midnight Mayhem" in a Disney Channel Original Movie. Seventeen year-old Pete Riley (Taylor Handley) and the other employees (Richy Mabe, Julia Cantrey, Joanne Boland, J.J. Stocker, and Lisa Ng) of the megaplex have been told their jobs are on the line if anything goes wrong by the theatre manager (Rich Hutchman). Naturally, things begin to go wrong, and the staff must fight back against the Phantom before the final reel.

Phantoms of the Opera

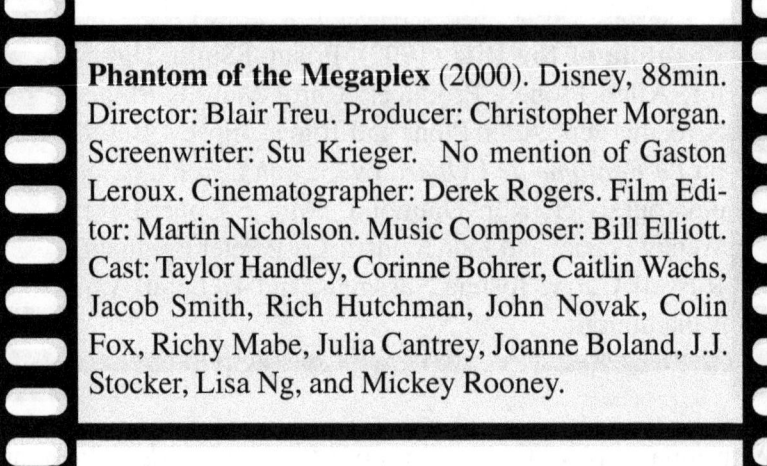

Phantom of the Megaplex (2000). Disney, 88min. Director: Blair Treu. Producer: Christopher Morgan. Screenwriter: Stu Krieger. No mention of Gaston Leroux. Cinematographer: Derek Rogers. Film Editor: Martin Nicholson. Music Composer: Bill Elliott. Cast: Taylor Handley, Corinne Bohrer, Caitlin Wachs, Jacob Smith, Rich Hutchman, John Novak, Colin Fox, Richy Mabe, Julia Cantrey, Joanne Boland, J.J. Stocker, Lisa Ng, and Mickey Rooney.

Sweet with very little bite behind it, "Phantom of the Megaplex" is yet another confection like "Popcorn." The references to Lon Chaney and his original 1925 version of "The Phantom of the Opera" demonstrate a love of movies, and casting loveable Mickey Rooney as the Movie Mason was a stroke of real genius. Catch it some night on the Disney Channel.

John L. Flynn

~ 8 ~
Trap Doors on a Hollywood Back Lot

Phantom: *"To destroy the back lot is to destroy yourself!"*
 —*"The Phantom of Hollywood" (1974)*

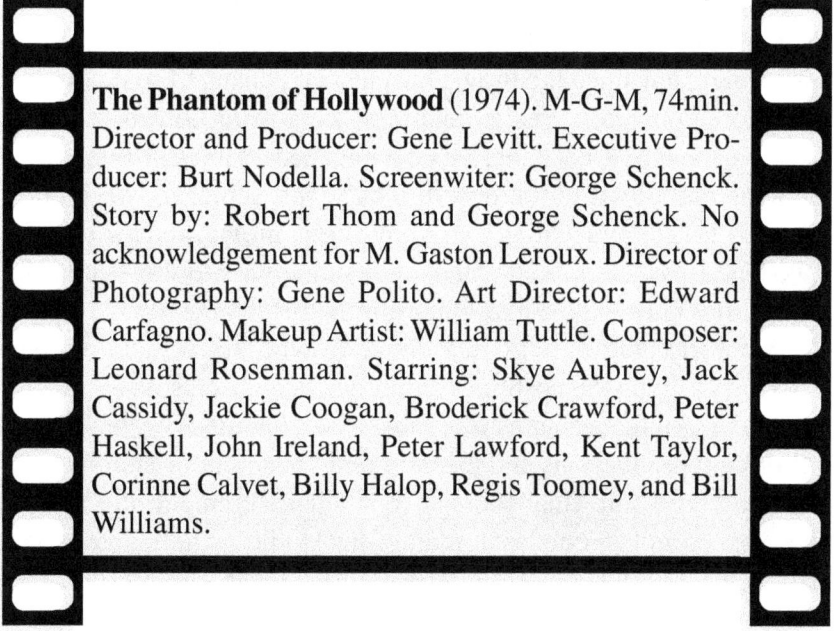

The Phantom of Hollywood (1974). M-G-M, 74min. Director and Producer: Gene Levitt. Executive Producer: Burt Nodella. Screenwiter: George Schenck. Story by: Robert Thom and George Schenck. No acknowledgement for M. Gaston Leroux. Director of Photography: Gene Polito. Art Director: Edward Carfagno. Makeup Artist: William Tuttle. Composer: Leonard Rosenman. Starring: Skye Aubrey, Jack Cassidy, Jackie Coogan, Broderick Crawford, Peter Haskell, John Ireland, Peter Lawford, Kent Taylor, Corinne Calvet, Billy Halop, Regis Toomey, and Bill Williams.

Released the same year as Brian De Palma's "Phantom of the Paradise" (1974), this television movie-of-the-week was yet another retelling of the familiar story. Encouraged by the success of "Frankenstein: The True Story" (1973) and "Dracula" (1973), small screen adaptations of classic horror novels which had performed admirably well in the ratings, producer and director Gene Levitt hired George

Phantoms of the Opera

Schenck and Robert Thom to develop an number of horror properties. One of those properties was a contemporized version of the Gaston Leroux tale. Levitt thought that, by placing its setting not in an opera house but in a deteriorating movie studio and by making the Phantom an aging, disfigured film star, television audiences would have better access to the character and his plight. And although the credits fail to acknowledge the 1911 novel as source material, no one could possibly fail to identify with the efforts of a masked avenger to preserve his home of thirty years and his right to privacy.

The Screen Story

The seventy-four minute telefilm opens with W-KDF reporters boarding a helicopter to complete a feature story for their nightly news on the closing of a major studio. The internationally famous Worldwide Studios (in actuality, Metro-Goldwyn-Mayer) has hit hard times, and has been forced to sell its back lot to Hollywood property developers. The studio (as we are told) has been making movies for forty years, but since the movie business has changed so much, with audiences demanding reality and producers being forced to film on location, the movie back lots are no longer necessary. As the reporter's cameras pan down to the deserted back lot, actual movie footage, from "A Tale of Two Cities," an Andy Hardy movie, and a World War Two feature, is intermixed with their documentary to show audiences what things once looked like. Gone now, with lot three, are the "castles in Spain, the jungles of Africa, Small Town, U.S.A., and old New York City." Even the costumes and props have been sold to the largest bidder. All that remains is a ghost town, haunted by the spirits of a thousand productions and the very real "phantom of Hollywood. "

Shooting some final footage for their assignment, the W-KDF reporters complete one last circuit of the studio by helicopter just as two teenage punks are scaling the security fence into lot two. They fail to notice the intrusion, but the ever-watchful visage of the "Phantom" doesn't. He follows the two interlopers on their violent journey through the back lot, as they break statues and props, tear down walls, and smash windows. Annoyed by their wanton acts of vandalism, the "Phantom" suddenly appears from behind one of the broken windows. Wearing an executioner's mask, leather tunic, and cape (looking much like "Dr. Doom" from Marvel Comics), he is the image of an avenging spectre. He grabs one of the teenagers and bludgeons him to death with a mace, then moves swiftly on the other and kills him as well.

Sometime later, Captain O'Neill (Broderick Crawford) and Lt. Gifford (John Ireland) of the Los Angeles Police Department examine the bodies of the "leather-jacketed punks" and inform Executive Publicity Agent Ray Burns (Peter Haskell) that the deaths were not accidental. The two boys had split skulls and broken necks—the work of "some deranged psychopath." Burns finds their conclusions hard to believe: the back lot is completely deserted, and no one could have gotten in or out without alerting the security police. Worldwide Studios CEO Cross (Peter Lawford) orders the police away and demands that his publicist keep the deaths out of the newspaper, so as not to blow a multi-million dollar deal with Westside Financial. Lot two, along with the remaining costumes and props, is to be sold in a couple of days.

Financial consultants from Westside arrive for an impromptu tour of the forty-acre facility, and Ray Burns reluctantly takes them on a tour of the lot. They drive past Andy Hardy's house, visit the sets of the Brother's Grimm and "The Three Musketeers," and walk through old London of the Dickens novels. The financiers are not interested in the history of the lot, just where they can begin building their condos. Behind the scenes, the "Phantom" watches their every move.

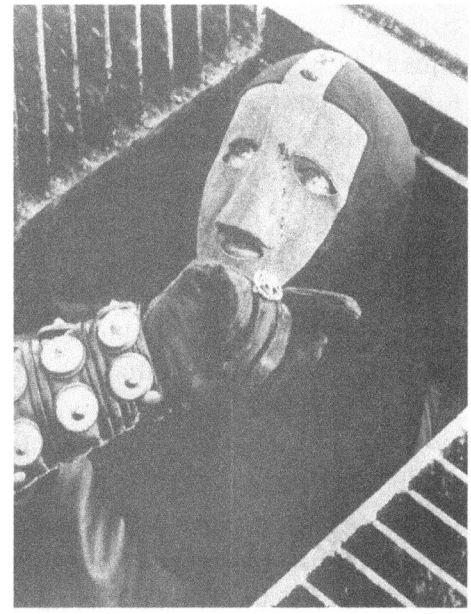

Back in the CEO's office, Burns and Cross discover a note from the "Phantom," which reads "To destroy the back lot is to destroy yourself!" Cross tries to trivialize the message, by quickly dismissing it as a prank, in order to prevent panic among the new buyers. He then orders his secretary Betty to arrange a survey team to review the property. But the note is no prank. The "Phantom" intends to prevent the sale of lot two at all costs, including murder. When the two men arrive to conduct their survey, he carries out his threat, bludgeoning them to death and burying their bodies in the back lot graveyard.

When Los Angeles police detectives arrive the next day searching for the lost men, they begin questioning employees of Worldwide Studios. Joe, the aged watchman, tells them about the legend of the "Phantom"—a mysterious figure who has been living on the back lot for years. No one really knows who he is, or if he is real, but they all seem to have their own private speculations about him. (Ironically, as the police continue their line of questioning, the "Phantom" looks on from the shadows and listens to their idle talk.) The police have searched every storeroom, every building, every bush, and have found nothing! Ray Burns begins to believe that the "Phantom" is real, and warns his girlfriend Randi Cross (Skye Aubrey) to be very careful.

Later that night, while Cross and Burns are reviewing the forty-year retrospective created by editor Jonathan (Jackie Coogan), utilizing clips from "Ben-Hur," "Grand Hotel," "Bringing Up Baby," "Mutiny on the Bounty," and "San Francisco,,. the screening room phone rings. The "Phantom" demands that the sale of lot two be canceled under threat of more deaths, then hangs up. Cross is furious and orders Ray Burns to find out who this "Phantom" is. Burns begins by consulting Otto Vonner (Jack Cassidy), the film genius who maintains all the records and trivia about the studio. Otto claims "the Phantom is just a rumor" and dismisses the matter as wholly superstition. But as the scene ends, the camera focuses on Otto's ring—a ring that is identical to the one that the "Phantom" wears. Could the doddering old man be the illusive, masked avenger?

When a night watchman is murdered (while straying too far into the domain of the "Phantom"), the police again are called. Lt. Gifford has had enough of the studio bigwigs and demands that Cross start cooperating with their efforts to find the murderer. Cross refuses, then, in the same breath, announces that lot two has been sold to Westside Financial for real estate development. Worldwide Studios will host a final all-star party to announce the sale of the studios, with the hopes that the party will lure the "Phantom" out into the open for capture. If not, he will be buried in the rubble of the back lot when it is bulldozed to the ground. Captain O'Neill and Lieutenant Gifford concur with Cross's plan, unaware that the "Phantom" has been listening to their conversation in the sewer grate below their feet.

"The end of an era," Otto remarks to the gate watchman as he remembers "the ghosts of a thousand pictures" who made films there. He is unhappy with the news of the sale but attends the big gala nonetheless. Other studio personnel, including Cross and his daughter Randi, extras in costume, movie stars, and executives of Westside Financial are all in attendance. During the elaborate festivities, a man wearing an executioner's mask, leather tunic, and cape appears from one of the old buildings and startles Otto. The old, doddering film archivist approaches the strangely costumed man and demands that the murders cease, or he will expose Karl, his younger brother, to the police. Horrified with the prospect of exposure, the "Phantom" drops a heavy sign on Otto that kills him
instantly. Police pursue the masked man, but he easily evades capture by moving though the honeycombed sewer system.

Moments later, he reappears on a, soundstage, which resembles the Paris Opera House. and startles Randi Cross. His awful visage is too much for her, and she falls to the floor unconscious. Taking her gently in his arms, he carries her to his lair below the cemetery. When the daughter of studio head Cross finally awakes, Randi discovers

that she is in an underground cavern which has been decorated to look like an actor's dressing room. She soon comes upon the "Phantom," who is unmasked, sitting in the center of a dining area, reciting lines from "Hamlet."

He hides his scarred features from her and forces Randi to write a ransom letter to her father: in exchange for the deed to the property, he will spare her life. Cross momentarily concedes to his demands, but then recants when Lt. Gifford and Ray Burns discover a secret crawl passage which has allowed the "Phantom" to move around the studio unnoticed. Perhaps they can follow the passage to his lair? Meanwhile, bulldozers have already begun to tear down the back lot.

Returning to his lair, the "Phantom" accidentally reveals his face to Randi. She is not horrified by the disfigurement and in showing genuine pity asks him how it happened. Thirty years before, Karl Vonner (Jack Cassidy, in a dual role) was a famous actor whose face was badly burned when an explosive charge went awry during the filming of "The Three Musketeers." One day, he had been the dashing D'Artagnan, and the next, a hideous, disfigured monster. His brother Otto had convinced him to take a job as a night watchman, and while working at such a demeaning occupation, he conceived of the plan to live his life in the shadows of the studio back lot. Karl reveals his old press photos, and Randi is moved to tears by his pitiful story.

Suddenly, the ground begins to tremble as bulldozers begin trashing his home. Arming himself with the bow and arrows he once carried as "Robin Hood," Karl Vonner goes out to fight with the wrecking crew. He attempts to shoot the workers down, one by one, with his primitive bow, but he is no match for the police's far superior weapons. Ray Burns arrives to rescue Randi just as the walls to the lair come crashing down. He then chases the "Phantom" to the top of a Medieval castle, where Karl Vonner is finally gunned down. As his body falls to the pavement below, the bulldozers continue to push buildings down. His death is inexorably connected to the death of the back lot and the end of old Hollywood.

Production Notes

Every bit as unrelenting as the 1925 silent Lon Chaney classic, "The Phantom of Hollywood" demonstrates exceptional skill in the use of both camera and editing to sweep the audience into the nightmarish world of shadows that is the studio back lot. Had Gene Levitt remained there, focusing on the comings-and-goings of the Phantom, the telefilm might well have supplanted "The Night Stalker" (1972) as the most horrific movie made directly for the small screen. But instead, the producer-director feels compelled to show us the mundane world of the movie executives. Thus, the weakest part of the piece has to do with the background details and set-up of the studio sale. The audience needs this information to understand the

Phantom's motives for killing six men; but, at the same time, these scenes actually dilute the wonderfully haunting and evocative world of the Phantom. Particularly effective, though, is the early fly-over by the W-KDF reporters, in which actual movie footage is combined with shots of the back lot. This lends an even more nightmarish tone to the bizarre proceedings, and provides enough informational set-up that make the other lackluster scenes superfluous.

The latest in a long line of Phantoms, Karl Vonner (as portrayed by veteran character actor Jack Cassidy) is certainly the most deranged, lacking all other rationale de compri. Disfigured in an accident that occurred nearly thirty years before, the arrogant, Shakespearean thespian has tragically never come to terms with what he is. He lives in the past with memories of his association with Clark Gable, Douglas Fairbanks, and Errol Flynn, and deludes himself into thinking that time has stood still. By maintaining an "altar" of publicity photos from some of his past films, he perpetuates the illusion. In Vonner's mind, he is still playing the role of a leading man—either the role of an impetuous, young Gaston from "The Three Musketeers." or the notorious robber-baron of  Sherwood Forest from "Robin Hood." or an avenging angel. Even when he sits alone in his underground lair, he recites lines from "Hamlet," portraying the melancholy Dane. Like Lon Chaney's fanciful interpretation of Erik the Phantom, Karl Vonner cannot function in the real world with his handicap. He finds it much easier to hide behind masks of other parts, unaware that thirty years of role-playing has stripped him of his humanity. Without the back lot, his world of illusion would shatter, and he would at last have to see his own reflection in the mirror.

The Phantom of Hollywood is a tragic man crippled more by his pride than his disfigurement. He longs to be the elegant hero, and tries to use his fantasies as a shield from reality. In the end he looses everything, but dies seemingly in triumph. Perhaps more than anything this film version elevates the homeless and tragically destitute to the level of humanity that they deserve.

Unlike Gaston Leroux's mad musical genius, however, the "Phantom" of Hollywood has no object of desire, no obsession, no young opera star (or. in this case, movie starlet) to enrich with his vast talents. Part of the motivation, which made Erik the Phantom a more fully realized character, has been dropped for the sake of simplicity. Karl Vonner has no other motivation beyond simple revenge. This, unfortunately, underlines one of the weaknesses in recent adaptations, and reveals how much of a complete transformation the story of *Le Fantôme de l'Opera* has undergone. In the sixty, or so, years since Monsieur Leroux first penned his tragic variation on the Beauty and the Beast fable, the central character has changed beyond all recognition. A closer examination of the ingredients used by Levitt, Thom, and Schenck to concoct their version more than bears this out. Instead of the elegant venue of the Paris Opera House, with the master architect's secret panels and chambers, the new story takes us backstage to a crumbling movie studio (the deteriorating M-G-M back lot at Culver City). Instead of the haunted and obsessed Phantom, who has been scarred since birth, it casts a disfigured actor as the "anti-hero" whose one-dimensional course of action is to prevent the destruction of an already crumbling back lot. And in place of Erik's mysterious death and burial in the labyrinthine world below the theatre, the telefilm executes Karl Vonner in an anti-climatic cops-and-robbers shoot-out. Is it any wonder why Gaston Leroux's name has been omitted from the credits when what remains of Le Fantôme de l'Opera is a flawed, paint-by-the-numbers version which seems drawn from a *Classic's Illustrated* comic book rather than the original novel?

"The Phantom of Hollywood" does occasionally rise above the standard movie-of-the-week fare, particularly in three key areas: makeup, cinematography, and a fine performance by Jack Cassidy in a dual role. Credit for the excellent makeup belongs solely to William Tuttle. Long associated with imaginative thrillers, including the award-winning "Seven Faces of Dr. Lao" (1964), Tuttle went outside the traditional realm of horror makeup to study victims at a hospital burn unit. His eye for detail and expert sculpting render a design that achieves a high level of verisimilitude. Though hardly in the same class with Lon Chaney's brilliant "death's head," it is less horrific than the makeup worn by Herbert Lom in the Hammer version and more believable than that evoked by William Finley in "Phantom of the Paradise" (1974). Regrettably, the same amount of careful consideration was not placed on costume design. The Executioner's garb appears to be purchased right off the rack from Frederick's (Frankenstein?) of Horrorwood.

Director of Photography Gene Polito demonstrates superb craftsmanship in his selection of camera angles and his evocation of Karl Vonner's dark, shadowy world. He also knows exactly what not to show, and realizes that much of the power of horror lies in suggestion rather than overt grue and gore. In spite of the many gruesome deaths - five men bludgeoned to death by a mace and a sixth crushed by a heavy sign - there is, surprising, very little blood. While Polito (and director Levitt, to a lesser extent) may be simply honoring the concerns of the network's standards and practices, he is also creating a taunt, little thriller that does not have to rely on grue-and-gore (like the same year's "Texas Chainsaw Massacre") to arouse and titillate audiences. Regrettably, scenes focusing on the "Phantom" are fewer than those that focus on the corporate executives who run the studios, but that has more to do with poor scripting than with Polito's fine camera work.

Veteran actor Jack Cassidy is brilliant as both the aging archivist Otto and the vain but troubled Karl Vonner. He brings a lonely pathos to the role of a sociopathic Phantom. Driven to commit murder in order to protect his world, he shows little or no remorse, yet there is still an underpinning of deep melancholy in his character. The husband of Shirley Jones and father of David Cassidy, Jack was certainly no stranger to unusual film or television roles. He had more than a dozen motion pictures and one television series ("He and She," 1967) to his credit. Although he died suddenly in 1976, he

left a long legacy of underplayed yet outstanding characters, including a philandering husband in "A Guide to the Married Man" (1967), a homicidal homosexual in "The Eiger Sanction" (1975), and, of course, "The Phantom of Hollywood." Regrettably, his fellow actors pale in comparison. Peter Haskell and Peter Lawford seem to sleepwalk through their roles. Broderick Crawford reprises his familiar police detective from "Highway Patrol" (1955-58) and a half dozen other films, and adds nothing new to the part. Skye Aubrey is good in the role of Randy, portraying a daughter mostly ignored by her father and courted by the studio's ad executive. She is determined to have her own life though, and when she realizes her own father would bulldoze her for profit, she accepts the fact and moves on. Jackie Coogan and John Ireland, two genuine Hollywood stars, are totally wasted in what amounts to cameo performances.

Flawed and faded today, "The Phantom of Hollywood" (1974) is still a worthy entry to the other cinematic translations of Gaston Leroux's classic. All in all, it's a film that is more important than it would have been otherwise, just because of the historic film sets in it that can't be seen anymore. The seventy-four minute telefilm is currently unavailable on videocassette, but surfaces regularly on Turner Home Entertainment's two cable networks (TNT and TBS). (Note: when M-G-M sold its entire stock of films to Ted Turner. "The Phantom of Hollywood" was one of the many acquisitions.)

Other Related Productions

The Mystery of the Hollywood Phantom (1977) for "Hardy Boys/Nancy Drew Mysteries." Universal, 2-Part, 60min. Director: Steven Stern. Producer: Joe Boston. Executive Producer: Glen Larson. Writer: Michael Sloan. Cast: Parker Stevenson, Shaun Cassidy, Pamela Sue Martin, William Schallert, Susan Buckner, Edith Atwater, Edmund Gilbert. Guest Stars: Robert Wagner, Jaclyn Smith, Dennis Weaver, Ruth Cox, Harry Rhodes, Lou Antonio, Casey Kasem, James Wainwright, J.D. Cannon, and Clive Revill.

When the young sleuths search for three kidnapped detectives - Arlo Weatherly (James Wainwright), Phil Bronson (Clive Revill) and Fenton Hardy (Edmund Gilbert) - Frank (Parker Stevenson) and Joe (Shaun Cassidy) Hardy and Nancy Drew (Pamela Sue Martin) follow the clues from a detective's convenion to a deserted Hollywood soundstage (actually a stage on the Universal Studios back lot tour). According to the legend, Stage 24 (not the real Stage 28) is haunted by the Phantom of Hollywood; he has been responsible for strange accidents, missing props, fires, and all sort of other mischief. Now the "ghost" demands a ransom of $500,000 for the release of the three top detectives, but of course Frank, Joe and Nancy are on his trail. First aired on October 2 and October 9, 1977, respectively, on the ABC network, Sunday night during the family hour, the two-part episode featured lots of celebrity guest cameos, including Bruce the shark (from "Jaws"), Robert Wagner (from "Switch"), Jaclyn Smith (from "Charlies' Angels"), Dennis Weaver (from "McCloud"), Harry Rhodes, Lou Antonio, Casey Kasem, and J.D. Cannon. But the show was little more than a retelling of "The Phantom of Hollywood," with a tour of the famous Universal Studios thrown in as filler.

Phantom of the Studio (1985) for "Knight Rider." NBC/Glen Larson Productions for Universal Television, 54min. Producer: Glen Larson. Assistant Producer: Bernadette Joyce. Creator: Glen Larson. Cast: David Hasselhoff. Edward Mulhare, and William Daniels. Guest Star: Robert Englund.

Several years before Robert Englund took on the role of Erik in "Gaston Leroux's Phantom of the Opera" (1989), he played an angry, disfigured actor who was haunting a major film studio. Though the plot is borrowed almost scene for scene from "The Phantom of Hollywood," the efforts of David Knight (David Hasselhoff) and his supercar KITT to uncover the mysterious Phantom help to raise this television show above the commonplace. The episode was shot largely in-house and made use of the famous Universal Studios' back lot tour. Ironically, sixty years before, Lon Chaney walked upon the very same sets in the classic 1925 silent film.

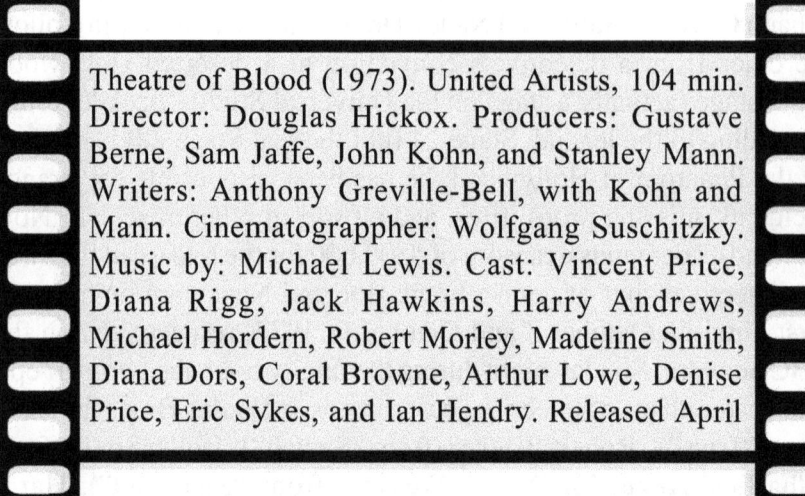

Theatre of Blood (1973). United Artists, 104 min. Director: Douglas Hickox. Producers: Gustave Berne, Sam Jaffe, John Kohn, and Stanley Mann. Writers: Anthony Greville-Bell, with Kohn and Mann. Cinematograppher: Wolfgang Suschitzky. Music by: Michael Lewis. Cast: Vincent Price, Diana Rigg, Jack Hawkins, Harry Andrews, Michael Hordern, Robert Morley, Madeline Smith, Diana Dors, Coral Browne, Arthur Lowe, Denise Price, Eric Sykes, and Ian Hendry. Released April

Although not strictly based on Gaston Leroux's work, "Theatre of Blood" (1973) borrows so liberally from the Frenchman's work that it deserves to be recognized here. Humiliated by the nine members of the London Theatre Critics Circle (including Jack Hawkins, Harry Andrews, Michael Hordern, Robert Morley, Ian Hendry, among others) who bestow the top prize to a lesser actor at an awards ceremony, Shakespearean actor Edward Lionheart (Vincent Price) commits suicide by throwing himself into the Thames. Unbeknownst to the public, he survives drowning by being rescued by homeless vagrants who live by the river. Like the dwarf and the street denizens in the 1962 Hammer version of "The Phantom of the Opera," they pledge their allegiance to Lionheart, and vow to help him carry out his revenge. A mysterious young woman named Edwina (Diana Rigg), who has been tutored as an actress by the great Edward Lionheart, throws her lot in with them. She is later revealed to be Edward's daughter. The group takes up residence at a dilapidated playhouse, the Burbage theatre (which was actually the Putney Hippodrome), in a less fashionable section of London, and begin plotting their revenge. Two years later, Edward Lionheart emerges from the theatre, and begins killing each of the drama critics in a variety of innovative ways, copied from famous death scenes in Shakespeare plays.

John L. Flynn

~ 9 ~
In the Cellars of the Budapest Opera House

Once, when they were passing before an open trapdoor on the stage, Raoul stopped over the dark cavity. "You have shown me over the upper part of your empire, Christine, but there are strange stories told of the lower part. Shall we go down?" "Never!...Everything that is underground belongs to him!"
—*Gaston Leroux, Le Fantôme de l'Opera*

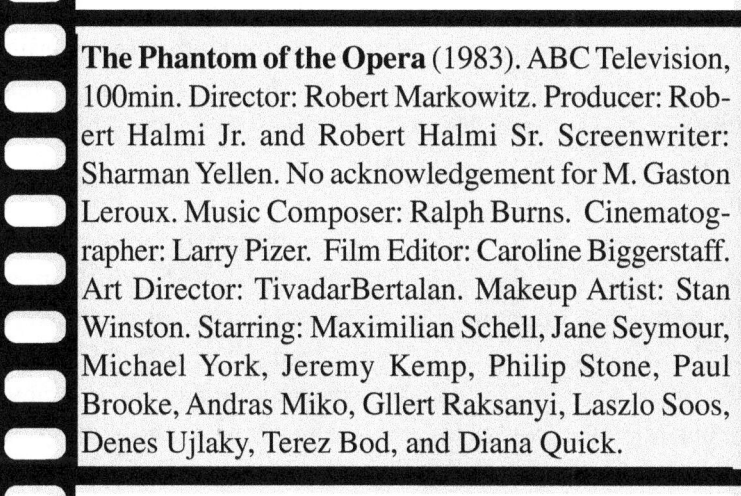

The Phantom of the Opera (1983). ABC Television, 100min. Director: Robert Markowitz. Producer: Robert Halmi Jr. and Robert Halmi Sr. Screenwriter: Sharman Yellen. No acknowledgement for M. Gaston Leroux. Music Composer: Ralph Burns. Cinematographer: Larry Pizer. Film Editor: Caroline Biggerstaff. Art Director: TivadarBertalan. Makeup Artist: Stan Winston. Starring: Maximilian Schell, Jane Seymour, Michael York, Jeremy Kemp, Philip Stone, Paul Brooke, Andras Miko, Gllert Raksanyi, Laszlo Soos, Denes Ujlaky, Terez Bod, and Diana Quick.

Not so much a new adaptation of Gaston Leroux's 1911 classic but a remake of the 1943 and 1962 versions, "The Phantom of the Opera" (1983) was a further departure from the familiar story. Filmed entirely in Budapest, Hungary, the telefilm exhibited a talented international cast, lush photography, and extravagant production values, but not a faithful script. In fact, the credits fail to recognize M. Leroux or acknowledge his novel as source material. Television has produced a number of first-rate, expensive adaptations of classic novels, including "The Hunchback of Notre Dame" (1982), "A Tale of Two Cities" (1982), and "The Scarlet Pimpernel" (1983), for its prime-time sweeps, and "The Phantom of the Opera" was to have been the next in its popular series. However, when it debuted on January 29, 1983, audiences, familiar with the tragic tale of a disfigured composer and his love for a young opera singer, were treated to a number of other unfortunate changes and omissions.

The Screen Story

Set in Budapest, Hungary, prior to the outbreak of the First World War, the telefilm opens, predictably, with a beautiful, young singer completing a beautifully executed aria in the private chambers of a musical tutor. Elena (Jane Seymour, in the first of two roles), the wife of a noted conductor has been rehearsing for years behind closed doors in an effort to perfect her singing abilities. On the eve of her debut at the Budapest Opera House (actually the József Katona Theatre in Kecskemét), she is understandably nervous, and seeks comforting words from her tutor-husband. Shandor Korvin (Maximilian Schell), who believes she is very talented, tries to relieve her fears with words of reassurance. He, too, has invested years of his life in training her. and wishes to see her succeed.

Unfortunately, those individuals who want to see her fail - a spurned lover and a jealous theatre critic – arrange for her debut to be a disastrous one. The manager of the opera house Baron Hunyadi (Jeremy Kemp), a pompous Hungarian aristocrat, once showered Elena with riches as his sign of affection, but she rejected his materialistic vision of love for a much deeper one with Korvin. He never forgave her rejection, and now seeks to get even with the help of a local drama critic Kraus (Philip Stone), who was also jilted by the pretty young singer. Together, they conspire to have her declared an incompetent talent. The two men seek not only to embarrass her but also to humiliate her popular and famous conductor-husband.

A series of bad reviews, proclaiming Elena's debut as Marguerite in "Faust" a failure, drive the young singer to suicide, and she drowns herself. Enraged to the brink of madness by her death Korvin confronts the two individuals who are responsible. While struggling with the drama critic, he accidentally knocks over a heater and sets his clothes ablaze. His rage very literally consumes him as the skin on his face, hands, and body is instantly burned away by the fire. Disfigured, permanently scarred beyond recognition, he crawls away from the conflagration. With a rat catcher as his accomplice, he then flees underground into the labyrinthine world below the city, there to heal his body and plan an elaborate scheme of revenge.

Five years later, a young, Italian singer named Maria Gianelli (Jane Seymour, in the second of her two roles) arrives in Budapest, Hungary, seeking employment with the local opera company. Michael Hartnell (Michael York), a noted British conductor who assumed the role of opera director when Korvin disappeared, is taken with her beauty and talent. He hires her, over the objections of the resident diva Madame Bianchi (Diana Quick), and assigns Christine to understudy the female lead. When La Carlotta takes ill during one of the performances, Miss Gianelli triumphs in her place, bringing her to the attention of both Shandor Korvin and the Manager. To the former conductor, she is both the reincarnation of his dead wife and the perfect tool to execute his plan of revenge. To Baron Hunyadi, the Hungarian aristocrat, she represents, simply, a second opportunity for sexual conquest.

Korvin emerges from the shadows as Orpheus, the musical angel of the Budapest Opera House, and abducts Maria from her dressing-room. He takes her to his mysterious, subterranean world below the city. He warns her not to look behind the mask, then kneels at her feet in worship, praising the gods for her return from the dead. When she demands her freedom, he confesses his undying affection. His madness clouds the reality of her identity. For

Korvin, he truly believes Miss Gianelli is his wife Elena. The Phantom then sits down at his piano and begins at the point where he left off five years before, determined that she will become successful.

Maria Gianelli is so overwhelmed that she pretends to play along with his madness in order to gain her freedom. But while rehearsing the song, she tears the mask from his face and exposes his disfigurement. The young singer is, at first, frightened by his horrible face, then, seeing his sorrow, looks upon him without fear. Feeling sorry for him, she continues to sing. The Phantom tutors her by day, and at night she becomes the toast of Budapest, upstaging La Carlotta with her superb playing of secondary characters. The Manager attempts to shower her with affection, buying her gifts and flowers, but she is not fooled by the charlatan. Hartnell also tries to court her, but she remains very distant, as if held captive by some unseen force.

Before long, the Phantom is ready to launch his terrifying plan to destroy his enemies in order to make certain Maria enjoys the success denied his wife. Luring the resident diva, the theatre critic, and several other hapless figures to his lair, he dispatches them one-by-one with his own brand of retributive justice. He acts as judge, jury, and executioner, and hands out sentences that fit each person's crime. To prevent La Carlotta from ever singing poor notes again, he slits her throat. To prevent the drama critic from writing future poor reviews, he cuts off the man's hands, then strangles him. No one must stand between his wife Elena (actually Miss Gianelli) and success.

When the first murders are discovered, members of the theatre company are thrown into a panic. The British director attempts to allay their fears, but his words provide little comfort. Maria recognizes his frustration and feels not only compelled but guilt-ridden to reveal all that she knows. She proceeds to tell him the sordid truth about the Phantom, his subterranean world, and her daily visits to him. Hartnell is totally aghast by the story and vows to take her to safety as soon as the police are notified. Unbeknownst to the two young lovers, the Phantom is perched on a scaffold, high above their heads, and has been listening to every word of Maria's betrayal.

The local police are summoned, but they can find no evidence of the murderer or his underground lair.

Later that night, prior to the evening's performance, Korvin uses Miss Gianelli unwittingly to ensnare the Manager in his trap. The

Hungarian aristocrat follows the young singer to her dressing room with the thought of seduction in mind, only to be grabbed by the Phantom. The former conductor leads his two victims down into the cellars of the Budapest Opera House to exact his revenge, but Hartnell and several police officials discover a trap door in her dressing room, and follow after them. Surprised by the sudden appearance of the police, Korvin slips away, and climbs to the rafters above the theatre.

In the climatic conclusion, Korvin stands atop the chandelier and cuts the suspending chain above his head. It is apparently an act of suicide, but when the chandelier plummets down into the screaming audience, the Phantom's actions become more clear. He has purposely timed the fall to murder his true nemesis, the manager of the opera house. Smiling faintly, the Phantom turns his last glance to the young singer and bids a fond and lovely farewell to his "wife" before dying himself.

Production Notes

Far less concerned with the original Victorian conceit, which focused on the metaphysical opposition of beauty and ugliness, good and evil, sanity and madness. Robert Markowitz's movie concentrates - as did several other versions before it - on simple melodrama. As a result, the made-for-television movie has rejected most of the key elements that made the 1911 novel as well as the 1925 silent film so endearing, in favor of another revenge fable. Like the 1943 and 1962 versions, this incarnation of the Phantom has been wronged by his contemporaries and must struggle against impossible odds to right the injustice. The single connecting thread to the Frenchman and his work, which was the main theme of the novel - that of the Phantom's obsession with the young singer and his desire to see her become a great star - survives simply as an afterthought. This would certainly explain, though hardly excuse, the reason why Gaston Leroux's name does not appear in the credits. Director Markowitz and screenwriter Yellen seem to have "borrowed" his book title and the barest essence of a storyline to create their own exploitative vision.

The Phantom of their story is neither a menace nor a mad musical genius with a hidden agenda; he is simply insane. Disfigured by a freak accident, the Phantom inflicts his own brand of vengeance upon those responsible. He becomes judge, jury, and executioner, and proceeds to eliminate his rivals one-by-one. When. in the course of standard television melodrama, a woman appears resembling his dead wife, he shifts the focus of his revenge to make her a star. While these plot contrivances may seem highly dramatic, they are certainly not Leroux! His Erik had been scarred from birth, and lives in the labyrinthine world below the Paris Opera House because members of French society view him as a freak. He labors on his opera "Don Juan Triumphant" and tutors a young singer in an attempt to achieve acceptance. Only when his world of privacy is threatened does he commit murder and other acts of violence. Very little of this character remains in the Markowitz-Yellen version.

Other obligatory shock elements, found in all previous adaptations, have been either eliminated or down-played in favor of a script that is long on talk and short on horror. Besides the title, just about the only ingredients remaining from the original story are the opera house setting, the obsession-revenge theme, and the famous unmasking scene. The film pretends to be very literary, relying primarily on the acting skills of the cast rather than the cinematic abilities of its director, but finds itself trapped by its own uncinematic conventions. Rather than allowing the camera to build atmosphere and tension by weaving its own spells, Markowitz simply follows the characters around as they recite their lines. Like a stage play that has been recorded on video, the pacing is slow and pedantic, and suspense is reduced to a few sensationalist images, like the unmasking, which themselves are handled ineptly.

Although most of the major set-pieces of the novel are missing from the film, the unmasking scene remains somewhat intact. Regrettably, our glimpse behind the mask is handled rather clumsily by the director, as poor camera angles diminish instead of enhance the shock value. Then, too, the make-up is less than convincing. Stan Winston, who would later achieve wonderful results with "The Terminator" (1984) and "Aliens" (1986), spent several months studying victims at a hospital burn unit, much like Tuttle before him. Yet his eye for detail is not as sharp, and his make-up appliances for Maximilian Schell look like left-over masks from an after-Halloween sale. His phantom is the least convincing of all the phantoms that came before him.

The Hungarian setting is interesting, but contributes very little that is new. The tragic story of the Phantom is so universal that it could be set in Paris, London, New York, or outer Mongolia, for that matter. Producer Robert Halmi choose to shoot on location for financial rather than artistic reasons, and sent his film crew to Budapest, Hungary, in order to save costly production dollars.. The opera house is actually the József Katona Theatre in Kecskemét. He could afford lush scenery, expensive costumes, and hundreds of extras because Hungarian craftsmen work for considerably less than their Hollywood counterparts. Scenes meant to evoke the dark, subterranean world of the Phantom were actually shot in tunnels under a brewery.

"The Phantom of the Opera" fails miserably in other areas as well, most notably in the much ballyhooed international cast. Maximilian Schell, a fine character actor, is the least acceptable of all the Phantoms, due in large part to his limited range. He does not have the depth of Lon Chaney, the charm of Claude Rains, or the menace of Jack Cassidy. He does, however, bring a certain degree of madness as well as devotion to duty that are somewhat typical of the dozens of roles he has played over the years. Born in Austrian in 1930, he played in many international films, but his breakthrough role was in "The Young Lions" (1958) as a tough, sadistic soldier. Three years later, after winning the Academy Award for supporting actor in "Judgment at Nuremberg" (1961), he became typecast as a German officer or aging Nazi war criminal in a hand full of films, including "Counterpoint" (1967), "The Odessa File" (1974), "The Man in the Glass Booth" (1975), "Cross of Iron" (1977), and "Julia" (1977). His thick, Austrian accent was a hindrance to his career, and caused him to be cast as a character actor in minor roles in "Krakatoa" (1968), "Avalanche Express" (1979), and "The Black Hole" (1979). Today,

he continues to be a popular stage and screen actor, his role of the Phantom long since forgotten.

The very lovely Jane Seymour, who is easily recognized in the United States as the queen of television movies and miniseries, is also out of her depth as a young opera singer. Totally believable as a concentration camp survivor in "War and Remembrance" (1988), a prostitute in "East of Eden" (1977), an industrialist in "Seventh Avenue" (1977), or a widow and star warrior's wife in "Battlestar Galactica" (1978), Jane simply cannot sing opera and convince the audience that she is a budding diva (in either role). Born in 1951, the British leading actress made her feature debut as the tarot-reading Solitaire in "Live and Let Die" (1973). That role as a James Bond girl was followed by another brainless heroine in Ray Harryhausen's "Sinbad and the Eye of the Tiger" (1975). Miss Seymour made the transition to television the very next year with a featured role in "Captains and the Kings," and cemented her reputation with one stunning performance after another. She played a Victorian actress, opposite Christopher Reeve, in "Somewhere in Time" (1980), and seemed entirely suited for period costume dramas. Unfortunately, her roles in "The Phantom of the Opera" leave much to be desired.

Other members of the cast, including Michael York and Jeremy Kemp, try valiantly to rise above the material but seem trapped like Schell and Seymour. In all fairness to Mister York, the role of Hartnell is simply not in the same caliber as other leading men that he's played. No matter how one plays the part, as Raoul or a renowned orchestra conductor, the character is still a lovesick youth. His actions are all predetermined even before the female lead is kidnapped by the Phantom, and his character is regrettably the least interesting one in the love triangle.

At one hundred minutes, which was the longest version of the story to date, "The Phantom of the Opera" emerges as a stillborn piece of television melodrama, barely watchable today. When it first aired in January 1983, the telefilm seemed like it would be the last word in murdering musical phantoms. Thankfully, the musical by Andrew Lloyd Webber and two other adaptations appeared to restore dignity to the time-honored tale.

John L. Flynn

~ 10 ~
The Torture Chamber

> ***Erik Destler:*** *You love the music. I am the music. Now you are married to the music. You cannot serve two masters. Do not see another.*
> ***Christine:*** *I promise.*
> ***Erik Destler:*** *Tonight, you shall be my bride.*
> —*"Gaston Leroux's Phantom of the Opera" (1989)*

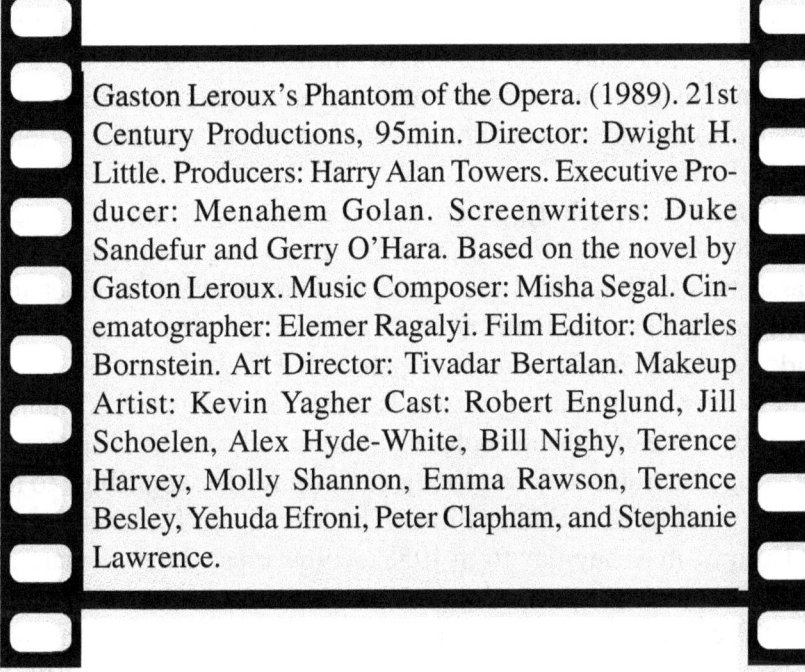

Gaston Leroux's Phantom of the Opera. (1989). 21st Century Productions, 95min. Director: Dwight H. Little. Producers: Harry Alan Towers. Executive Producer: Menahem Golan. Screenwriters: Duke Sandefur and Gerry O'Hara. Based on the novel by Gaston Leroux. Music Composer: Misha Segal. Cinematographer: Elemer Ragalyi. Film Editor: Charles Bornstein. Art Director: Tivadar Bertalan. Makeup Artist: Kevin Yagher Cast: Robert Englund, Jill Schoelen, Alex Hyde-White, Bill Nighy, Terence Harvey, Molly Shannon, Emma Rawson, Terence Besley, Yehuda Efroni, Peter Clapham, and Stephanie Lawrence.

"Gaston Leroux's Phantom of the Opera" (1989), one of the few ambitious low-budget projects from Menahem Golan's 21st Century Productions, emerges as a surprisingly faithful, if somewhat gruesome, adaptation of the time-honored classic. Hurried into production to capitalize on the dark enchantment (as well as the mega box office take) of the Andrew Lloyd Webber musical, this film manages to transcend its cynical origins with superior craftsmanship and lush cinematic values evocative of the best of Hammer films. The single drawback is the perfunctory slasher violence which modern audiences have come to expect from a horror film; though it is kept to a minimum, the routine bloodletting detracts rather than enhances the material. Otherwise, it is superbly realized, capably directed, and well-acted, with Robert Englund contributing a haunting performance as the Faustian Phantom.

"My intent was not to try and make the definitive 'Phantom of the Opera,'" the classically trained Englund revealed in a 1989 interview. "What we all had in mind was to reinterpret it. We wanted to cross breed the best of the previous films and play up the elements of the supernatural, the Faustian side of the story. Bookending the film with a contemporary framing device was also intriguing and very smart. It's a device that will attract an older, Broadway theater crowd as well as the Freddy and the classic horror film audiences. We've combined many elements, and I think they ultimately serve the movie well. I also like the idea that the film we're making has a heavy Hammer influence."

Filmed in New York, London, and Budapest, Hungary, (where the 1983 version was filmed), this motion picture has the look of a classic horror film. Dwight H. Little, who had directed the much underrated "Halloween Four" (1988), endows the production with a dark, brooding atmosphere of fog-shrouded English streets, rat-infested caverns, and damp graveyards. Lush period sets and costumes, impressive use of light and color to create mood, and the proper mixture of gothic romance and bloody violence further contribute to his loving pastiche of Hammer Films. The legendary "Hammer House of Horror," in its hey-day from 1958 to 1969, created the standard by which many contemporary horror films are often compared. Pictures like "The Curse of Frankenstein" (1957), "The Horror of Dracula" (1958), and Terence Fisher's own "Phantom of the Opera" (1962), supplanted their American counterparts by treating the famous monsters of filmland with respect and realism. Their production values were unusually high in quality, and they employed some of the finest talent of the British cinema. When the studio finally folded in 1975. it had produced nearly a hundred and fifty motion pictures (which meant seven to eight major films a year). While not all the films were successful at the box office (as in the case of the 1962 version), these motion pictures always represented excellence. On his own, without the backing of a large studio like Hammer, Little achieves much with this new adaptation.

The Screen Story

"Pray for them who giveth their immortal soul unto Satan. ..for each is damned to relive that wretched live ...throughout all times," the epigraph, written by St. Jean Vitius of Rouen on the day of his execution March 7, 1544 warns viewers as the credits roll on the tenth cinematic version of Gaston Leroux's tale. The film proper opens in present-day New York where aspiring actress Christine Day (Jill Schoelen), a second year student at Julliard, hails a taxi-cab for the Bennett Music Library. Once at the library, she stumbles upon a rare piece of music from a long-deceased composer and decides to use it in an upcoming audition. Her friend Meg (Molly Shannon), the resident librarian, tells her the piece is actually part of a much longer work and reads her the biography of the man who wrote it: "Know primarily for his unfinished opera 'Don Juan Triumphant.' Erik Destler's music reputation is overshadowed by his infamy. He was said to be obsessed with a young opera singer who disappeared without a trace the night of his death. Authorities believe but were never able to prove that the composer was a psycho pathic killer responsible for the brutal murders of at last a dozen London residents."

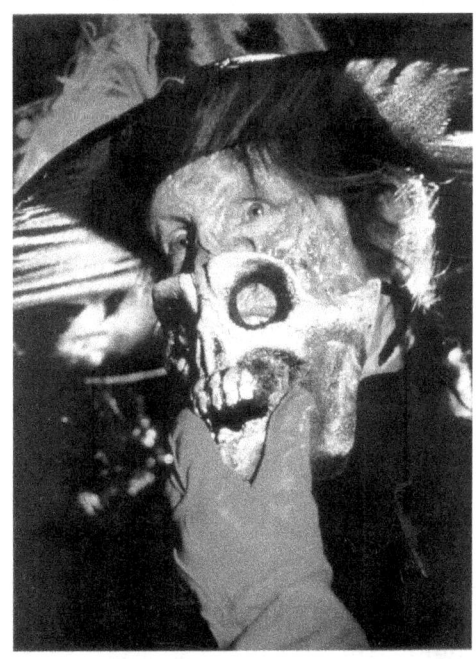

Intrigued by the romantic nature of the music, the two women search the stacks of the library for several hours until Christine discovers the complete manuscript buried under several other works. When she begins to sing the notes, the manuscript bleeds, or does it? On the following day, she captivates the audience with her superior voice and the haunting lyrics of the piece, and easily wins the part. After the tryout, however, Christine is accidentally struck by a falling prop; while unconscious, she imagines hearing Erik say, "Christine, come back to me," and is transported back to London, circa 1889, to meet Destler as the Phantom.

When Christine regains consciousness, she assumes her encounter with the Phantom was only a nightmare, until she discovers that she has indeed been sent back in time one hundred years. Joseph Buguet (Terence Besley), frightened by a ghost, accidentally released a sand bag which struck Christine on the head. Rehearsals continue on "Faust," as Meg (played now by Emma Rawson) takes her by the hand, leads the dazed singer to her dressing room, and tries to help her remember who she is. Christine is an American singing with the London Opera, understudy to the diva; she is having an affair with Richard Dutton (Alex Hyde-White), one of the theatre managers, and has been taking vocal lessons from a private tutor.

Meanwhile, in the dark labyrinthine world below the opera house, amidst hundreds of candles, Erik gingerly sews several pieces of human skin tissue onto his face to cover his deformity. He does not wear the traditional mask of leather or porcelain. Once finished. he hunts down and murders Joseph Buguet for having injured Christine; then the Phantom pays a visit on his naive young student. She greets him as her "Angel of music," and the two rehearse the role of Margarita from "Faust," Christine singing in the place of La Carlotta (Stephanie Lawrence)!

Several hours later, Martin Barton (Bill Nighy), the other theatre manager, brings roses and a contract to the resident diva. La Carlotta is not happy about her accommodations, and jealously demands that Christine be returned to the chorus. Barton is enraged by her outrageous demands and leaves her abruptly. Satisfied she has had her way with him, La Carlotta vainly looks into the mirror before dressing. When she opens her closet, the diva discovers the flayed body of Joseph Buguet. The shock causes her to loose her voice, and the theatre managers have no choice but to give Christine the lead.

"Faust" opens on schedule with Christine Day singing the role of Margarita. Several patrons. including Harrison the Gazette Opera Critic (Peter Clapham), are disappointed by the last moment substitution. But as Erik Destler takes his seat in Box Five and begins to listen to her sing, he becomes enraptured with her voice. Unfortunately, scenes from the opera recall his unholy past. Flashback: Erik remembers a time, long ago, when he was a young man playing piano in a whore house. One customer. taken by his work, offered him a Mephistophelian pact: in exchange for his soul. Erik's music would last forever. Destler agreed to the bargain, unaware that the Devil planned to disfigure him: "The world will love your music. but that's all that it will love you for!" Christine's singing brings him out of his reverie, and he rises to his feet, with the rest of the audience, to salute her excellent performance. Her triumph is his triumph.

Following the performance. Richard confesses his love for Christine and proposes marriage, while Erik makes love to a prostitute in her name. She has captured the hearts of both men, but refuses to choose between her manager or her tutor. She wishes to remain free to pursue her acting career. Across the dining room, Barton conspires with the opera critic to have Christine's debut panned, in order to satisfy his lover - La Carlotta.

After his rendezvous with the prostitute, Erik Destler arrives at a local pub for dinner. Several ruffians mistake him for a wealthy aristocrat and try to shake him down for money. He's much too busy eating his meal and working on his manuscript "Don Juan Triumphant" to be bothered, and demonstrates his annoyance by insulting

the locals. They don't take kindly to his superior behavior, and arrange to ambush him on his way home. Little do the ruffians realize that they are dealing with a psychopathic killer. Like Jack the Ripper, he cuts the men to pieces, then flays their skin for his own sinister purposes.

Unfavorable reviews from the *Daily Gazette*, which point out Christine's "lack of discipline and training." further insight the Phantom to violence. Erik follows the opera critic to the steam baths and kills Harrison after failing to convince him to reconsider his review. When the body is discovered by the police, Inspector Hawking (Terence Harvey) of Scotland Yard begins to recognize a pattern. Someone is committing untold acts of murder on behalf of Ms. Christine Day.

That night, as the young singer seeks solace at the grave of her father Philip Day, she is visited by the "Angel of Music." He begins playing "The Resurrection of Lazarus" (a favorite tune of her father's) on a violin, and she is lulled into a trance by the notes of the music. Richard interrupts their tranquility, trying to lure Christine away from the Phantom, but he is unsuccessful. She boards Erik's waiting cab, and rides off into the night with him. The Phantom leads her to his dark, labyrinthine world below the theatre, with seductive promises to make her an opera star. She is, at first, fearful, not quite certain by what she sees around her; but Christine allows herself to be further lulled into a false sense of security by Erik's charming words and romantic music. At his dimly-lit organ, he plays several selections from "Don Juan Triumphant" which she easily sings with heart-felt passion. Erik exclaims, overwhelmed with feelings of passion and ecstasy, that she will be his voice, his inspiration. He then forces his Satanic ring upon her finger, symbolically joining his fate to hers, and takes her in his arms as his bride.

Overwrought, Richard prays to the Blessed Virgin for help and understanding in a local cathedral. His prayers are interrupted by Hawking, who believes "the Phantom is real! " "He sold his soul to the Devil so the world would love him for his talent," the inspector further explains, but Richard dismisses the story as myth. Inspector Hawking has been following leads to the whereabouts of Erik Destler for years, and he is convinced that Christine Day knows more than she is saying.

At the masked ball, Christine tries to avoid Richard so she doesn't have to explain the ring (which she cannot remove from her finger) or where she has been for the last few days, but the young manager persists in finding her behind one of the many masks. When the two lovers are finally united, she confesses her undying love for Richard and warns him to stay away from her. Meanwhile, Erik has made his entrance as Edgar Allan Poe's "Mask of the Red Death," and begins dancing with La Carlotta. The diva is overwhelmed by his charm and elegant moves, and forces him into a back room so that she can look upon the man behind the mask. Once La Carlotta has seen the sight of his unholy visage, the Phantom slits her throat deeply with a knife and places her decapitated head in the dinner soup (which has yet to be served). In the mass of the confusion that follows the arrival of dinner, Erik abducts Christine from the arms of her lover.

Richard, Hawking, and several of his men follow the rat catcher (Yehuda Efroni) into the sewers that run beneath the opera house. The Phantom soon learns intruders have entered his dark world and imprisons Christine before killing them one-by-one. He dispatches the rat catcher first, then several of Hawking's men. When Richard and the inspector from Scotland Yard finally break into Erik's music room to rescue the girl, the Phantom attacks and kills the manager, and injures Hawking. Horrified and angered by her fiancee's death, Christine pushes several candelabras over to set Erik's world ablaze. She then acquires Richard's pistol, and fires it point-blank at the Phantom. He falls forward, taking her down into the hellish conflagration.

After the fiery finale in which both Destler and the young singer die, Christine once again "awakens" in the present from what appears to have been a dream. The cast and crew hurry to her side to make certain that she has not been injured by the falling prop. Mr. Foster (Englund), the producer and major backer who looks like Erik Destler , offers Christine the role, and takes her back to his recording studio to celebrate their fortune. While he steps into the bathroom to freshen up, she recognizes a familiar piece of music on a computer disk. It is a selection from "Don Juan Triumphant!"

"I knew we'd find each other again. Love and music are forever," he explains, revealing that he was been waiting over a hundred years for her. Christine tears his skin-mask away to expose fresh beneath that has been rotting for decades. She then stabs Erik and burns his music which, in essence, destroys him. Weeks later, as she is walking down a New York City street, she pauses to listen to a street violinist. Christine gives him a few coins. and as she turns to walk away, he begins to play a selection from "Don Juan Triumphant." Startled, she realizes that the Phantom has somehow survived, as the screen begins to darken and the closing credits roll.

The Film's Release and Aftermath

"Gaston Leroux's Phantom of the Opera" was released on November 4, 1989, and grossed a respectable $3,953,745 in its first two weeks. Menahem Golan decided to add a disclaimer at the end of the credits, which stated, "This Motion Picture is not associated with any current or prior stage play or motion picture of the same title," in order to deflect any legal action on the part of Andrew Lloyd Webber and the Really Useful Group. None was forthcoming. Most critics thought the movie was far too violent, and turned a thumbs down.

Richard Harrington in *The Washington Post* called the film "an old-fashioned melodrama with a twist of gore, a match not likely to work in either Heaven or Hell." Christopher Null wrote that "from its tired and unnecessary setup to its laughable finally, this is one remake the world is probably better off without. David Nusair voiced a concern that was heard in most cinematic circles: "It's difficult to know just who the film is meant to appeal to – certainly not fans of the source material...or gorehounds (who) won't find much here worth embracing," while Richard Scheib defended the more horrific elements, stating, "The slasher element is not as incongruous with the story of The Phantom as might initially seem."

A sequel, entitled "The Phantom of New York," was planned by Golan and Little (with Englund) as a follow-up for 1990, but then never shot. However, Robert Englund did reprise his role as the Phantom in a low-budget, Filipino movie titled "Dance Macabre" (1991).
Production Notes

With the exception of a few dubious revisions, all the key elements, which have made Gaston Leroux's novel an enduring classic, have been lovingly recreated by Little. Characters, like Meg Giry, Joseph Buquet, the rat catcher, the detective, and the theatre managers, who have been curiously absent in previous adaptations have been restored to importance, and scenes often eliminated (like the masked ball, which has not been portrayed on film since the 1925 version) have been reintroduced. In fact, the staging of the masked ball, in which Erik appears as the "Red Death," demonstrates Little's impeccable sense of dramatic timing. Costumed characters move rhythmically across the dance floor or seem to float majestically up-and-down the staircase. When the Phantom arrives, however, the dancers move tensely and the proceedings slowly begin to unravel. His presence is larger than life, and he commands attention, particularly when he wrests La Carlotta from the arms of Barton. Finally, as dinner is served, the tense atmosphere turns to one of chaos and terror. Beautifully mounted, the sequence is pure Leroux, while at the same time classic horror.

Similarly, Christine's midnight rendezvous with Erik at the grave of her father is both haunting and romantic. Like the famous balcony scene from Zeferilli's "Romeo and Juliet" (1967), Little's camera remains in tight focus on the young singer as she kneels on the mist-shrouded soil, then pulls back to reveal the presence of the Phantom in deep shadow. The soft musical notes of the violin, which seem to follow the clouds across the sky, cast a hypnotic spell upon the young singer, and she floats, like the camera, toward Erik's waiting carriage. The director's impressive use of light and color to create atmosphere further contribute to a powerful scene -perhaps the best in the entire film. Other scenes in the London Opera House (actually the József Katona Theatre in Kecskemét, Hungary), are bright, flamboyant, and colorful, whereas the Phantom's world is dark, somber, and illuminated only by candle. While these settings fulfill our expectations, Little brilliantly undercuts each by adding an unexpected element of tension or romanticism with a slight tilt of the camera or a soft focus of the lens.

Unlike the Frenchman's original story conceit, however, the Phantom here has not only sold his soul to the Devil (for the sake of his music) but also been disfigured as a result of that bargain. Although the novel portrays him as a struggling, passionate artist who will do anything to see that his music survives, he does not literally sell his soul to Satan, Mephistopheles, or anyone else for that matter. Leroux's Erik was also born with his physical deformity, and developed his keen, highly resourceful personality in order to compensate for his poor features. But once again, filmmakers have chosen to portray him as a normal man who has suffered unjustly at the hands of other, lesser men.

His origin aside, the latest incarnation of the Phantom does demonstrate a multiplicity of conflicting facets which seemed culled from the previous cinematic adaptations as well as the novel. Though conflicting, however, they contribute much to making the Victorian character believable. Too often, previous attempts to render a credible Phantom have meant either rejecting the original source material to create an entirely new, one-dimensional character or restricting the original character to a simple, single motive. Screenwriters Gerry O'Hara and Duke Sandefur have wisely returned to the 1911 classic and added substance to a fictional creation that has been played in a dozen different ways. Like Lon Chaney, this Phantom is dark and menacing; he dispatches street ruffians, like an 1890's "caped crusader," and forces Christine (among others) to look upon his unholy visage. Like Claude Rains and Herbert Lom, he works selflessly (behind the scenes) so that the young diva can ascend to greater glory. Like Michael Crawford, he commands a strong sense of sexuality when dealing with what is obsviously his unrequited love for Christine. Charming. confident, and seductive, he easily whisks the young singer away from the lovesick Richard. Unlike the other phantoms, this Erik ventures out beyond the cellars of the playhouse and attempts to conduct business like a normal human being. His mask is a patchwork guilt of human skin tissue that has been sewn together to hide his disfigurement. He is also short-tempered and prone to acts of ultra-violence. Part of the credit for this multi-faceted character belongs to Robert Englund, who contributes a sinister yet touching performance as the Phantom.

"Coming up with a complete Erik Destler really tested me as an actor," Englund confessed in a 1989 interview. "At first, I was very nervous because I knew I wasn't just doing Freddy again. I needed time to work into the role, to create a character that could be menacing one moment and romantic the next." He worked very hard during the several weeks of rehearsal, practicing "a seasoned British accent" and learning to how to appear "natural" in period costumes.

The end result - a thoroughly convincing, three-dimensional mad musical genius -transcends many of the best and worst performances before him. "I liked the idea that I would be in the company of great actors like Herbert Lom, Claude Rains, Max Schell, and Lon Chaney, who all played the Phantom and I liked the idea that the film had such a well written central character."

Robert Englund, certainly no stranger to horror films or imaginative thrillers, follows in the familiar footsteps of another long line of actors from a bygone era - Lon Chaney, Boris Karloff, Bela Lugosi, Vincent Price, and Christopher Lee - who devoted most of their careers to playing monsters and madmen. For nearly a decade, Englund has played either an alien, a psychopathic killer, or a demented composer. Born in 1948, the classically trained actor did not start his career with the notion of becoming a horror movie icon. He studied Ibsen and Shakespeare with the hopes of playing an angst-ridden, tragic hero, but talent agents insisted on casting him as either a street punk or the boy-next-door in a handful of low-budget quickies. His breakthrough role came in 1983, when Kenneth Johnson hired him to play Willie the good lizard in the phenomenally successful miniseries "V." Au-

diences identified with this awkward stranger in a strange land, much as they had identified with the half-Vulcan Mr. Spock fifteen years earlier on "Star Trek." He reprised his role as Willie for "V-The Final Battle" (in 1984) and the short-lived television series (in 1985). He also played a disfigured actor hiding out on a Hollywood back lot in "Phantom of the Studio" (1985), an episode of "Night Rider."

In between the two "V" miniseries, he originated the role of Freddy Krueger, the child molester who refuses to stay dead, in the first "Nightmare on Elm Street" for Wes Craven in 1984, and gained an overnight cult following. Robert has played him in every subsequent film, including "Freddy's Dead: The Final Nightmare" (1991), and as the horror host (and sometime director) of "Freddy's Nightmares," an anthology spun from his famous series. Even though playing Freddy Krueger for six films and a television series has occupied much of his time in the last seven years, he has managed to garner other plum assignments, including the title role in "Gaston Leroux's Phantom of the Opera." Englund also directed the popular "976-EVIL" (1987), and played a bad guy opposite Andrew Dice Clay in director Renny Harlin's "Adventures of Ford Fairlane" (1990). Today, the forty-three year old actor lives and surfs in Laguna Beach, and hosts (as well as appears in numerous segments of) "Nightmare Care." His future plans include a role similar to the one Anthony Perkins played in "Psycho" and a desire to star or play a supporting role in a historical miniseries, opposite Jane Seymour.

Though many critics were quick to draw comparisons between his menacing musical genius and the child molester from his "Nightmare on Elm Street" films, Englund maintains "they're two very different characters." In an interview given in 1989, Robert responded to negative criticism by explaining, "The Phantom character has much more going on psychologically than Freddy. Erik Destler's obsession is more artistic, while Freddy is on this sort of purgatory plane. The Phantom is on much more of a survival guest, while Freddy's guest is based primarily on revenge. Age is also a major factor in the difference between Erik and Freddy. The Phantom is a little younger and much more of a swashbuckler. Freddy's this ugly old man who's set in his ways."

Regrettably, the film is flawed by the sadistically brutal actions performed by the Phantom - the very aspects that sold Menahem Golan on the project. The pointless beheadings, impalements, and murders take away from what may have been the definitive screen adaptation. Yes, Gaston Leroux's mad musical genius did kill individuals in the original novel but only to advance the career of his young protégé or to protect his dark, subterranean world. The street murders seem to have been added, as an afterthought, in order to appeal to the cult audience that made Freddy Krueger a household name. Indeed, when Englund removes his flesh mask, Kevin Yagher's makeup reminds us that Freddy's spirit is not far away.

Besides the gratuitous and largely unneeded violence, the only real disappointment is the ending, where the film seems unable to make up its mind whether or not the action was all simply a dream. "Gaston Leroux's Phantom of the Opera" seems to resolve itself in a dissatisfying series of false endings, which recall the shocking conclusions of "Carrie" (1976) and "Fatal Attraction" (1987). Does the Phantom survive his contemporary demise at the hands of Miss Day? Was the action in Victorian London real or part of a hallucination? Who is it - really - that is playing? The film is currently available on home video.

Other Related Productions

Dance Macabre (aka The Phantom of the Opera) (1991). Phillipines, 97min. Director and Writer: Greydon Clark. Producer: Menahem Golan. Music Composer: Dan Slider. Film Editor: Earl Watson. Cast: Robert Englund, Michelle Zeitlin, Marianna Moen, Julene Renee, Nina Goldman, Irina Davidoff, Alexander Segeyev, Nastash Fesson, Vadim Zajtsev, and Greydon Clark.

Producer Menahem Golan revisits *Le Fantôme de l'Opera* with Robert Englund as the Phantom in this low-budget, Filipino production. Simply titled "Dance Macabre," the story follows a choreographer and his dance troupe to a small, abandoned theater in St. Petersburg, Russia, for some much-needed rehearsals. What his dancers don't know, however, is that Anthony Wagner (Englund) he has a dual personality—and his hidden personality is a serial killer. At one point, he confesses that "tortured people do things in this world no one understands," and when the prima ballerina rebuffs his amorous advances, he begins striking at members of his own troupe. He pauses only long enough to romance Jessica (Michelle Zeitlin), a small town girl whose rich father wants her to become a ballerina, but when she rejects him, Wagner descends even lower into the depths of depravity. Robert Englund plays this Phantom like a lovesick Norman Bates, and completely misses the mark. Golan would have been better off spending his money on "Phantom of New York," the proposed follow-up to "Gaston Leroux's Phantom of the Opera," than this horrid, direct-to-video mess.

John L. Flynn

~ 11 ~
An Opera Ghost's Love Story

***The Phantom:** [about Christine] For as long as I can remember... ever since I was a child, I have dreamed of her. People are born for many things, Gerard. I was born to live, if one can call this living, down here. But I've never known quite why. I was born so she could save me. That's what she's done! She's the reason I was born... I love her, Gerard.*
—*"The Phantom of the Opera" (1990)*

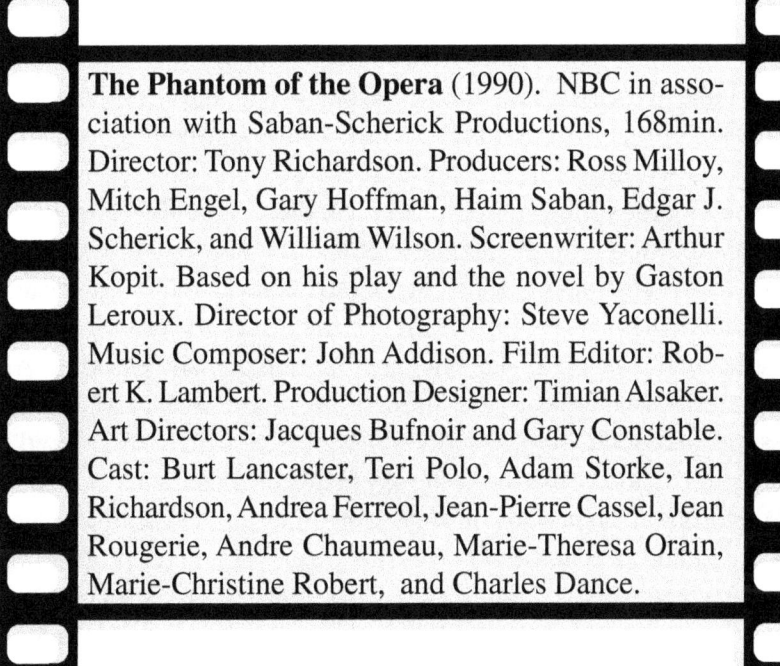

The Phantom of the Opera (1990). NBC in association with Saban-Scherick Productions, 168min. Director: Tony Richardson. Producers: Ross Milloy, Mitch Engel, Gary Hoffman, Haim Saban, Edgar J. Scherick, and William Wilson. Screenwriter: Arthur Kopit. Based on his play and the novel by Gaston Leroux. Director of Photography: Steve Yaconelli. Music Composer: John Addison. Film Editor: Robert K. Lambert. Production Designer: Timian Alsaker. Art Directors: Jacques Bufnoir and Gary Constable. Cast: Burt Lancaster, Teri Polo, Adam Storke, Ian Richardson, Andrea Ferreol, Jean-Pierre Cassel, Jean Rougerie, Andre Chaumeau, Marie-Theresa Orain, Marie-Christine Robert, and Charles Dance.

"The Phantom of the Opera" (1990), the third attempt to bring the Frenchman's work to the small screen' is a stylized, beautifully-rendered but flawed retelling of the classic by Gaston Leroux (with an equal mixture of "Beauty and the Beast") that sometimes manages to transcend the limited medium of television. NBC spent millions producing and promoting the two-part miniseries in an effort to exploit the success of the Andrew Lloyd Webber musical, then curiously dumped the production in mid-March (1990), weeks after the ever-important, February ratings period. Arthur Kopit's script (based on his original play) provides a most faithful translation of the gothic romance while keeping the horror elements to a minimum. Unfortunately, the four hour block of time, usually reserved for adaptations belonging to Danielle Steele or James Clavell, is much too luxurious for the story. Burdened with much unnecessary dialogue, expository flashbacks, and literarily narrative structure, the film lacks the fluid dramatic consistency that have distinguished the better adaptations. Still, the miniseries is not without its merits. The magnificent sets and costumes (which easily rival those of the 1943 version) and the sincerity of the three central performances (Erik, Christine, and hia father) are well worth the investment of time.

The Screen Story

Part one of the two-part miniseries opens with the arrival of Christine (Teri Polo) at the famous Paris Opera House. She has been singing at country fairs for several years, and a chance meeting with Philippe Georges Marie (Adam Storke), the Comte de Chagny, has led to an audition with the manager of the playhouse. Unfortunately, her arrival is ill-timed. Monsieur Gerard Carrier (Burt Lancaster), the man who has guided the theatre for the last thirty years, has been replaced by Alan Coletti (Ian Richardson) and his wife Carlotta (Andrea Ferreol), who believes that she can sing opera. When La Carlotta's dressmaker Joseph Buquet suddenly vanishes, Christine is hired to replace him. Carrier suspects foul play in the disappearance of Buquet, and descends into the labyrinthine world below the theatre to warn Erik the Phantom (Charles Dance) that he can no longer protect him. (For thirty years, the former manager has guarded Erik's secret world from those who would destroy him; but now, his dismissal means that the Phantom is all alone.)

As rehearsals begin on Gounod's "Faust," Christine Daee {sic} is shown the duties of a costume assistant and dressmaker. The work is very hard, and the chorus girls make fun of her because they believe that she has fallen for the Comte. a well-known womanizer. But

Christine merely dreams of singing the role of Marguerite in a large scale production. At night, she wanders upon the stage, and sings happily to herself. The voice carries through the underground chambers and attracts Erik's attention. He has heard the Angel's voice before (when his mother used to sing to him in his crib), and he knows that Christine can become an important singer with his special help. The Phantom offers her a bargain; as long as he can wear a mask to remain anonymous, he will train her to oneday sing the role of Marguerite.

One month later, Inspector Ledoux (Jean-Pierre Cassel), who has been summoned by the new owners of the theatre to clear up a mystery, explains to Coletti and La Carlotta that the Paris Opera House has been haunted by a ghost for nearly thirty years. During the days of the Commune, he elaborates, there were torture chambers down below, and the "Phantom" has inhabited them since Ledoux first came to the police force. No one has ever seen the opera ghost, but he believes the Phantom wears a mask because he has no face. Coletti thinks that he is mad and refuses to honor Erik's latest note (requesting box five and insisting that La Carlotta be given singing lessons). He further demands that the Inspector do something to rid him of the pest. Ledoux promises to review the floor plans of the Opera House. Meanwhile, La Carlotta's debut as the reigning diva ends in disaster. Her grand entrance in "Norma" is marred by a lice-infected wig -courtesy of the Phantom. He warned them to keep box five open, but they continue to ignore his warnings. Disaster strikes on the second night, as Carlotta again makes a fool of herself on stage. Coletti orders Ledoux to inspect the chambers below the playhouse, but once again the Inspector declines.

Another month passes, heralding the arrival of Philippe de Chagny. All the chorus girls hurry to greet him, but he confesses that his heart has been stolen by a young country girl -Christine Daee. Having learned of his reputation with the ladies, Christine is cold toward him. She does not want to be another conquest. The young aristocrat announces he will throw a party at the Bistro for her and members of her company. While she reluctantly accepts his invitation, Erik believes that the party will provide the perfect opportunity to reveal her new voice. The Phantom dresses her in a gown which was his mother's, and sends her to Chagny.

At the Bistro, Christine demonstrates her incomparable talent -in spite of interference from La Carlotta -and wins her a place in the chorus. Philippe is enchanted by her voice, and takes her for a private carriage ride which, in turn, leads to a night-time picnic. (Outside the Bistro. the Phantom has heard her triumph. and watched with a heavy heart as the two have ridden off together in the Comte's carriage.) Their picnic rekindles old memories of the first time that they met as children. Christine was a serving girl in the Chagny home, and her father was the woodcutter and handyman. When she became too dependent on Philippe, Madame Chagny dismissed both her and her father. The two young lovers have not seen one another in years. Philippe attempts to romance her. but Christine breaks off their meeting, realizing that someone is waiting for her return. The young singer arrives at the Paris Opera House to discover that Monsieur Coletti wants her to sing the lead in their new production of "Faust." La Carlotta is enraged by this news, considering the part to be hers, and badgers the young singer into revealing that Christine's teacher wears a mask. The resident diva now knows that Miss Daee has been learning her craft from the Phantom, and devises a way with her husband to have him caught. With Carlotta's departure, the Phantom appears to congratulate Christine on her triumph at the Bistro. She first lies about her date with Philippe, then confesses all, throwing her arms around him. Erik is so overwhelmed by her affection he does not know how to respond.

Prior to the opening of the new production of Gounod's "Faust," both Philippe and La Carlotta pay a visit on the young singer. While the Comte de Chagny offers her words of love, the vengeful diva slips Christine a potion of herbs that causes her to loose her voice.

Unaware of the treachery, Miss Daee confidently enters the stage, then discovers she cannot sing. The members of the audience, who have been dubious of the young costume girl's talent, begin to "boo" her. Refusing to let the humiliation continue, Erik leaps from his box seat and races backstage to drop the main chandelier on their ignorant heads. Gerard Carrier tries to stop him, but it is too late, as the chandelier's tremendous weight comes crashing down.

Part two of the miniseries repeats the fall of the chandelier, then focuses on the aftermath of destruction and chaos. As bodies are carried from the theatre and the police begin their investigation, the Phantom abducts Christine and takes her down into his dark, labyrinthine world below the playhouse. There, in the world of broken props and broken dreams, he conveys her across his stygian lake by boat, and finally carries the young singer to her own bed. Erik sings a lullaby that relaxes Christine and allows her to sleep. He then rushes off, and to make certain the police are unable to trace him, he murders two of the men. No one must ever enter and disturb the Phantom in his world!

Next day, Christine awakes and begins to investigate Erik's world. She discovers a painting of his mother, who resembles Miss Daee, and dresses in a wedding gown that has been left for her. Meanwhile, the Phantom, who has learned that Christine was poisoned by La

Carlotta, pays a visit on the resident diva. She tries to bargain for her safety, but he simply pours a box full of rats on her. (The rats drive her to insanity.) Upon his return to the underworld, Carrier confronts Erik and warns that he will never be able to keep Christine captive. The Phantom ignores his warnings and begins to fortify his defenses, pouring gunpowder and aiming an ancient catapult. Gerard Carrier offers to take Christine to safety, but she is not afraid of Erik. In flashback, the former manager tells her the truth about the Phantom. He was born in the catacombs and has lived there all his life because his face was so hideously disfigured at birth. Carrier and Erik's mother Bella (also played by Polo) were once lovers, but since he could not marry her, she tried to take her own life. That attempt deprived her unborn baby and caused the deformity. She saw nothing ugly about his face, and sought the safety of the underworld to raise her child away from ignorance and prejudice. One day she died, and Carrier began to raise him. Erik's love of music helped the former manager make the right decisions about the opera house, and for nearly thirty years, it prospered and grew to greatness because of the man behind the mask. Now that the father has been dismissed, he must leave the playhouse and his son behind.

Christine is moved by his story, and offers to stay with Erik herself. She believes that she loves him and will see only goodness in him. Both the Phantom and Miss Daee go on a picnic in an enchanted forest (with plastic animals) that he has created in the catacombs. Erik calls the world his "dreamery" and claims that all his dreams come true there. The young singer promises to stay with him and to love him if only she could see the face behind the mask. At first, he resists, but then -after numerous requests -he removes the mask. Christine is horrified by his unholy visage, and faints dead away. She was totally unprepared for what she saw.

Enraged, the Phantom begins tearing his enchanted forest apart, demanding to know (from the gods) why he cannot have love. Christine awakens and tries to run away from him. Erik pursues her through the labyrinth of tunnels. Finally, she reaches the playhouse, and falls into the arms of Philippe. Carrier calls for a hansom cab, and the three ride away to the young aristocrat's home in the country. Christine blames herself for Erik's great unhappiness, claiming she is unworthy of his love and knowing that he will die without her. Jealous, the Comte de Chagny only wants to kill the Phantom, but she convinces both men that she must return to the theatre and make amends. If she can perform Marguerite in "Faust," Erik will know how much his help has meant to her. Gerard Carrier has something else in mind.

Descending once again into the dark, labyrinthine world below the opera house, Carrier discovers his son's shattered world. He also learns that Erik is very sick and dying. The Phantom is aware that Christine no longer loves him, but he is satisfied by the knowledge that he once had someone's affection. Carrier reveals that he has loved Erik for thirty years as his son, and the Phantom explains that he has always known Gerard was his father but he has waited for him to say it. "Twice in my life I have been touched by an angel," he confesses happily, then makes his father promise that his body will not end up in some freak circus when he is dead. At the same moment, Christine begins to sing the role of Marguerite in the theatre above, and her lovely voice provides Erik with renewed strength. He must travel one last time to his reserved box in order to witness her triumph.

Her triumphant performance moves the lonely Phantom to tears and causes him to begin singing the role of "Faust" from his box seat. The audience is overwhelmed by both of their wonderful voices and rise to greet them with a standing ovation. Above, in the catwalk over the stage, Inspector Ledoux's men advance into positions to obtain a better shot at him. From his vantage point in box five, the Phantom suspects that he has been lured into a trap. Instinctively, he leaps onto the stage, takes hold of Christine's hand, and races to the safety of the roof above the playhouse. Philippe follows after them, with Carrier and the police

in hot pursuit. Moments later, the young aristocrat grabs Erik, and the two rivals struggle with one another; the Comte looses his footing and tumbles to the ledge of the building. At Christine's request, the Phantom pulls Chagny to safety. He then finds himself surrounded by the police. Remembering that his son did not want to be captured alive (or dead, for that matter), Carrier fatally wounds Erik with a gunshot. With his last breath, Erik calls to Christine, who removes his mask and kisses him gently on the forehead. The Phantom dies happily, cradled in the arms of his father, while the young singer walks off into the night with Philippe.

Production Notes

"The Phantom of the Opera" (1990) invokes mystery and romance rather than the traditional elements of horror in its retelling of the tragic tale of a disfigured composer and his love for a young opera singer. Filmed in Paris, France at the actual Paris Opera House and in the Caves of Mello, the miniseries has a number of wonderful elements working for it, including impressive sets and lavish costumes. But the most important element is the three-dimensional portrait of its central character.

For the first time since Gaston Leroux imagined his mad musical genius, the "Phantom" of the Opera is portrayed with the origin that was initially written. Whereas Lon Chaney's character was an escapee from Devil's Island and other phantoms have been ordinary men whose lives have been scarred by acid, this Erik was born with his physical deformity. Like the Elephant Man, he has hidden away in the depths of the theatre, developing a highly intelligent, resourceful, and creative personality in order to adjust to his isolation and loneliness. Though he scorns the world above (referring to it as "hell"), the Phantom does not seek revenge upon others for some real or imagined wrongdoing. Unlike previous phantoms, he simply does not have an axe to grind. He has been watched over for years by a loving father. and has been allowed to contribute to the growth of the theatre. When he first hears Christine sing, her voice reminds him of the "angel" that used to sing to him -his mother. He tutors the young opera star in an attempt to recapture the lost love and happiness of his childhood. Only when that "angel" is taken from him does Erik begin his journey toward madness.

Similarly, in his journey toward madness, he becomes the tragic figure that the Frenchman first imagined. Like Sophocles' Oedipus or Shakespeare's Othello, his anger manifests itself in violent actions that ordinary would not seem possible by his temperament. Pushed to the limits of tolerance, he strikes back at the world above in the only terms that they can understand. The simple fact that the "shocking" violence of the Phantom's actions - with the exception of the famous chandelier scene - is never visualized on screen contributes much to the mystery of his character. Gratuitous violence is simply not part of Erik's nature. He kills to protect his world of privacy and the woman he loves. Any other reasons would challenge the audience to reconcile the central character's sweetly gentle nature with his hideously private actions. Thus, by exploring the world between what makes us "human" and what makes us a "monster," the miniseries raises the question that has been central to the novel since its inception: Is Erik still "human" after he has revealed his features to Christine? Ultimately, the strength and overall beauty of the production reveals itself with the answer to that question in the denouement.

Charles Dance, a soft-spoken and distinguished actor of both stage and screen, is perfectly cast in the role of Erik the Phantom. Having played many classical characters on the British stage, Dance brings a certain charisma to the part that projects both sympathetic desperation and lonely introspection. Co-star Teri Polo endows Christine with enough innocence and sexuality that a hundred love-starved phantoms would be unable to resist; but the real casting coup is Burt Lancaster as Gerard Carrier, Erik's father. The former circus acrobat, dancer, and leading man provides the perfect balance for the other two' acting as both father and counselor. All three characters are finely drawn, and represent the singularly important high point of the production.

Unfortunately, screenwriter Arthur Kopit has removed several of Gaston Leroux's key sequences in order to more fully develop his three central characters. By eliminating a number of important plot elements, including the famous masked ball, Christine's nightly visit to her father's grave, the lover's rendezvous on the roof of the Paris Opera House, and the torture chamber, he has taken away many of the scenes that made novel so interesting. Literary critic Eugene La Biche once compared the novel to film, claiming that the former was like a trip by carriage and the latter was like a journey by a high-speed train. Kopit's script refutes that comparison by trying to tell a novel-length story in dramatic form. Regrettably, in his attempt to tell the whole tale, he sacrifices suspense and pacing -s o vital to past productions of the Phantom - for greater character development. While the many flashbacks provide the audience with valuable information en medias ' that has never been revealed about the Phantom, those flashbacks also slow the action of the story down to a snail's pace. The added interruption of commercials every fifteen or twenty minutes makes this production (at 200 minutes) seem intolerably long. Without Leroux's memorable sequences to keep the plot moving along, his gothic romance fails to rise above the commonplace.

Like the 1943 version, the operatic sequences are also overly long and unnecessary. Gounod's "Faust," curiously missing from the Andrew Lloyd Webber version and other recent adaptations, has been restored (along with its important subtext), and the biblical opera "Norma" has been added as a companion piece. While the music is extremely beautiful (conducted by John Addison and performed by the Hungarian State Opera Orchestra), the pieces contribute very little to whole; in fact, by the fourth time that "Faust" is played by the company, one begins to wonder how the Paris Opera House has survived all these years, offering the same opera. Trimming the operatic sequences to a bare minimum might have actually improved the pacing of the drama.

The flamboyant, over-the-top performance of Andrea Ferreol as La Carlotta provides a wonderfully comic touch to the production, but also reduces Christine's chief rival to a mere caricature. Her character must be a strong one, so that when the young singer triumphs in her place she has truly succeeded in replacing a great diva. Their "dueling voices" at the Bistro provides little suspense or doubt as to who will win the competition. Similarly, La Carlotta's manager-husband is little more than a caricature. Whereas Leroux created two interesting yet diverse characters in Richard and Moncharmin, the managers who take over the opera house, the character of Monsieur Coletti (as played by Ian Richardson) is exaggerated to ridiculous lengths. His scenes with Inspector Ledoux (Jean-Pierre Cassel), a character borrowed from the 1925 silent, are extremely predictable and remind one of comic opera. They also add very little to the production, except to provide padding for its four-hour running time.

Director Tony Richardson tries his best to keep the production moving, but seems burdened by the limitations of television. The British director who won critical acclaim for "The Loneliness of a Long Distance Runner" (1962) and an Academy Award for "Tom Jones" (1963) never manages to create an atmosphere of terror and menace. The Phantom's haunting of the Paris Opera House is never fully explored, and his world beneath the playhouse - though wonderfully evocative of the 1925 version - lacks the frightful or mysterious qualities that are necessary for the central character. Richardson does manage to minimalize the grue and gore which had made the 1989 version so repulsive. His best sequence, on the roof of the Opera House in which Christine kisses and embraces the dying Erik, is smartly conceived and executed. By positioning the camera above and behind the Phantom, his disfigured features remain a complete mystery at the close of the miniseries. Too bad that many of the other key sequences were not handled with the same finesse.

"The Phantom of the Opera" (1990) is a lush, lavish production, beautiful to the eye but overwrought with minor problems. A good editor might have been able to trim the extraneous material in order to make it into a tight, little two-hour movie; perhaps, in the production's next incarnation, those problems will be eliminated. The miniseries is currently available on home videoe but (at the time of this writing) NBC had yet to broadcast the four hour film a second time. Since the network spent millions producing and promoting the two-part tele-film the first time around, then curiously dumped the production in mid-March (1990), it is anyone's guess where and when the miniseries will be re-broadcast.

The Film's Release and Aftermath

"The Phantom of the Opera" miniseries played on American television on March 18 and 19, 1990, repectively. One year later, it played in Europe as a three-hour film. The miniseries was nominated for two Golden Globe awards, one for Best Mini-Series and one for Best Performance by an Actor in a Mini-Series (for Burt Lancaster). The 1990 series also won Two Emmy awards, for Outstanding Achievement in Hairstyling and for Outstanding Art Direction for a Miniseries.

Because of the show's huge popularity, a theatrical version of Arthur Kopit's play, complete with an original score by Maury Yeston, debuted in Texas in 1991 and played to capacity crowds at Houston's Theatre Under the Stars. The play also had an extended run at the California Theatre in San Bernardino with Richard White as the Phantom and Glory Crampton as Christine. It has since played in Chicago, Westchester, Kansas City, St. Petersburg, and many other cities. This musical version was actually written in 1982 by Kopit and Yeston, but remained unproduced until 1991. The miniseries was based on Kopit's libretto, with real operatic sequences in place of Yeltson's score. When it played as a live musical, audiences were thrilled to hear the original score, and have remained a popular favorite, second only to the Webber version.

Other Related Productions

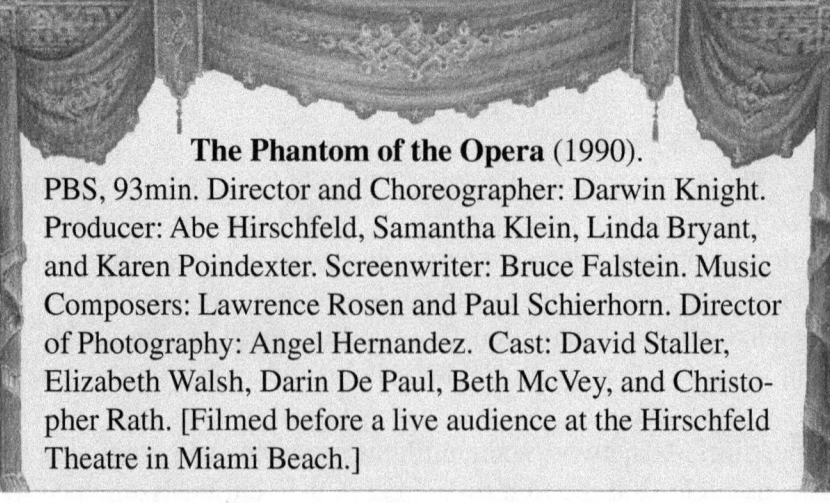

The Phantom of the Opera (1990).
PBS, 93min. Director and Choreographer: Darwin Knight. Producer: Abe Hirschfeld, Samantha Klein, Linda Bryant, and Karen Poindexter. Screenwriter: Bruce Falstein. Music Composers: Lawrence Rosen and Paul Schierhorn. Director of Photography: Angel Hernandez. Cast: David Staller, Elizabeth Walsh, Darin De Paul, Beth McVey, and Christopher Rath. [Filmed before a live audience at the Hirschfeld Theatre in Miami Beach.]

Commissioned by Abe Hirschfeld, the New York City real estate magnate, for a Miami Beach Hotel (which was later condemned), the Hirshfeld Theatre production of "The Phantom of the Opera" is one of the most literate, engaging, and faithful adaptations of the Leroux novel. David Falstein's script, with music and lyrics by Lawrence Rosen and Paul Schier horn, reintroduces several important characters, including Harsh Nayyar as the Persian, and concentrates on the struggle of the three central characters to come to terms with their romantic triangle. But unlike the previous incarnations of the Phantom, who seems to crumble with rejection, this Erik is arrogant, self-assured, and wholly pragmatic. When Christine Daae dumps him for her childhood sweetheart, he quickly turns his attention to a young dancer. The Phantom's decisive actions reveal that his life will continue without the young singer, and seem to add an extra dimension to the character that has not been previously explored.

The play opens in Calais, France, 1901, and focuses on the childhood romance of Raoul and Christine. He met her on the beach while returning her scarf that had blown away into the surf, then shifts ten years later to the events at the Paris Opera House. Having successfully eluded the assassins of the Shah of Persia, Erik has hidden in the dark, labyrinthine world below the theatre for nearly twenty years. The appearance of beautiful Christine Daae frees him from despair, and sets him again upon the reckless course of intrigue, seduction, and murder. When he finally takes the young singer to his lair, Falstein's underlying theme becomes clear: the world above is terrified of genuine passion (creavity, love, etc.), and the Phantom, or other artists like himself, cannot exist in the world which fears individual expression. Raoul does not understand creativity or passion, and opposes Erik. Between them, Christine is torn by her love of music and her passion for Raoul.

David Staller is perfectly cast as Erik the Phantom; Elizabeth Walsh is his musical protege; Christopher Rath portrays the lovesick Raoul, and Beth McVey plays Carlotta much more sympathetically than any other actress has. But it is Darin De Paul and Richard Kinter who both turn their comic portraits of Moncharmin and Richard into truly scene-stealing performances. A video version, co-directed by Darwin Knight and Angel Hernandez, was shot live at the Hirschfeld Theatre in Miami Beach, and was shown on PBS several times. The production is available on home video. Not long after its debut on Public Broadcasting, the musical moved from Miami to New York, and played at the West 57th Playhouse Theatre for four weeks.

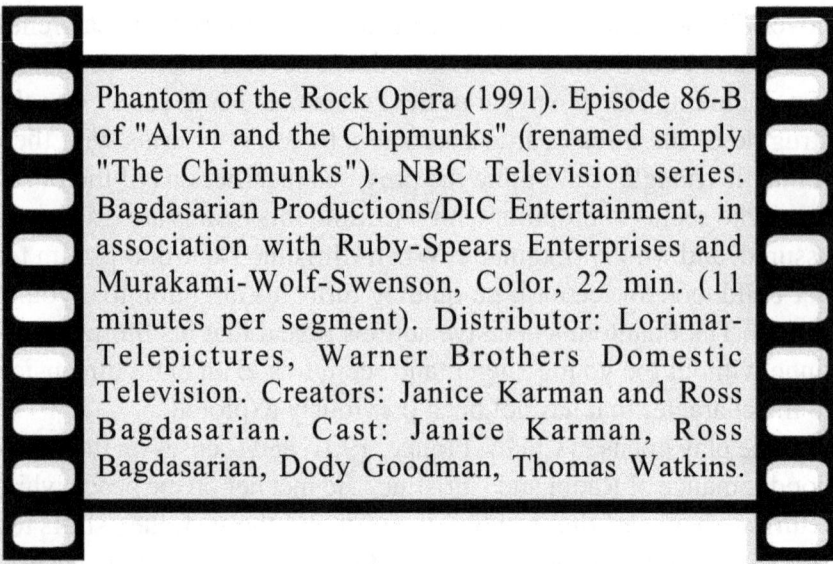

Phantom of the Rock Opera (1991). Episode 86-B of "Alvin and the Chipmunks" (renamed simply "The Chipmunks"). NBC Television series. Bagdasarian Productions/DIC Entertainment, in association with Ruby-Spears Enterprises and Murakami-Wolf-Swenson, Color, 22 min. (11 minutes per segment). Distributor: Lorimar-Telepictures, Warner Brothers Domestic Television. Creators: Janice Karman and Ross Bagdasarian. Cast: Janice Karman, Ross Bagdasarian, Dody Goodman, Thomas Watkins.

On a 1991 episode of "The Chipmuks" cartoon series, Alvin, Simon, and Theodore parody Gaston Leroux's classic, much to the chargrin of their handler Dave Seville (Bagdasarian). They perform "Alvin! - A Rock Opera," and cast the school janitor, a forgotten man, as the Phantom. The janitor shines brightly in the role, despite Alvin's initial reluctance to give him a part. This 11-minute short is played mostly for children who probably have no idea who Gaston Leroux or the Phantom was. [In a 2017 animated children's book, titled The Muppets Meet the Classics: The Phantom of the Opera, author Erik Forrest Jackson tries to make Leroux's classic hip for elementary school kids, and most of his pop culture references fall similarly flat. Parodies and pastiches simply don't resonate with children who have never been exposed to the original classic.]

~ 12 ~
Apollo's Lyre and the Song of Orpheus

The Phantom: *[singing softly to Christine] Say you'll share with me one love, one lifetime. Lead me, save me from my solitude. Say you want me with you here beside you, anywhere you go let me go too, Christine that's all I ask of...*

—*"The Phantom of the Opera" (2004)*

> **The Phantom of the Opera** (1986).
> The Really Useful Group, 153min. Director: Harold Prince. Producers: Andrew Lloyd Webber and Cameron Makintosh. Music by: Andrew Lloyd Webber. Lyrics by: Charles Hart (with additional work by Richard Stilgoe). Inspired by the Gaston Leroux novel. Production Designer: Maria Bjornson. Musical Director: Michael Reed (with orchestrations by David Cullen and Andrew Lloyd Webber). Makeup Artist: Tiffany Hicks. Original Cast: Michael Crawford. Sarah Brightman. Steve Barton. John Savident. David Firth. Rosemary Ashe. Mary Millar. Janet Devenish, and John Aron.

Beautifully rendered, Andrew Lloyd Webber's "The Phantom of the Opera" is the definitive version (to date) of Gaston Leroux's classic 1911 novel. Though the musical builds upon his success with "Jesus Christ-Superstar," "Evita," "Cats," and (to a lesser extent "Starlight Express," the adaptation represents the composer's most elaborate, beguiling score and his most operatic, with parodies of period works of such composers as Salieri and Meyerbeer. Director Hal Prince's evocation of the uncanny atmosphere surrounding the Phantom, and his haunting of the Paris Opera House, aided by Maria Bjornson's lush scenic and costume designs, skilfully relies upon that sweeping, romantic score to give the production a spellbinding rhythm. His imaginative use of visuals is engaging but never overpowering, as he allows the musical motifs to carry the audience away on its journey to the darkside. Principal among the highlights are a boat trip through an underground lake with a sea of rising candles, a rooftop rendezvous between lovers, and a chandelier that appears to crash onto the audience at the end of Act One. The stage musical was so popular that it inspired the 2004 film, also by Andrew Lloyd Webber. But the real strength of the production lies in the sympathetic portrait of a creative genius who simply yearns to be loved.

The Story of the Musical

During the prologue, set at an auction on the stage of the Paris Opera House twenty-four years after the main action, Raoul-the Vicomte De Chagny (Steve Barton from the original cast, Patrick Wilson in the film version) purchases a poster from "Hannibal" and a papier-mache musical box. Both items evoke memories of his beloved Christine, the brief love that they shared, and the incidents that brought them together so many years ago. When lot 666 - a chandelier in pieces - is brought to the auction block, the portly auctioneer (Barry Clark, Paul Brooke) reminds Raoul and the gathered company of the famous disaster which may have been caused by the Phantom of the Opera. "The mystery was never fully explained," he concludes, switching on the chandelier (refitted with new electric lights). An enormous flash, like thunder, sweeps over the chandelier and through the theatre, and the Overture begins. (During the main theme, the chandelier "rises magically" from the stage to its original place, high above the seats, as the playhouse is restored to its earlier grandeur, seemingly by magic.)

Twenty-four years earlier, in 1881, rehearsals for "Hannibal" by Chalumeau eventually come to highlight the singing talents of Christine Daae (Sarah Brightman from the original cast, Emmy Rossum in the film version) for the two new managers. After a backdrop crashes to the floor, ruining her rehearsal, Carlotta Guidicelli (Rosemary Ashe, Minnie Driver) storms off stage in protest. She refuses to continue singing until the "opera ghost" has been exorcised from the playhouse. Without their diva to perform, Monsieurs Firmin (John Savident, Ciaran Hinds) and Andre (David Firth, Simon Callow) are beside themselves; they have not only just purchased a theatre with a curse on it but also one in which the whole company is obsessed with a "phantom." Madame Giry (Mary Millar, Miranda Richardson), the ballet mistress, attempts to explain the Phantom's contract, but they dismiss her words as insane, worrying instead about Carlotta's replacement. Both Meg Giry (Janet Devenish from the original cast, Jennifer Ellison in the film version) and her mother recommend one of the chorus girls and they reluctantly agree to hear her sing. Instantly, Christine picks up the great aria (where Carlotta left off) and demonstrates excellant vocal command. Several nights later, she is singing before an large audience.

Her performance at the Gala receives high praise from the audience members, including applause and bravos from a young aristocrat. Raoul remembers rescuing a scarf when he was fourteen for "Little Lotte" and asks Madame Giry take a note to Miss Daae. (As the Vicomte de Chagny, he has become a patron of the theatre, and enjoys each performance from the manager's private box.) He goes backstage to pay tribute to his childhood sweetheart, but Christine has little time for reminiscing. Beyond the walls of her dressing-room, "the Angel of Music" (actually the Phantom) awaits her return. The former friends exchange a brief embrace, then Christine hurries off unexpectantly to keep her dark rendezvous.

Confused, Raoul follows behind her, and pauses outside her door to listen at the keyhole.

From behind the mirror in Miss Daae's dressing-room, the Phantom (Michael Crawford from the original cast, Gerard Butler in the film version) praises her triumph, then reaches through the glowing, shimmering glass to take her hand. His touch is so cold that Christine reacts in fear, but she does follow after him, like Alice through the looking-glass, drawn by his lyrical voice. (Raoul bursts in moments later to find the room empty.) The Phantom and Christine journey to the dark, labyrinthine world below the playhouse, walking down several corridors and crossing the misty waters of an underground lake. Once there, in his subterranean lair, amidst several hundred candles, he asks that she "surrender" to her darkest dreams. The young singer tries to accommodate the coldness of his touch, but when he unveils a wax likeness of her wearing a wedding gown. The image is too much for her to bear! Miss Daae faints into his arms, and he subsequently carries her to bed.

The next morning, Christine awakes to the sound of an organ, and she follows the musical notes in a half trance' to the Phantom, who does not see her. Overwhelmed with curiosity, she tries several times to remove his mask. When she finally succeeds, he springs up in terror to face her. "Damn you!" he shouts in anger. "You little demon - is this what you wanted to see?" His unholy visage is so much more than Christine can bear that she quickly returns the mask to him. The Phantom puts it back on; then, realizing the singer will be missed by the "two fools" who run his theatre, he returns her to the stage.

Several notes, instructing Andre and Firmin to replace La Carlotta with Miss Daae, have arrived at the Paris Opera House. The resident diva is outraged by the request, and accuses Raoul of trying to advance his girlfriend's career. The Vicomte de Chagny pleads innocence, and encourages the managers to proceed with the production with La Carlotta in the lead. Arriving late for the staff meeting, Madame Giry and her daughter warn them that the Phantom's orders must be obeyed or there will be dire consequences. The two managers decide to ignore these warnings.

During the overture of "Il Moto" by Albrizzio, Raoul, Andre, and Firmin take their respective seats -with the young aristocrat in Box

Five and the managers in a box opposite. When production actually begins, Miss Daae is made to appear foolish as the mute Serafimo opposite Carlotta's wealthy Countess. Watching from the catwalks above the stage, the Phantom realizes that the owners must be taught a lesson in terror. First, he arranges to have the diva "croak" like a frog; then, he causes the lights in the chandelier to blink on-and-off; finally, the Phantom drops the garrotted body of Joseph Buguet upon stage, causing the theatre to erupt into pandemonium.

Raoul rushes on stage to embrace Christine, then the two lovers flee to the safety of the roof. High above the Paris Opera House, the singer confesses her fear of the Phantom and pleads with Raoul "to hold me and to hide me..." The young aristocrat agrees, and they share a loving embrace. Unbeknownst to them, the Opera Ghost is perched on a statue of "La Victoire Ailee," high above their heads, and has been listening to every word of the young woman's betrayal. Enraged by what he has heard, the Phantom curses the two young lovers, and follows them back to the theatre. Once there, he cuts the cable that holds the crystalline chandelier, and it crashes onto the stage at Christine's feet. (In the 2004 film version, he cuts the cables to the chandelier near the end of the motion picture.)

Six months later, at the merry, mad Bal Masque de l'Opera, the Phantom appears in crimson cloak and white skull (as Edgar Allan Poe's "Red Death") with a copy of "Don Juan Triumphant." He has been working for the last few months to complete his opera, and now demands that Andre and Firmin produce the work. He also warns Christine that she still belongs to him. When he finally departs, the company is all aghast. The managers are afraid the Phantom will destroy another chandelier; Carlotta still suspects Raoul is responsible, and the Vicomte is worried about his beloved Christine. They all seem to agree that his opera is not very good.

Frightened, and fearing that he may have learned about her secret engagement to Raoul, Miss Daae tries to run away to her father's grave. But she is followed by her tutor and the Vicomte. (Her father "once spoke of an angel," and for months she has believed that the Phantom was her "angel of music.") When Christine attempts to speak to her father's spirit, the Phantom emerges from behind a cross and speaks to her like a ghost. Bewildered, she addresses him in the same manner she would address her father. Raoul suddenly appears from the shadows' embracing her protectively; he is not fooled by the ruse, and easily defends himself against a flurry of fireballs thrown from the madman's staff. As the two lovers flee into the darkness, the Phantom exclaims, "So be it! Now let it be war upon you both." (In the 2004 film version, the Phantom actually crosses sabers with the Viconte, and does not hurl fireballs.)

Before the premiere of "Don Juan Triumphant," Raoul convinces Andre and Firmin to let Christine sing the lead role so that they may lure the Phantom into the theatre for capture. The ghost has heard every word and is prepared for their betrayal. On the set of the final scene from his opera, the Phantom strangles Piangi (John Aaron, Victor McGuire) and takes his place as the masked Don Juan. When his character emerges from the curtains, the young singer suspects that there is something different about him, his voice, and his appearance. He begins to sing, pleading with Christine to share a lifetime of love with him, handing her a ring. By now, everyone in the theatre realizes that the Phantom has traded places with Piangi, who may be dead. Thinking fast, Miss Daae tears the mask from his face and reveals his unholy visage to the audience. As the police close in on the horrifying skull, the Phantom sweeps his cloak around Christine and vanishes. (In the 2004 film version, the Phantom then sends the chandelier crashing into the audience as a distraction to get away.) Madame Giry informs Raoul where the Phantom has taken her, and warns him to hold his hand up (to the level of his eyes) in order to avoid the deadly effects of the Punjab lasso. Moments later, as the Vicomte de Chagny descends into the underground labyrinth, an angry mob with burning torches gathers on stage to follow him.

Beyond the lake, the Phantom drags Christine roughly out of the boat into his subterranean lair. The young singer tries to resist, but he is determined to make her his bride before the others arrive. The Phantom suddenly senses Raoul's presence (as the young aristocrat climbs from the water), and catches him around the neck with his deadly Punjab lasso. He plans to strangle the Vicomte unless Miss Daae will agree to be his bride. She reflects for a moment, then with resolution moves slowly toward her captor. He has never known true love or compassion, and Christine offers herself willingly to him (in the form

of a kiss and a loving embrace). "The Pitiful creature of darkness" is so overwhelmed by her love that he releases Raoul. "Take her, forget me, forget all of this," he urges the Vicomte, then turns to look at his mask as the music box plays "Masquerade." Christine removes the ring (he has given her in the previous scene) and hands it to the opera ghost. As she hurries off to join Raoul, the Phantom places the ring on his finger. He then walks slowly towards his throne and disappears, leaving only the mask. When the mob finally arrives, the Phantom is nowhere to be found. Meg Giry crosses to the throne and picks up his mask in her small hands. (The 2004 film version concludes with Raoul taking the music box he has purchased at auction to Christine's gravesite, and discovering that the Phantom has left her the ring and a rose.)

Production Notes

Inspired by a review he had read in the *Daily Telegraph* of the 1985 production of "The Phantom of the Opera" (see Chapter Thirteen for details), Andrew Lloyd Webber contacted his long-time friend and associate Cameron Mackintosh to arrange a screening of the 1925 silent. They also went to the Theatre Royal, Stratford, in East London, to evaluate the Ken Hill version in light of the current offerings on the West End. Both Lloyd Webber and Macintosh were impressed by what they saw, in spite of its many flaws, and soon commissioned Hill to write a new treatment. When the two producers first conceived their "Phantom of the Opera," they envisioned a camp spectacular, with adventurous chases through an underground labyrinth and a silly, frivolous score. "We had something like 'The Rocky Horror Show' in mind," Lloyd Webber explained in a 1987 interview. But nine months into preproduction, he changed his mind and convinced Cameron Macintosh that he had a much more interesting direction in mind. (The composer would later say that he was inspired by his wife Sarah Brightman to write such a lush, romantic piece.)

"I was actually writing something else at the time, which I may still do again - a treatment of 'Aspects of Love' by David Garnett," the composer revealed, "and I realized that the reason I was hung up was because what I was trying to write was a major romantic love story, and I had been trying to do that ever since I started my career, but I had never been able to find the plot that could be my -er -as it were – 'South Pacific.' Then, with the Phantom it was there! I called Cameron and said, 'I think if I follow the romance in the novel it could be the plot I'm looking for—I'll give it a go.'"

Once he had completed the score, Andrew Lloyd Webber began a search for the right creative team who could bring the music to life.

The diminutive composer offered the project to veteran producer and director Harold (Hal) Prince first. Prince, the director of such legendary musicals as "West Side Story," "Fiddler on the Roof," "Cabaret," and Lloyd Webber's own "Evita," seemed the ideal choice for such a great romantic musical, and he was very interested in directing the piece. "I said 'Yes' immediately, ,. Hal remarked candidly. "I don't usually say 'yes' right away, but it was exactly the sort of show I wanted to do (and see, for that matter, as a theater-goer)."

Lloyd Webber then began looking for a lyricist who could add words to his music. He first tapped the accomplished song writer and musician, who had provided the words for his 1984 hit "Starlight Express," Richard Stilgoe. Stilgoe wrote a first draft of act one, early in 1985, that reflected the music's operatic nature but was not very romantic. Disappointed with Stilgoe's work, Lloyd Webber asked Alan Jay Lerner, who had written the lyrics for "Brigadoon," "My Fair Lady," "Gigi," and "Camelot," to help rewrite the first act and create a second. Lerner agreed. but then three weeks into the collaboration had to withdraw because of illness. (He was to die a few months later of cancer.) Undaunted, the diminutive composer then turned to his long-time friend and former partner Tim Rice, but the man who had written the lyrics to "Jesus Christ-Superstar" and "Evita" declined. Not only was he still upset with Andrew over their previous collaboration but Rice was busy with his own show "Chess" (scheduled to open in May 1986). As the principal lyricist, Lloyd Webber finally selected Charles Hart, 25, a novice who had only one previous, unpreformed musical to his credit.

Still uncertain with his choice, the composer decided to test market part of the

"Phantom" score with a music video that would capture the essence of the story as he then saw it. He approached modern expressionist Ken Russell (who had directed the rock opera "Tommy"), and hired the lead singer of Cockney Rebel, Steve Harley, as the Phantom. Based on a rock version of "The Phantom of the Opera," the stylish video was an overnight success, and the single reached an impressive seventh place in the charts. A second music video, featuring Sarah Brightman and Cliff Richard singing "All I Ask of You," was quickly prepared and released, and a third one, with Michael Crawford singing "Music of the Night," followed. Four songs have since made the British charts, and several have appeared in Billboard's pop listing.

Andrew Lloyd Webber then decided to debut a rough draft of the first act of "The Phantom of the Opera," at his summer music festival at Sydmonton. Maria Bjornson, from the Royal Shakespeare Company, provided the costumes and sets, and Colm Wilkerson, who had been preparing for the role of Jean Valjean in Cameron Macintosh's "Les Miserables," was asked to sing the part of the Phantom. Since Lloyd Webber had composed the role of Christine for his second wife, Sarah Brightman was the logical choice for the female lead. The show was a tremendous success, and encouraged the composer to pursue financing for the production's important London premiere.

The Musical's Debut and Critical Commentary

Following a period of favorable reviews, "The Phantom of the Opera" opened on the West End at Her Majesty's Theatre on Thursday, October 9, 1986. Less than a year and a half later, the show crossed the Atlantic, and grossed $500,000 in its opening week in January 1988 at New York's Majestic Theatre. The Broadway production went onto to win several prestigious Tony Awards, including Best Musical and Best Actor (Michael Crawford), as well as other important awards. Productions have followed in Tokyo, Vienna, Los Angeles, Toronto, Chicago, Washington D.C., Paris, and other popular venues throughout the world. Currently, the show averages ten million dollars a month, and is the biggest theatrical draw in history. It also continues to inspire countless imitators, spoofs, and new adaptations of the Frenchman's work.

Although the Andrew Lloyd Webber version comes the closest in capturing the true spirit of the Leroux novel, several distinct revisions have been made in its transition to the stage. Some of these revisions make sense, while others remain questionable. The decision to concentrate on the romantic triangle between Raoul, Christine, and the Phantom meant restructuring the final chapters of the book. Both the Persian and Philippe de Chagny, who figure predominantly in those chapters, were eliminated from the drama, and the whole sequence in the torture chamber had to be removed in order to feature a more personal confrontation between the three principals. The character of Madame Giry was also changed from an anonymous box attendant to the mistress of the ballet; this alteration visible to the entire audience. Like the 1925 silent, the shock of the Phantom's unholy visage is doubled. First, we see the horror reflected in Christine's eyes; then, when his horrendous features are revealed during "Don Juan Triumphant," we see what she has seen earlier. The two sequences are cleverly directed by Hal Prince, and add much to the original production.

Besides these few revisions, other questionable changes have also been made. Gounod's "Faust," utilized in the original novel to suggest that Erik's dark powers were tied to a demonic pact, has been dropped to favor two pastiche operas – "Hannibal" by Chalumeau and "Il Muto" by Albrizzio - both actually written by Lloyd Webber. While the production numbers are exquisite (and demonstrate the creator's disdain for overblown, grand opera), the pieces contribute very little thematically to the whole. Similarly, the Phantom's own "Don Juan Triumphant," which "intoxicated" Christine in the original novel is considered ludicrous, a lamentable mess, by all who read it. If his opera is truly horrendous, then it remains unclear how this musical adaptation can refer to Erik as a such gifted composer? Lyricist Charles Hart defended these changes to the novel (in a 1987 interview) by claiming that he never intended to create a "storyline which would make the musical seem like a faithful, classic serial for the BBC"; but neither did he want to "tamper (like the many movie versions) with the tragic tale" of a disfigured composer and his love for a young opera singer.

Like Gaston Leroux's mad musical genius, the "Phantom" of the Lloyd Webber musical is a multifaceted character who embodies many attractive virtues as well as several hideous flaws. Charming, confident, and seductive, he proves more than a match for the lovesick Raoul and nearly succeeds in winning Christine with his "music of the night." However, quick to anger and exceedingly arrogant, the Phantom often fails to consider the feelings of others (particularly Christine) in his pursuit of happiness. No matter how kind, gentile, and well-intentioned he appear, the soul of an impatient sociopath lurks just below the surface. Only after Christine accepts his unholy bargain to save Raoul's life does his character change. Even though he does not become a "handsome prince," Erik begins to understand the real meaning of love, and allows the woman he loves to leave with his rival. Like his other literary forerunners (the Beast in "Beauty and the Beast" and "Faust" in Goethe's drama), he is transformed by the love and self sacrifice of a beautiful woman.

The Lloyd Webber version also maintains the ambiguous nature or mystique of the Phantom established in the original novel. Joseph Buquet's words, late in act one, ("Like yellow parchment is his skin, a great black hole served as the nose that never grew,") provide a rudimentary physical description (worthy of Leroux) but precious little else. The opera ghost has apparently been living in the labyrinthine world below the playhouse for some time, but it is unclear how he came to acquire/inherit such a wondrous lair. He watches every performance from his private seat in Box Five, and collects twenty thousand francs a month for his "informative criticism." He has the ability to throw his voice (like a ventriloquist), performs tricks of magic, and on occasion commit murder (like an assassin) with a deadly Punjab lasso. Not once is he referred to as "Erik" in the entire production. Madame Giry appears to be the only person (at the theatre) who knows about his subterranean home, and the way in which she guards his many secrets suggests the two have been friends for many years. (In the 2004 film version, Lloyd Webber makes Giry's connection to the Phantom very clear. Apparently, as a young girl, she was a dancer in training at the Opere House, and rescued Erik after he had killed the sadistic owner of a sideshow carnival in which he had been held captive.) The only other departure from the book, which concerns the Phantom's ultimate demise, has also been deliberately kept ambigious.

Part Valentino, part Bluebeard, and part gifted but demented composer, this Phantom also represents an amalgamation of his cinematic precursors. Like the 1943 and 1962 incarnations, he is portrayed as a wholly sympathetic character. While Erik secretly desires to have his musical talents recognized by the managers of the theatre, he works selflessly (behind the scenes) so that the young soprano can ascend to greater glory. However, when Christine gives the affection he so desperately needs to another man, the Phantom goes mad, declaring war on all those who oppose him. Like his 1925 antecedent Erik, becomes the monster that they believe him to be (dressed appropri-

ately as Edgar Allan Poe's "Red Death"). Arriving at the Bal Masque de l'Opera uninvited, he first strikes terror into the hearts of the costumed revelers, then expects Andre and Firmin to happily produce his "Don Juan Triumphant." Later, like his 1974 equivalent, he kidnaps Christine; even though she has made her feelings toward him clear, he tries again to seduce her with his music, then bullies her with empty threats. To accomplish this wide range of emotions, believeably, the Phantom has been portrayed by some of the finest stage actors in the world, from Kevin Gray, Dave Willetts, Mark Jacobs, and Colm Wilkerson to Timothy Nolen, Jeff Keller, Cris Groenendaal, and Robert Guilliane. But the person commonly associated with the role is Michael Crawford.

Crawford, the actor who originated the role in London, New York, and Los Angeles, has been performing on stage, in film, or on television for over forty years. Born Michael Smith in 1942, he grew up in post-World War Two England. His first appearance was at the age of eight years old in "Soap Box Derby" (1950), followed by "Blow Your Own Trumpet" (1954). Young Michael developed his singing voice with the English Opera Group, when Benjamin Britten cast him in the world premiere of "Noah's Flood" and "Let's Make Opera." In 1962, he played "Sir Francis Drake" in the noted television serial about the famous explorer, then turned to acting as the comic lead in films like "Two Living One Dead" (1962). Michael was the romantic lead in film versions of "A Funny Thing Happened on the Way to the Forum" (1966) and "Hello Dolly" (1969). He played clumsy Frank Spencer in the long-running television series "Some Mothers Do 'ave 'em" (1974-79). Crawford then starred as a comic superhero in Disney's "Condorman" (1979), and originated the title role in the London production of "Barnum." He was taking a much-needed vacation in the West Indies when Andrew Lloyd Webber offered him the role of a lifetime. Today, in retrospect, he fondly refers to "The Phantom of the Opera" as "the greatest adventure of my career," while it is very difficult for many to imagine anyone else in the role.

"I had only to hear the first eight or so bars to know that 'Phantom' was something quite special," Crawford notes. "The score sent chills down my spine the first time I heard it, and still does. Andrew's got me singing from the bottom of my heart to the top hair on my head."

Michael Crawford's tender and hypnotic singing voice not only endows the character of the Phantom with beauty and charm but also reveals his silent desperation. Even when he is not on stage, his haunting presence pervades the atmosphere like a lost spirit, or ghost, who has not been put to rest. He also has the physical ability to express himself even though his face is covered by layers of makeup and a half-mask. Like the great Lon Chaney, Crawford demonstrates all the tortured body movements of a man who is both emotionally and physically scarred. His hands easily glide over Christine's body, but he cannot bring himself to actually touch her (fearing that she may crumble or disappear with his slightest touch). When she finally takes him into her arms and kisses him, the Phantom does not know how to react. He is totally dumb-founded, and falls limp in her embrace. Yet, moments earlier, he has shown great agility and fearlessness, by balancing precariously on the statue which hangs overheard. Because the Phantom's character (as played by Crawford) is comprised of so many contradictions, he emerges as very real person—not an angel, or a devil, but simply a man. Too many of the actors who have played him in the past forgot that they should have been playing men, not horrible monsters.

From Stage to Screen

The Phantom of the Opera (2004). Warner Brothers, in association with The Really Useful Group, 143min. Director: Joel Schumacher. Producers: Andrew Lloyd Webber. Screenwriters: Andrew Lloyd Webber and Joel Schumacher. Inspired by the Gaston Leroux novel. Music by: Andrew Lloyd Webber. Lyrics by Charles Hart (with additional work by Richard Stilgoe). Film Editor: Terry Rawlings. Production Designer: Anthony Pratt. Art Directors: John Fenner and Paul Kirby. Cast: Gerard Butler, Emmy Rossum, Patrick Wilson, Miranda Richardson, Minnie Driver, Ciaran Hinds, Simon Callow, Victor McGuire, Jennifer Ellison, and Kevin McNally.

Phantoms of the Opera

Since its debut in London's West End at Her Majesty's Theatre on October 9, 1986, "The Phantom of the Opera" has reached an estimated audience of 80 million people. More than 65,000 performances of the popular musical have been staged for theatergoers in 18 countries around the world. In August of 2003, the show marked its 7000th performance. Productions of have also earned over 50 major awards, including three Olivier Awards, seven Tony Awards, seven Drama Desk Awards and three Outer Critic's Circle Awards. The first Broadway production ofopened at New York's Majestic Theatre in January of 1988, and has since gone on to become the second-longest running musical in Broadway history (after Lloyd Webber's "Cats"), playing to more than 10.3 million people. Current productions on Broadway at the Majestic, in London at Her Majesty's and the United States tour continue to set records, thrilling audiences and garnering critical acclaim.

For composer Andrew Lloyd Webber, the continued success of his musical version of "The Phantom of the Opera" has given him the much-deserved recognition and attention that he had - for so long - been denied. Even though he has demonstrated his creative abilities time-and-again with a string of unprecedented theatrical successes, including "Jesus Christ-Superstar," "Evita," "Cats," and "Starlight Express," both critics and the Hollywood community have treated him unfairly. Because the film version of his New Testament rock opera was such a critical disaster, Lloyd Webber's compositions about Eva Peron, cute-and-cuddly singing cats, and talking trains have all been optioned by studio executives but never produced. For nearly twenty years, the cinematic adaptation of "The Phantom of the Opera" also seemed in doubt. Paramount, Warner Brothers, M-G-M/UA, and Universal had all expressed an interest in producing the musical version, but not one of them had put together a production package that was suitable to the diminutive composer. Both Steven Spielberg, who plans to make an animated version of "Cats" and Michael Jackson have tried unsuccessfully for years to secure the rights from Lloyd Webber. But he had retained those rights with Cameron Macintosh through their own production group, the Really Useful Company, with the hope that the right offer would come.

Early in 1989, Gary Luchessi, a top-level executive at Paramount Pictures, introduced the multi-millionaire composer to the work of

Joel Schumacher (notably "D.C. Cab," 1983, and "Cousins," 1989). Apparently, he liked what he saw, and screened two of the director's important films, "St Elmo's Fire" (1985) and "The Lost Boys" (1987).

"I thought Joel had an incredible visual sense and his use of music in the film was exceptional," Lloyd Webber recalls. "One of the great joys of collaborating with Joel is that he has a great ear for music; he really gets it, he understands how the music drives the story." Webber was so impressed by Schumacher's blockbuster vampire thriller "The Lost Boys" that he asked to meet with him. Then, following several preliminary meetings between Andrew Lloyd Webber and Schumacher in London and Los Angeles, the composer offered Joel the chance to direct the film version of the musical theatre's all-time money maker.

"The prospect is thrilling," Schumacher told the press hours after the contracts had been signed in 1989. Later that same year, he and Webber wrote the screenplay in the South of France. Schumacher was to have been "very actively involved" in preproduction, with the composer and Cameron Macintosh serving as executive producers. Both Michael Crawford and Sarah Brightman were set to reprise their stage roles, and construction of the elaborate Paris Opera sets was scheduled to begin in a few months. But then, weeks away from the start of shooting in 1990, the bottom fell out of the production. Webber announced that he was divorcing Sarah for another woman, and that

young soprano would no longer be available for the role of Christine.

While Macintosh, Schumacher and others scrambled around looking for a replacement for Ms. Brightman (considering Patti Cohenour, the American singer who had performed the role of Christine in New York and Los Angeles), the start date was pushed back several times. Finally, the production ground to a dead hault. Contractually bound by Columbia, Joel Schumacher went off to direct both "Flatliners" (1990) and "Dying Young" (1991), both with Julia Roberts. Cameron Macintosh left to oversee Bruce Bereford's film version of "Les Miserables," which also fell through, and Andrew Lloyd Webber went on an extended honeymoon with his new wife. The diminutive composer still retained control of his project, and was in no particular hurry to see a film version, considering the renewed success of the road company touring "The Phantom of the Opera" around the world.

Several years later, following the success of Francis Ford Coppola's big screen version of "Dracula" (1992), Schumacher and Webber began anew, sketching plans for a December 1994 or Summer 1995 release of their film.

"We haven't yet decided on what country to shoot the movie," Joel explained in a 1992 interview. "I'd like to shoot a couple of scenes in Paris. But it's a fantasy, an opera, and we're going to be anything but literal about it." He did reveal that the film version would certainly boast eye-popping special effects, elaborate set designs, and would feature the talents of Michael Crawford. But beyond that, he remained purposely ambiguous about the screenplay and the actress who would play Christine. Once again, the production was inexplicably put on hold, and Schumacher went onto direct "Falling Down" (1993), two Batman films, "Flawless" (1999), "Tigerland" (2000), "Veronica Guerin" (2001) and "Phone Booth" (2002), which he shot in a mere twelve days. Webber returned to the London stage to produce "Aspects of Love" (1993), "Sunset Blvd." (1995), and "Whistle Down the Wind" (1998).

Fate and good timing finally collided in December 2002, when the old friends met for dinner in London and Webber proposed they join forces to launch the long-awaited and twice-delayed production. "I had just done a series of gritty, more experimental films than the mainstream blockbusters I'd been associated with in the past," Schumacher explained in an interview in 2003. "I've done so many different genres, but never a musical. It seemed like a huge challenge and I like that." The success of "Moulin Rouge" (2001) and "Chicago" (2002), two musicals that had taken Hollywood by storm, furthered convinced them that the time was right for "Phantom."

Adapting the Musical

In adapting their screenplay from the musical's book, Schumacher and Webber delved further into the backstories of several key characters and incorporated the backstage world of the Paris Opera House into the main story. "In the stage musical, we touch on the Phantom's childhood, but we don't visually go back in time to explore it as we do in the film," Webber explains. "It's a very important change for us, because it makes the Phantom's plight even more understandable." Unlike previous adaptations of the Gaston Leroux novel, they take us back to the point in time when Erik was a caged freak in a sideshow carnival. Tortured by the sadistic owner, Erik kills him, and escapes to freedom where he is befriended and protected by a young Madame Giry. She actually leads him to the Paris Opera House, and helps him find a home in the dark, labyrinthine world below. While not entirely accurate to *Le Fantôme de l'Opera*, the sequence does capture the spirit of Leroux.

Joel Schumacher enjoyed fleshing out the backstory with Webber, but was far more interested in developing the love triangle as well as the historical backdrop."The stage show concentrates on the Phantom, Christine and Raoul," Schumacher elaborates. "Not only did we want to give the audience more insight as to how each of these characters arrived at the opera house, we also wove the backstage activity

– the plasterers, prop makers, wig makers, scenic artists, dancers and singers – into the fabric of the story." Webber concurs, ""While it doesn't deviate much from the stage material, the changes have given it an even deeper emotional center. It's not based on the theatre visually or direction-wise, but it's still got exactly the same essence. And that's all I could have ever hoped for."

In addition to the back story about the Phantom, they include several other sequences that have escaped other productions. When the Phantom escorts Christine to his subterranean lair, he places her on a black horse for a while. This is not part of the stage show, but is a nod to the original book, where the Phantom uses a horse named Cesar to transport Christine part of the way. Similarly, at the end of the Masquerade scene, Raoul briefly enters a circular chamber full of mirrors. This is yet another reference to the original novel, in which the Phantom used the mirrored chamber as a torture chamber to drive his victims insane. Regrettably, the role of the Persian which is featured so prominently in the novel is absent.

With the script finally complete, Webber and Schumacher settled on a budget and start date for "The Phantom of the Opera." Initially Schumacher wanted to film the production in Paris, but he later agreed with Webber to to build the sets they needed for the Paris Opera House at Pinewood Studios in Iver Heath, Buckinghamshire, England, on the same soundstage that had serviced so many of the James Bond films. The same lead sculptors who had made the set for the original stage show in London were used for the making of the film sets. Additional filming would be done in London, with locations redressed to look like Paris, and other sequences at Her Majesty's Theatre where "The Phantom of the Opera" had played since 1986. In fact, one audience of the stage version of was asked to stay behind at the end of the show in April 2004 and record the sound effects for the movie. (The sounds are played during the famous chandelier crash in the film adaptation.)

Casting the Film

The most difficult and stressful part of the production still lay ahead for director Joel Schumacher and producer-composer Andrew Lloyd Webber. Casting their film version proved to be an exceptional challenge. Michael Crawford and Sarah Brightman were now both too old for the production, but had cast a long-shadow over the musical with their exceptional portrayals of the Phantom and Christine. Over the years, Webber had considered John Travolta and Antonio Banderas for the role of the Phantom; in fact, Banderas spent several years in vocal preparation, and sang the role of the Phantom in "Andrew Lloyd Webber: The Royal Albert Hall Celebration" (1998). But by 2003, he was also considered too old for the production.

Schumacher envisioned the film as a sexy young love story, and set out to cast fresh new actors in the principal roles. This was especially vital in casting Christine, a naïve, orphaned teenager who believes the Phantom's voice calling to her from the dark shadows of the Paris Opera House is the "Angel of Music" her dying father promised to send her. "Part of the beauty of the character is her innocence, her attachment to her father and her belief that the Phantom might actually be a representation of him from beyond the grave," Schumacher noted. "We needed to find a young woman who could exude a genuine youthful innocence and longing, and at the same time, we had to find two wildly charismatic actors to play the two men she is torn between."

The role of the eponymous Phantom demanded an actor who could radiate a charismatic intensity, while at the same time being a bit

vulnerable to his love. "We needed somebody who has a bit of rock and roll sensibility in him," Webber explained. "He's got to be a bit rough, a bit dangerous; not a conventional singer. Christine is attracted to the Phantom because he's the right side of danger, so we had to find an actor who could deliver that vocal quality."

Webber and Schumacher saw dozens of potential Phantoms and Christines in the early stages of pre-production. The diminutive composer felt that one of his collaborator's trademarks was that he had the ability to find talented young actors who were just about to break through, and entrusted the acting aspect of the casting process to Schumacher while he strived to achieve the perfect "vocal balance" between the candidates who demonstrated they possessed the vocal chops to perform his libretto of sophisticated songs. They eventually settled on Gerard Butler, who they had seen in "Dracula 2000" (2000), and Emmy Rossum.

Gerard Butler makes an exceptional Phantom. Younger and more conventionally handsome than Michael Crawford, his chiseled features suggest a sexy Valentino or some other matinee idol from the 1920's. And while his Phantom may loose Christine to the fatuous Raoul, he wins the hearts and souls of every member of the audience with his tragic portrayal of the disfigured composer. Born in Glasgow, Scotland, to Margaret and Edward Butler, Gerard was raised (along with his older brother and sister) in his mother's hometown of Paisley, Scotland. His parents divorced when he was a small child, and though primarily raised by his mother, he had no contact with his father Edward till years later when he was sixteen years old, after which time they became very close. Butler studied to be a Solicitor at Glasgow University, but he decided to give up law school for acting after a chance meeting with actor Steven Berkoff, who gave him a stage role in "Coriolanus." Small roles in "Mrs. Brown" (1997), "Tomorrow Never Dies" (1997), and "Tales of the Mummy" (1998) fol-

lowed. While filming "Mrs. Brown" in Scotland, he rescued a young boy from drowning, and received a "Certificate of Bravery" from the Royal Humane Society. His two breakthrough roles came as Attila the Hun in "Attila" (2001) and Dracula in Wes Craven's "Dracula 2000" (2000). Since then, Butler has appeared in "Reign of Fire" (2002) as Creedy, "Lara Croft Tomb Raider: The Cradle of Life" (2003) as Terry Sheridan, and Andre Marek in "Timeline" (2003). His turn as the Phantom in the Andrew Lloyd Webber musical has garnered him much popularity in fannish circles, and also established him as an important leading man. His other recent projects have included "The Game of Their Lives" (2005), "Beowulf and Grendel" (2005), and "Burns" (2006).

Butler's co-star in "The Phantom of the Opera" (2004), Emmy Rossum, turns in the best performance of any previous incarnation of Christine, including Sarah Brightman who originated the role on the London stage. Rossum was only 16 when she screen-tested for the role in full costume and make-up, and was finally selected for the part by Andrew Lloyd Webber after singing for him at his home. Born and raised in New York City, she auditioned for the Metropolitan Opera when she was only 7 years old, and then performed in over 20 operas in six different languages at Lincoln Center, alongside renowned figures like Placido Domingo and Luciano Pavarotti. In 1999, she created the role of Abigail Williams on the daytime soap opera "As the World Turns," and branched out to play in other television

shows, including "Snoops" (1999), "Law and Order" (1999), and "The Practice" (1999). She played Audrey Hepburn as a young teenager in "The Audrey Hepburn Story" (2000). Emmy made her feature debut in "Songcatcher" (2000), and followed that with turns in "Nola" (2003) and "Mystic River" (2003). Just prior to making "Phantom," she played the female lead in "The Day After Tomorrow" (2004). Despite the fact that many, better-known and older actresses lobbied for the role of Christine, including Keira Knightley, Katie Holmes, Charlotte Church, and Anne Hathaway, the combination of Rossum's vulnerable, fragile beauty and fine, classically-trained singing voice ultimately proved that she was perfectly cast.

For the role of Raoul, the filmmakers cast Patrick Wilson, star of Broadway's "Oklahoma!" and "The Full Monty," and an Emmy nominee for his performance in the HBO miniseries "Angels in America." "I had seen Patrick on the stage and I knew he sang beautifully," says Schumacher. "He's a very talented actor and he has the voice of an angel." Webber was also pleased with the choice, stating, "Patrick is one of the great natural lyric tenors from the theatre." Wilson's turn as Raoul represents a more dynamic version of the character than audiences have seen in the theatrical production. He is often demoted to second-tier status in most of the other film versions, and plays the foil in the love triangle with the Phantom and Christine. But Webber and Schumacher imagined him as a "very aggressive, swashbuckling romantic hero," who is a far greater threat to the Phantom because of his appeal to Christine.

Versatile actress Miranda Richardson, an Academy Award nominee for her roles in "Tom & Viv" and "Damage," plays Madame Giry, the ballet mistress who knows more about the mysterious events at the Paris Opera House – and the Phantom – than she cares to reveal.

"Miranda has been one of my favorite actresses ever since I saw her in "Dance With a Stranger,'" Schumacher commented."I can't say enough about the brilliance she brought to the role of Madame Giry."

The only member of the Opera ensemble whose larger-than-life persona threatens to eclipse the Phantom's menacing presence is the company's temperamental diva-in-residence, La Carlotta. Minnie Driver, the talented actress known for her performances in the Oscar-winning drama "Good Will Hunting" and "Return to Me," portrays the volatile Italian soprano. Though a talented singer in her own right, Driver did not perform her own singing for the film. Her part was voiced by professional opera singer Margaret Preece, who had performed the role of Carlotta onstage.

Rounding out the "Phantom" cast were accomplished character actors Simon Callow (from "Shakespeare in Love") and Ciaran Hinds (from "Road to Perdition") as theatre buff Andre and the business-minded Firmin, respectively, Victor McGuire (from "Lock, Stock and Two Smoking Barrels") as the grand baritone singer Piangi, and Jennifer Ellison in the role of Christine's young friend Meg Giry.

The Film's Release and Aftermath

"The Phantom of the Opera" debuted in Spain at the Festival Internacional de Cinema de Catalunya on December 9, 2004, and then opened in the United States on December 22, 2004. With a budget of $60 million, the motion picture earned a respectable $150 million worldwide. The critics were mixed in their appreciation of the big screen adaptation of one of the most beloved musicals. Roger Ebert of *The Chicago Suntimes* wrote, "I love the look of the film, but I do not seem to like [the film] very much." Peter Travers of *Rolling Stone* called it "a rapturous spectacle," while Ed Morales in *The Village Voice* joked, "If Bob Fosse had a recurring nightmare of being forced to stage a flamenco

show in Vegas, this is what it would look like." Most of the critics agreed that they loved the look of the film, but generally did not like the cinematic adaptation.

Nominated for 3 Oscars at the 2005 Academy Awards, "The Phantom of the Opera" was trumped by lesser productions in the categories of Best Achievement in Art Direction, Cinematography, and Original Song. The film also lost Golden Globes for Best Motion Picture, Best Original Song, and Best Peformance by an Actress (Emmy Rossum). Clearly, the finest musical produced for film since Robert Wise's "Sound of Music" (1965), the 2004 film adaption of "The Phantom of the Opera" remains a favorite among fans of Andrew Lloyd Webber's productions.

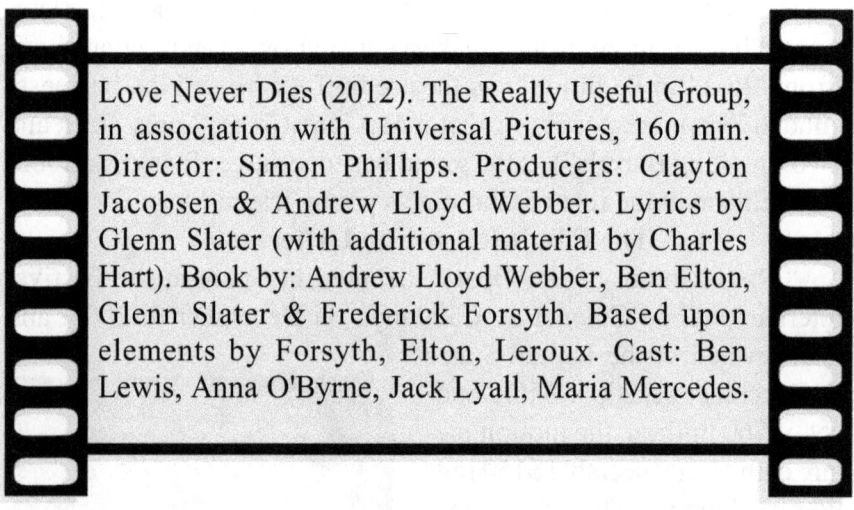

Love Never Dies (2012). The Really Useful Group, in association with Universal Pictures, 160 min. Director: Simon Phillips. Producers: Clayton Jacobsen & Andrew Lloyd Webber. Lyrics by Glenn Slater (with additional material by Charles Hart). Book by: Andrew Lloyd Webber, Ben Elton, Glenn Slater & Frederick Forsyth. Based upon elements by Forsyth, Elton, Leroux. Cast: Ben Lewis, Anna O'Byrne, Jack Lyall, Maria Mercedes.

The Phantom returned in Andrew Lloyd Webber's stunning musical sequel "Love Never Dies," filmed at the Melbourne Regent Theatre and screened in select theatres on February 28, 2012. Ten long years have passed. Christine, now a world-renowed diva, is married to Raoul, and they have a son named Gustave. Raoul has gambled their fortune away, and they travel to New York to claim money for one final performance for a wealthy but mysterious Mr.Y, unaware it is the Phantom. The Phantom now hides in plain site with the other freaks at his Phantasma on Coney Island. He still loves Christine, unaware that Gustave may be his son, and will do anything to win her affection. The sequel was good, when the production should have been great.

~ 13 ~
Interesting Vicissitudes

> Erik here rose solemnly. Then he continued, but, as he spoke, he was overcome by all his former emotion and began to tremble like a leaf: "Yes, she was waiting for me...waiting for me erect and alive, a real, living bride...as she hoped to be saved....And, when I...came forward, more timid than...a little child, she did not run away...no, no...she stayed...she waited for me...and...I...kissed her!"
> —Gaston Leroux, *Le Fantôme de l'Opera*

Although Andrew Lloyd Webber's version of "The Phantom of the Opera" (1986, 2004) represented the apotheosis of the seventy-year attempt to translate the Frenchman's work into drama, with its evocative richness, its use of musical numbers to convey character and meaning, and its technological achievements in special effects and make-up, there remained other avenues still unexplored. Many, who had found fault with the Tony Award-winning musical, believed that the definitive version of Gaston Leroux's 1911 novel had yet to be made.

Throughout the late Eighties into the Nineties and the new Century, numerous studios, independent filmmakers, and theatrical pioneers have produced their own variations on the theme. Most of the motion pictures and dramatic productions came and went with very little fanfare and even less box office appeal, but there were a number of notable exceptions that lured a younger, hip (and often punk) audience to the theatre and still received critical and commercial approval. To many, that mad musical genius who haunted a forgotten opera house was, after all, a popular draw. Films, like "Terror At the Opera"

(1988), "Phantom of the Mall: Eric's Revenge" (1989), and "Popcorn" (1991), attempted to re-interpret or re-invent the myth for contemporary audiences, while others, like "Batman" (1989), "Gremlins 2" (1990), "Darkman" (1990), and television's "Beauty and the Beast" (1987, CBS), paid loving tribute to one of the sources that spawned them. Still others felt obligated to tell the story over-and-over again.

Motion Pictures and Direct to Video

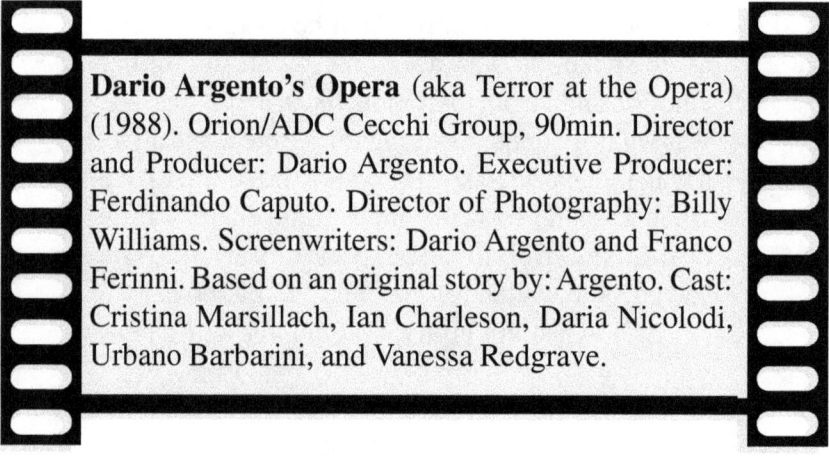

Dario Argento's Opera (aka Terror at the Opera) (1988). Orion/ADC Cecchi Group, 90min. Director and Producer: Dario Argento. Executive Producer: Ferdinando Caputo. Director of Photography: Billy Williams. Screenwriters: Dario Argento and Franco Ferinni. Based on an original story by: Argento. Cast: Cristina Marsillach, Ian Charleson, Daria Nicolodi, Urbano Barbarini, and Vanessa Redgrave.

Freely adapted from Gaston Leroux's classic tale, "Dario Argento's Opera" (released at the Cannes Film Festival as "Terror at the Opera") takes its voyeuristic approach to sadistic ends in order to shock his audience but fails, ultimately drowning in its own grue and gore. Set in an Italian opera house, the film chronicles the abduction, seduction, and terrorism of a talented but unknown opera singer (Cristina Marsillach) by a mysterious killer (Ian Charleson) into the joys of sado masochism. When Betty (Marsillach) and members of her acting troup enter a disused opera house to stage a new production of Verdi's "Macbeth," they are unaware that the the Shakespearian adaptation brings a curse upon those unlucky enough to perform it. In the days that follow, as the troup begins rehearsal for the opera, they become increasingly edgy, sensing that something is not quite right. Props disappear, then reappear somewhere else; elements of costumes are rearranged, and scenic backdrops are switched. Someone is deliberately causing them problems. Then, suddenly, the company's prima donna (Vanessa Redgrave) is struck dead by a mysterious car following an argument with the show's director (Ian Charleson).

Betty, the hopeful young ingénue, inherits the lead role of Lady Macbeth and uses the part to reveal her tremendous talent as a singer. Her triumph on opening night attracts a secret admirer, the "phantom," who will go to murderous lengths to see that she succeeds. Numerous brutal deaths follow, until the young singer is abducted by the psychopathic killer and made to watch his bloody retelling of "Macbeth." (Tied to a pillar, Betty's eyes are actually forced to remain open by needle-lined tape so that she can witness each death in gory detail.) Predictably, Inspector Alan (Urbano Barberini), a local constable, arrives just in the nick of time to rescue the young heroine and dispatch the murderous "phantom."

A box office failure in Italy, where it ran for less than three weeks in 1987, Orion Pictures introduced a slightly-altered, English-language version at the 1988 Cannes Film Festival which was literally laughed off the screen. "Dario Argento's Opera" has remained in the vaults ever since, where the distributor continues to debate its release. Poorly dubbed and cut to eliminate much of the hard-core violence, the eight-million dollar production represents one of the worst of Dario Argento's films. From the director who brought us "The Bird with the Crystal Plumage" (1969), "Suspira" (1976), and "Creepers" (1985), we expected something more from his homage to Gaston Leroux's classic novel.

> **Il Fantasma dell'opera** (Dario Argento's The Phantom of the Opera) (1998). Italy, 106 min, Director: Dario Argento. Producers: Giuseppe Colombo and Aron Sipos. Screenwriters: Gerard Brach and Dario Argento. Based upon Le Fantôme de l'Opera by Gaston Leroux. Music Composers: Maurizio Guarini and Ennio Morricone. Cinematographer: Ronnie Taylor. Editor: Anna Rosa Napoli. Production Designers: Massimo Antonello Geleng and Csaba Stork. Cast: Julian Sands, Asia Argento, Andrea Di Stefano, Nadia Rinaldi, Coraline Cataldi Tassoni, Istvan Bubik, Zoltan Barabas, Lucia Guzzardi, Aldo Massasso.

Phantoms of the Opera

After failing with "Terror at the Opera" (1988), Dario Argento went back to the original source material to produce yet another take on Gaston Leroux's *Le Fantôme de l'Opera*. "Il Fantasma dell'opera" begins in 1877 when rats rescue a small baby from the cold, cruel Parisian steets, and take him to their underground lair below the Opera de Paris. This child grows to manhood to become the Phantom of the Opera (Julian Sands), a half-human half-animal breed, who falls in love with Christine Daaé (Asia Argento), an opera singer initiating her career. He disputes her love for the aristocratic Baron Raoul De Chagny (Andrea Di Stefano), and demands that Christine love him. When she rejects him, the Phantom becomes enraged, and sets about on a course for revenge. In the nifty, little subplot, the Phantom invokes death upon anyone who dares harm his beloved rats. In fact, The Phantom's nemesis is the chief exterminator (Istvan Bubik) who develops a rat-catching machine.

While most fans of Dario Argento's other horror films have dismissed "Il Fantasma dell'opera" as a "Hollywood-influenced piece of garbage," the film is actually the gentlest and most romantic of all his other work. His legendary status in the genre, with films like "Suspira" and "Deep Red," is clearly evident as he moves his actors through the familiar story; in fact, his version with its own collection of splashy gore scenes reminds one of Terrence Fisher's 1962 adaptation. All of Argento's trademarks, including his cool camera angles, his creepy Goblin music, his use of color and suspense, make the film especially interesting. He also employs real operas, from Georges Bizet's "L'amour est un oiseau rebelle" from the opera "Carmen," Leo Delibes's "Lakmé: Air des clochettes," and Charles Gounod's "Faust," to good effect.

The only misstep Argento takes is making his "Phantom" so human. Without scars, without any kind of mutilation or disfigurement, Julian Sands plays this "Phantom" of the opera as an unwashed orphan abandoned in the sewers under the Paris Opera and raised by rats. In fact, this is the first film not to feature the Phantom wearing a mask. The tall and guant Sands, who has made a career out of playing British leading men in horror films like "Warlock" (1989) and "Boxing Helena" (1993), is far too "pretty" to play a convincing Erik. He'd actually make a more believable Raoul than Phantom, and without the mask to hide his face, one wonders why he is even referred to as a "phantom" in this opera house. His muse is played by Dario Argento's daughter Asia, who has very little to fear from her lovesick admirer. Forced to choose between the handsome Sands and the equally attractive Andrea Di Stefano as the Baron Raoul De Chagny, she faces a nearly impossible decision that was never explored by Gaston Leroux or any other film production. Currently available on home video.

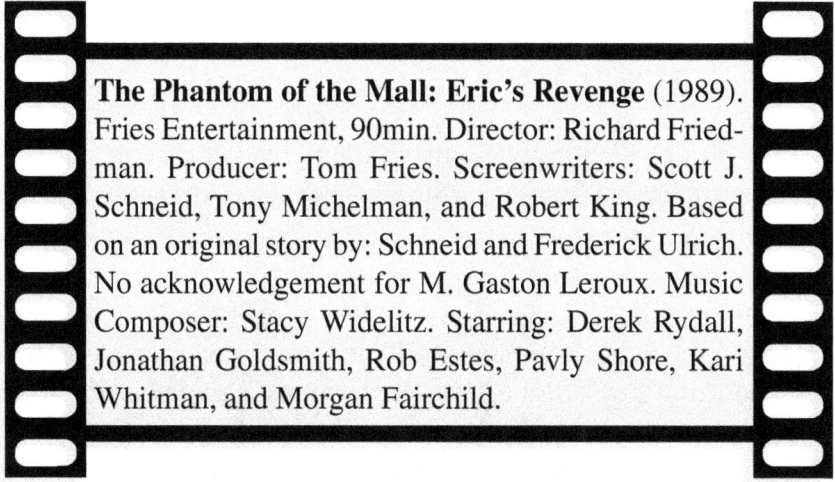

The Phantom of the Mall: Eric's Revenge (1989). Fries Entertainment, 90min. Director: Richard Friedman. Producer: Tom Fries. Screenwriters: Scott J. Schneid, Tony Michelman, and Robert King. Based on an original story by: Schneid and Frederick Ulrich. No acknowledgement for M. Gaston Leroux. Music Composer: Stacy Widelitz. Starring: Derek Rydall, Jonathan Goldsmith, Rob Estes, Pavly Shore, Kari Whitman, and Morgan Fairchild.

A belated and conspicuously low-budget addition to the teenage slasher cycle, which started with John Carpenter's "Halloween" (1978) and had already begun to wear thin by the fifth "Nightmare on Elm Street" film, the lackluster "Phantom of the Mall" contributes yet another twist to the already familiar Gaston Leroux tale. The advertisement for the motion picture read: "There was a nightmare at the mall; Eric the Phantom struck." But audiences already knew what they would be seeing.

The film opens in the rich, suburban community of Sherman Oaks, California. Childhood sweethearts Eric Matthews (Derek Rydall) and Melody Austin (Kari Whitman) vow their undying love to one another, but their promises for a post-high school wedding are shattered when the Matthews' home burns to the ground. Eric manages to rescue his love but is himself caught in the fire (which may have been set by an arsonist). One year later, memories of that terrible night overwhelm Melody as she begins work at a glitzy new mall that has been built over the site of her dead boyfriend's home. She has tried her best to recover from the trauma, including dating a handsome young photographer (Rob Estes). But reminders of Eric keep appearing out of nowhere at the mall. First, a fresh bouquet of flowers; then, the young lover's song keeps playing on the sound system. Finally, people begin to disappear. A badly-disfigured Eric Matthews is alive, hiding in the ventillation system, and he desperately wants to prove that a greedy land developer (Morgan Fairchild) was responsible for the fire.

"What I primarily liked about the script was that it's about kids - a sensitive screenplay, but still a horror story," thirty year-old Richard Friedman explained in an interview shortly before the film's debut. "It follows the classic story line of *The Phantom of the Opera*, but it's about a kid hideously disfigured in a premeditated fire who comes back only because he wants what he once had: to rekindle his relationship with the girl he loved and to be normal again. It's a traditional story, given a strong modern twist."

Friedman, the director of several low-budget quickies including "Doom Asylum" and "Scared Stiff" and three memorable episodes of "Tales from the Darkside," was very optimistic about his film when it was released in 1989 by Fries Distribution. Combining state-of-the-art makeup and special effects by Matthew Mungle with a very literate script by Scott J. Schneid, Tony Michelman, and Robert King, the production had all the necessary elements for a breakaway success. Regrettably, "Phantom of the Mall: Eric's Revenge," as one of a half dozen motion pictures inspired by the highly successful Broadway musical, premiered the same month as Robert Englund's far superior "Phantom," and did not fare well. However, the film has managed to survive theatrical distribution in another medium.

John L. Flynn

Home video has given new life to several "Phantom" films which ordinarily would have died at the box office and remained dead. Whereas the early Seventies witnessed a decline of the horror film, the VCR and cable explosion of the Eighties has opened the market up wide for low budget films, independents, or those that were simply too soft for theatrical distribution. Patrons across America, Japan, and a dozen other countries generally rent. at least, one film per night (from the local video store) and tape more than ten movies a week (from cable television); since the number of ..A" titles are limited, "B" (and even the lower grade "Z") movies are in the greatest demand. For example, "The Toxic Avenger" (1984), produced through independent Troma films, played in only a handful of movie theatres and would have disappeared entirely had it not been for home video. The motion picture has since become the most successful independent film ever released on videocassette and has inspired a sequel, which was released theatrically as "The Toxic Avenger II" (1988). All those films recently inspired by the 1911 Gaston Leroux novel, including Englund's "Phantom of the Opera" (1989) and "Popcorn" (1991), have found renewed interest with patrons of Blockbuster. "Phantom of the Mall: Eric's Revenge" (1989) has not only returned its modest two million-dollar investment but also achieved cult status on home video.

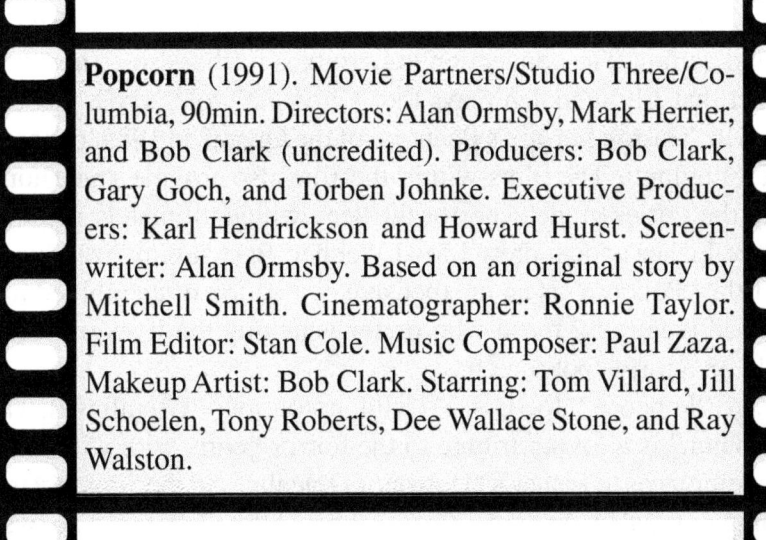

Popcorn (1991). Movie Partners/Studio Three/Columbia, 90min. Directors: Alan Ormsby, Mark Herrier, and Bob Clark (uncredited). Producers: Bob Clark, Gary Goch, and Torben Johnke. Executive Producers: Karl Hendrickson and Howard Hurst. Screenwriter: Alan Ormsby. Based on an original story by Mitchell Smith. Cinematographer: Ronnie Taylor. Film Editor: Stan Cole. Music Composer: Paul Zaza. Makeup Artist: Bob Clark. Starring: Tom Villard, Jill Schoelen, Tony Roberts, Dee Wallace Stone, and Ray Walston.

"Popcorn" (1991) is a wonderfully imagined, nine million-dollar spoof of Gaston Leroux's 1911 novel, with additional tributes to Roger Corman, Edward D. Wood Jr, and Hammer Films. Written and directed by Alan Ormsby (with assistance by Herrier and Clark), the film mixes a sick sense of humor with a stream of cinematic in-jokes to effectively parody and pay homage to the shlocky horror genre that inspired its creation. The principal action unfolds at an abandoned movie palace (Kingston's Ward Theatre in Jamaica), where a group of film students decide on put on a festival of horror movies from the Fifties. One of the films, which include "Mosquito," "The Amazing Electrified Man." "The Stench," and "Possesser," was never released because its director, Lanyard Gates, went crazy and killed his family live on stage fifteen years earlier. And now he's back to kill his daughter Sara (Jill Schoelen), now known as Maggie, who is coincidentally among the film students at the festival. While holding their all-night "horror-thon," the spirit of the insane auteur - thought to have perished in a fire twenty years before - returns to inhabit Toby (Tom Villard), also one of the students. Toby takes on the looks of the disfigured "phantom," wearing his leatherface, then begins stalking the audience members and killing them off one-by-one.

Although many ticket buyers passed when this was first released to theatres, "Popcorn" has achieved a major cult following on home video. More than a simple slasher movie, the many parallels to Gaston Leroux's *Le Fantôme de l'Opera* are nicely underplayed for both comedy and parody. The connection to Leroux is further driven home by the fact that Jill Schoelen plays the "Christine" role, a role that she played in "Gaston Leroux's Phantom of the Opera" in 1989, opposite Robert Englund. The films-within-the-film also provide a nice homage to the Fifties grade Z horror thrillers, which ultimately inspired Terence Fisher and Andrew Lloyd Webber. Best summarized by its own title, "Popcorn" is an inexpensive confection often nibbled in a darkened theatre by those who prefer watching the lives of others unfold on a forty-foot screen.

Like "Popcorn," Joe Dante's wild, uproarious "Gremlins II: The New Batch" is a loving tribute to the horror genre, with widely diverse references to Fisher's "Horror of Dracula" and the Tony Award-winning musical by Andrew Lloyd Webber. After Galligan's mogwai, which he calls Gizmo, produces a number of less friendly creatures,

Gremlins II: The New Batch (1990). Warner Brothers, 96min. Director: Joe Dante. Producer: Mike Finnell. Executive Producers: Steven Spielberg, Kathleen Kennedy, and Frank Marshall. Screenwriter: Charlie Haas. Based on characters created by Chris Columbus. Cinematographer: John Hora. Film Editor: Kent Beyda. Makeup Artist: Rick Baker. Cast: Zach Galligan, Phoebe Cates. John Glover, Dick Miller, Kenneth Tobey, and Christopher Lee.

known as gremlins, the latter proceed to go on a rampage through a New York City high rise. The little monsters soon invade the gene-splicing lab of Dr. Catheter (Christopher Lee), and start experimenting with his chemicals. In one sequence, inspired by Terence Fisher's "Phantom," one gremlin throws acid in the face of another. Moments later, the disfigured creature emerges with a "phantom"-like mask (designed after the one Michael Crawford wore). In another sequence, taken from the Lon Chaney film, a female gremlin unmasks the "phantom" gremlin in a hilarious send-up. The third, and final tribute to Gaston Leroux's *Le Fantôme de l'Opera*, finds the masked gremlin taking part in a musical number, clearly derived from some of Broadway's greatest hits. Dante's wholesale parody of horror films demonstrates great imagination and fun, and is certainly worth a second (or third) viewing on home video.

O Fantasma da Opera (The Phantom of the Opera) (1991). Brazil, Rede Manchete Productions, 100min. Directors: Del Rangel, Atillio Ricco, and Alvaro Fugulin. Screenwriters: Jael Coaracy and Paul Afonso de Lima. Based on the novel by Gaston Leroux. Cast: Daniela Aguiar, Gesio Amadeu, Isaac Bardavid, Sergio Britto, Rebeca Bueno, Olivia Byington, Mario Cardoso, Marcos Caruso, and Ariel Coelho.

Phantoms of the Opera

This Portuguese version of Gaston Leroux's *Le Fantôme de l'Opera* played as a miniseries on Brazilian television on October 15, 1991, and was a surprisingly faithful adaptation. Daniela Aguiar played Luciana, the young, aspiring opera singer, while her rival Carlota was played by Olivia Byington. The production is not currently available on home video.

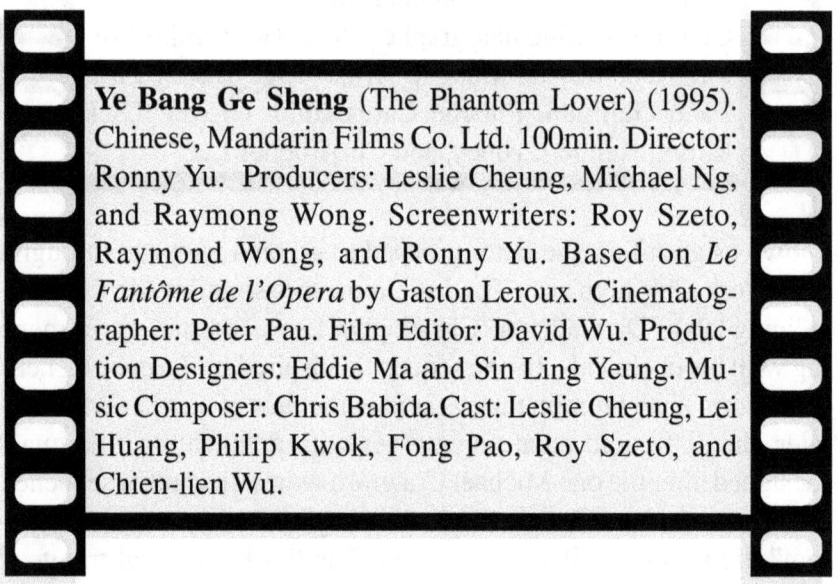

Ye Bang Ge Sheng (The Phantom Lover) (1995). Chinese, Mandarin Films Co. Ltd. 100min. Director: Ronny Yu. Producers: Leslie Cheung, Michael Ng, and Raymong Wong. Screenwriters: Roy Szeto, Raymond Wong, and Ronny Yu. Based on *Le Fantôme de l'Opera* by Gaston Leroux. Cinematographer: Peter Pau. Film Editor: David Wu. Production Designers: Eddie Ma and Sin Ling Yeung. Music Composer: Chris Babida. Cast: Leslie Cheung, Lei Huang, Philip Kwok, Fong Pao, Roy Szeto, and Chien-lien Wu.

This third, uniquely Chinese reinterpretation of Gaston Leroux's *Le Fantôme de l'Opera* finds a nearly bankrupt drama troupe performing at a burned-out theater, where the great actor Song Danping (Leslie Chung) was killed, in 1936 China. One of the actors, Wei Qing (Lei Huangi, from Chen Kaige's "Life on a String"), starts seeing strange apparitions. He soon comes to realize the mysterious figure who haunts the backstage area is the famed actor from the 1920s whose affair with the daughter (Jacklyn Wu) of a wealthy industrialist culminated in his death. Only he did not die in the terrible disaster that had consumed the magnificent theatre. Danping now lives amongst the ruins, a phantom-like recluse who hides his disfigured face from the world which once adored him. But the villainous factions which drove him and his lover apart are still active, and history begins to repeat itself, with potentially tragic consequences as the local villains who want the theatre to remain closed forever clash with the Phantom.

"Ye Ban Ge Sheng" ("The Phantom Lover," 1995) is one of the best films to come out of the Hong Kong cinema. With spectacular Gothic sets designed by the late Eddie Ma and swooping camerawork by world-class cinematographer Peter Pau (whose expansive images demonstrate the full potential of the wide Panavision frame), this sublime masterpiece represents a sensational marriage of old-fashioned storytelling and cinematic technique. The fast-moving narrative is heightened by director Ronny Yu's operatic film-making style, a style influenced by the horror films of the 1930s and one which he perfected two years earlier in the acclaimed fantasy "The Bride with White Hair" (1993), providing a near-perfect synthesis of plot, characterization and technical virtuosity. The film was recorded in sync-sound (a rarity for HK movies at the time) with the actors speaking Mandarin, but it was dubbed into Cantonese for domestic theatrical release. However, most DVD versions contain the original soundtrack, along with its dubbed alternative.

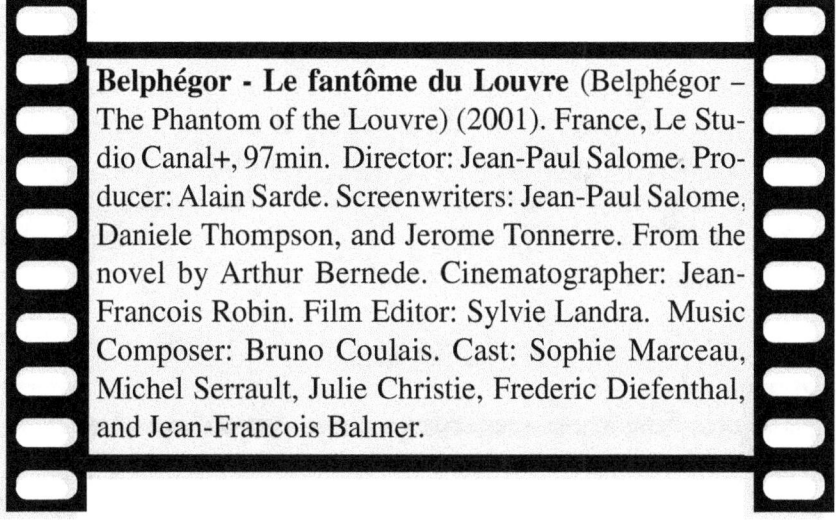

Belphégor - Le fantôme du Louvre (Belphégor – The Phantom of the Louvre) (2001). France, Le Studio Canal+, 97min. Director: Jean-Paul Salome. Producer: Alain Sarde. Screenwriters: Jean-Paul Salome, Daniele Thompson, and Jerome Tonnerre. From the novel by Arthur Bernede. Cinematographer: Jean-Francois Robin. Film Editor: Sylvie Landra. Music Composer: Bruno Coulais. Cast: Sophie Marceau, Michel Serrault, Julie Christie, Frederic Diefenthal, and Jean-Francois Balmer.

"Belphégor - Le fantôme du Louvre" ("Belphégor – The Phantom of the Louvre," 2001) combines equal parts of "The Mummy" (1932) and "The Phantom of the Opera" (1925) to tell a chilling tale of possession and revenge. When a collection of artifacts from an archeological dig in Egypt are brought to the famous Louvre museum in Paris, a phantom spirit escapes the ancient sarcophagus and makes its way into the museum's electrical system. Museum curator Faussier (Jean-Francois Balmer) brings in a noted Egyptologist,

Glenda Spencer (Julie Christie), to examine their new acquisitions, and she announces that the mummy inside the coffin was actually the evil spirit Belphegor. That spirit takes possession of Lisa (Sophie Marceau), a local who lives near the museum, and soon she is haunting the Louvre. Just as "Belphegor" proves more than a match for the Louvre's security forces, renowned detective Verlac (Michel Serrault) is brought out of retirement to counter her evil ways.

Le Fantôme De L'Opéra (The Phantom of the Opera) (2006). French TV Mini-series. Director-Volker Schlöndorff. Producers: Nora Melhli and Jerome Minet. Based on *Le Fantôme De L'Opéra* by Gaston Leroux. Cast: Jeremy Irons, Marie Gillain, August Diehl, and Klaus Maria Brandauer.

At the time of this writing, Director Volker Schlöndorff was shooting a French miniseries, based upon Gaston Leroux's *Le Fantôme De L'Opéra* in Belgium and Romania. Featuring Jeremy Irons as Erik-The Phantom, Marie Gillain as Christine Daaé, and August Diehl as Raoul de Chagny, the production boasted that it was to be the most faithful adaptation of the Frenchman's work.

Television

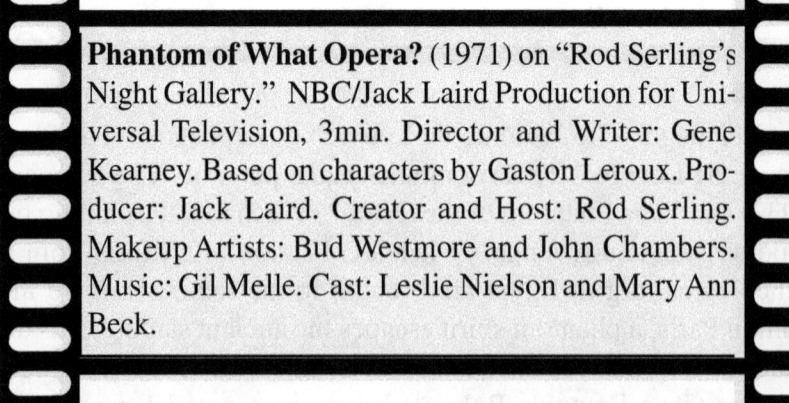

Phantom of What Opera? (1971) on "Rod Serling's Night Gallery." NBC/Jack Laird Production for Universal Television, 3min. Director and Writer: Gene Kearney. Based on characters by Gaston Leroux. Producer: Jack Laird. Creator and Host: Rod Serling. Makeup Artists: Bud Westmore and John Chambers. Music: Gil Melle. Cast: Leslie Nielson and Mary Ann Beck.

Years before television attempted its first adaptations of Gaston Leroux's classic novel, Gene Kearney wrote and directed a little known and rarely seen parody, entitled "Phantom of What Opera?." The three-minute short (produced for "Rod Serling's Night Gallery") finds our favorite Opera Ghost abducting Christine Daae from the stage of the Paris theatre and taking her to his dark, labyrinthine world below. Once there, he begins to play Bach's "Tocatta and Fugue in D-minor" on his pipe organ. while waiting for the young singer to recover from her faint. When Christine does finally awaken, she quickly removes the Phantom's mask to reveal his unholy visage. Then, in a marvelous parody of Lon Chaney's unmasking in the 1925 silent, Miss Daae reveals a startling secret of her own. Beneath her beautiful, young features, Christine has also been hiding a facial disfigurement. Leslie Nielson, who plays Lieutenant Drebin in the "Police Squad" movies, is ideally cast as the Phantom, with television actress Mary Ann Beck providing an acceptable Christine. But the real stars of the short piece are Bud Westmore and Academy Award-winner John Chambers for their wonderful makeup. A must viewing for Phantom fans!!

The Phantom of the Opera (Animated) (1987). HBO Cable Television in association with Emerald City Productions. No additional information is available. [55 minutes.]

An animated version of "The Phantom of the Opera" was created by Emerald City Productions for HBO Cable Television. Although produced with a potential audience of children in mind, the fifty-five minute short provides worthy entertainment for adults. It is also surprisingly faithful to the 1911 novel, and well-worth the investment of time.

Based on a premise that combined elements from the original fairy tale, the 1945 film classic by Jean Cocteau, and Andrew Lloyd Webber's "The Phantom of the Opera," CBS's "Beauty and the Beast" was one of the most remarkable shows to debut on network television in twenty years (since the original "Star Trek"). Not surpris

Beauty and the Beast (1987). Witt/Thomas Production with Ron Koslow Films in association with Republic Pictures Corporation for CBS. 60-min. Producers: George R.R. Martin and Ken Koch. Executive Producers: Raul Witt, Tony Thomas, and Koslow. Creator: Ron Koslow. Cast: Linda Hamilton, Ron Pearlman, Roy Dotrice, and Jay Acovone.

ingly, the series barely survived three short seasons against such mindless dribble as "Baywatch" (NBC), "Perfect Strangers" (ABC), and "Roseanne" (ABC) before cancellation. However, this intelligent and romantic series, which has recently appeared in other venues, deserves special attention.

Opening with the traditional lines of a fairy-tale - "Once upon a time..." - the first episode focused on up-and-coming, assistant district attorney Catherine Chandler (Linda Hamilton) and her struggle to find joy and happiness in an empty yuppie lifestyle. Engaged to a Donald Trump-like developer, named Elliot Birch (Edward Albert), she feels that he life is somehow incomplete. Late one evening, after a quarrel with him, Catherine is kidnapped, beaten (nearly to death), and robbed by an unknown group of assailants. Her body (with disfigured features) is found by a strange "phantom" and taken to a dark, labyrinthine world below the city. When she awakens several weeks later, Catherine finds herself in an unknown world, attended by a "beast-man, named simply Vincent (Ron Pearlman), who

prefers to remain in shadow. She eventually gains his trust, returns to the surface to start a new life as a public defender, and continues a long-distance love affair with him. Subsequent episodes further detail Beauty's romance with "the Beast," culminating (by the third season) in the birth of their first child and the untimely death of Catherine.

"Beauty and the Beast" abounds with elements that seem drawn from Gaston Leroux's gothic romance, including the subterranean lair, the tragic love affair, and a "cloaked" man who has been disfigured from birth. Since the Frenchman had been inspired by the original fable, the circle of inspiration returns completely to its source. Even though the second season ratings dropped precipitously and the series returned for a perfunctory ten-episode run as a mid-year replacement, this stylish show has found renewed life on cable television (The Sci-Fi Channel).

Phantom of the Court House (1991) for "Night Court." 2-30min. Creator: Reinhold Weege. Director: Jim Drake. Writers: Chris Cluess and Stuart Kreisman. Cast: Harry Anderson, Markie Post, John Larroquette, and Richard Moll. Guest Star: Gilbert Gottfried.

Writers of the popular sitcom "Night Court" (1991, NBC) turned to Gaston Leroux's classic 1911 novel for inspiration to produce the two, funniest segments of its final season. Authorities searching for Assistant District Attorney Dan Fielding (John LarroQuette) believe that he may have committed embezzlement, fraud, and grand larceny. Dan is no only innocent of the charges but has adopted an elaborate disguise in order to capture the real culprits; Dan is also slightly crazy. In his present dementia, he believes that he is "the Phantom of the Court House" and loosens the screws to the courtroom chandelier in preparation for his grand entrance at the masquerade ball. When that fateful evening finally arrives, Dan drops the chandelier on a sleazy detective and kidnaps Christine Sullivan (Markie Post). Predictably, he takes the beautiful public defender below to his subterranean lair and serenades her with his accordion. In a marvelous sendup of the unmasking scene from the Lon Chaney silent, Christine pulls the mask from Dan's face and forces him to confront his accusers. Brilliantly staged and written, the two episodes are marvelous additions to the "Phantom of the Opera" canon.

Live Shows At Theme Parks

The Phantom of the Opera Make-Up Show (1990).
Universal Studios, Florida -Hourly, live-action show.

In the early Nineties, Universal Studios Florida devoted an entire show to special effects makeup, and the attraction was hosted (appropriately) by the Phantom of the Opera. Upon entry into the marvelous reproduction of a Thirties theatre lobby, guests are greeted by a bronze, life-like statue of Lon Chaney as the Phantom. Moments later, the lights suddenly dim, and the (real) Phantom bursts through a poster from the 1925 film. He then ushers audience members into a circular theatre, and treats them to both a retrospective and live demonstration of makeup effects. Although the show only lasts about forty minutes, it is one of the most entertaining live action features on the back-lot tour.

Theatrical Productions

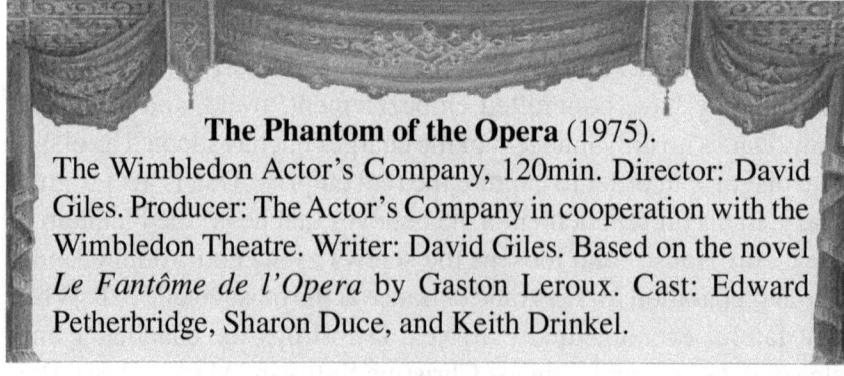

The Phantom of the Opera (1975).
The Wimbledon Actor's Company, 120min. Director: David Giles. Producer: The Actor's Company in cooperation with the Wimbledon Theatre. Writer: David Giles. Based on the novel *Le Fantôme de l'Opera* by Gaston Leroux. Cast: Edward Petherbridge, Sharon Duce, and Keith Drinkel.

Nearly a decade before Andrew Lloyd Webber created his Tony Award-winning musical, the Actor's Company presented the first British stage version of *Le Fantôme de l'Opera* at the Wimbledon

Theatre, in South-west London. Much more faithful to Gaston Leroux than any of the previous cinematic adaptations, the production featured Sharon Duce as Christine, Keith Krinkel as Raoul, and Edward Petherbridge as the tortured Phantom. Ironically, the Wimbledon Theatre (doubling as the mythical London Opera House) was the setting for Terence Fisher's 1962 film version.

> **The Phantom of the Opera** (1984).
> The Theatre Royal. Stratford, 120min. Director and Writer: Ken Hill. Producers: Allen Spivak and Larry Magid. Music Director: Donald Chan. Music Superviser: Alasdair Macneill. Based on the novel by: Gaston Leroux. Cast: Robert Ousley, Sylvia Rhyne, Robert Jensen, David Cleveland, Steve Blanchard. Suzanne Grodner, David Thomas Hampson, Wayne Hoffman, and Tony Lawson.

A rousing, rambunctious, and unashamedly camp adaptation of Gaston Leroux's 1911 novel was mounted nine years after the Wimbledon Theatre's production by the Theatre Royal, Stratford, in East London. Utilizing generous portions of classical opera from Gounod, Verdi, and Offenback, the Ken Hill version tells the familiar tale of a disfigured composer and his love for a young opera singer. What makes this theatrical production different from others is the humorist approach to the tragic story of love and loss. Hill sends his lovers on silly, adventurous chases through the Phantom's lair that are truly funny. Following its successful run in England, "The Phantom of the Opera" played in Europe and the United States. Interestingly, both Sarah Brightman and Andrew Lloyd Webber were involved with the Ken Hill production in 1984. Sarah was offered the role of Christine, which she had to decline because of other commitments, and Lloyd Webber commissioned Hill to write a new treatment, prior to creating his own. Both he and Cameron Macintosh had seen Hill's production at the Theatre Royal, and were impressed. They liked the campy approach, and envisioned their version as a kind of "Rocky Horror Picture Show." Thankfully, they reconsidered.

Phantoms of the Opera

The Phantom of the Opera (1987). Baltimore Actors Theatre, 120min. Director: Helen Grigal. Producer: Oregon Ridge Dinner Theatre in cooperation with The Baltimore Actors Theatre. Music Composer: Eugene Anderson. Lyrics and Book Written By: Helen Grigal. Based on the novel by: Gaston Leroux. Choreographer: Helen Grigal. Cast: Ricardo Chiapetta, Meg Genevese, James Katchko, and Linda Inauzzi.

No relation to the Andrew Lloyd Webber musical, the Baltimore Actors Theatre production of "The Phantom of the Opera" has been playing successfully to capacity crowds both here and abroad since 1987. The show, with a twenty-six member cast headed by four classically-trained singers, played for five years at the Oregon Ridge Dinner Theatre in a Northwest suburb of Baltimore, Maryland. Featuring eighteen original songs written by Helen Grigal based somewhat literally on Gaston Leroux's novel, the musical tells the familiar tale of a disfigured composer and his love for a young opera singer. Ricardo

Chiapetti plays a wonderfully sympathetic Phantom; Meg Genevese is his young musical protege; James Katchko portrays the lovesick Raul, and Linda Inauzzi is the show-stealing Carlotta. The current production toured Great Britain in the summer of 1990, culminating in a two-week engagement at the International Edinburgh Theatre Festival in Scotland, and spent several weeks during the summer of 1991 at the Hill Theatre in Sydney, Australia.

Phantom: A New Musical (1991). Drury Lane Theatre in Oakbrook Terrace, Illinois, 120min. Director and Choreographer: David H. Bell. Producer: Travis L. Stockley. Music Composer: Tom Sivak. Adaptation and Book Written By: David Bell. Lyrics Written by: Cheri Coons and Bell. Based on the novel by: Gaston Leroux, and the melodies of Peter Ilyich Tchaikovsky. Cast: Larry Adams, Jamie Dawn Gangi, Stephen R. Buntrock, Carol-Ann Edwards, Ronald Keaton, and Thaddesu Valdez.

"Phantom: A New Musical" (1991) features a few good melodies, several decent performances, and some nice looking costumes, but regrettably no strong central character. By reducing the importance of the lead, David Bell's script makes the same mistake that the 1943 version made. Erik the Phantom (as played by Larry Adams) resembles Caspar the Friendly Ghost rather than the menacing Opera Ghost Leroux imagined. He rarely appears during the production, and when he does make an appearance, the Phantom is simply part of the ensemble cast. But the production is not without its strengths. A sub-plot finds Raoul as a half-brother to the Phantom, and one of the two presentations of the Paris theatre is an operatic version of "Beauty and the Beast. With Gaston Leroux's novel in the public domain, many new productions will inevitably follow this one.

* * * * *

Clearly, "The Phantom of the Mall," "Popcorn" and "Dario Argento's Phantom of the Opera" were the most serious attempts by filmmakers to impose new, contemporary ideas on the familiar tale. Even though only one of the three films demonstrated any skill or intellect, not one was a serious competitor for box office revenue. They succeed as straight horror films to the degree to which they fail as successors to the large commercial success of Andrew Lloyd Webber's musical. [Notation: "Popcorn" was moderately successful as a late winter entry, but business dropped off dramatically by the time the big spring and summer releases arrived.] The three films were, in fact, squarely opposed to the traditions of previous adaptations, while attempting to advance a style and spirit of their own. On the other hand, the various theatrical productions were closer to the traditions and substance of Gaston Leroux's 1911 novel, but they were even less successful. The only successor to that tradition (and box office revenue) was the road company version of the Tony Award-winning musical, featuring Kevin Gray as the Phantom. Future productions of *Le Fantôme de l'Opera* will have to chart an uncertain course between the two extremes in order to satisfy the audience and be commercially viable. Only then, may we finally enjoy the definitive version of "The Phantom of the Opera."

Appendix One
Novels and Other Written Media

1988 –The Complete Phantom of the Opera by George Perry. Research by Jane Rice. Special Photography by Clive I Barda. New York: Henry Holt and Company, 1988.

The Complete Phantom of the Opera by George Perry is a richly designed, coffee-table edition about the origins and translations of Gaston Leroux's most famous work. Chapter one features a behind-the-scenes look at the construction of the famous Paris Opera House, and chapter two a biographical portrait of Leroux. Both are interestingly written and reveal a great deal of painstaking research. Although the two later chapters which deal with the cinematic adaptations of the Frenchman's story are extremely weak, the background material on the staging of the Andrew Lloyd Webber musical more than makes up for it. The book also includes the complete libretto and some spectacular photographs of the costumes, sets, rehearsal, and production of the Tony Award-winning musical.

1989 – The Phantom of the Opera, Illustrated By Gaston I Leroux, with illustrations by Greg Hildebrandt. New Jersey: Unicorn Publishing House, 1989.

The classic 1911 novel by Gaston Leroux is reproduced in its original brilliance with beautiful color and black-&-white illustrations by fantasy artist Greg Hildebrant. The book also boasts a brand new forward by Sarah Brightman.

1989 - The Phantom of the Opera Pop-Up Book. Based on the original stage design by Maria Bjornson. New York: Harper and Row Publishers, Inc, 1989.

Andrew Lloyd Webber's award-winning musical comes to life in this breathtaking, three-dimensional pop-up book (produced by Harper and Row). Some of the most beautiful and memorable scenes from the theatrical production, including the elaborate staging of "Hannibal," Christine's disappearance through the mirror, the masquerade ball, and the Phantom's final confrontation with Raoul, are lovingly recreated. In the final scene, set deep in the labyrinthine world beneath the playhouse, LED lights and a musical microchip bring the book to a haunting close. A must for "Phantom" fans.

1989 –Phantoms: An anthology of original stories edited by Martin and Rosalind Greenberg. New York: DAW Books, Inc., 1989.

Featuring thirteen original stories and an introduction by Isaac Asimov, *Phantoms* by Martin and Rosalind Greenberg is an ambitious attempt to further delineate the tale of Gaston Leroux. Set in locations ranging from the Paris Opera to New York's Broadway to a place completely outside of time, the short stories offer a varied assortment of interpretations. Some are really quite good and actually compliment the original source material; others are fair. and still others are quite bad. In "The Opera of the Phantom" by Edward Wellen. Erik watches from the shadows as members of the Paris Opera House rehearse his new creation. Henry Slesar's "The Phantom of the Soap Opera" finds the titular character haunting the set of a popular New York soap opera "Before the Dawn." In "The Other Phantom" by Edward Hoch, journalist Franz Vinding accepts a challenge from Bernard Mosaven to spend a night in the darkened theatre in order to discover if there really is a "phantom of the opera. " Lounge lizard Richard Hanratty, in "Dark Muse" by Daniel Ransom, becomes a popular sensation at Kenny's Lounge thanks, in part, to musical gifts from a mysterious composer who wishes to remain anonymous. J.N. Williamson's "Too Hideous to Be Played" focuses on a group of old people who decide to revive the familiar story when a young Chris Day appears. Meg Giry comes face-to-face with the Phantom in "The Final Threshold" by K. Marie Ramsland. On the return trip from Jupiter, crew members of the Balboa experience "Marian's Song" by James Kisner. In "The Light of Her Smile" by Karen Haber, New York model Christine discovers that Erik the Phantom, her fashion photographer, has been secretly dabbling in child pornography. "Time-Tracker" by Barry Malzberg features murder, madness, and mayhem involving a man who has inherited the legacy of the Phantom. In "Dark Angel" by Gary Alan Ruse, terrorists attempt to kidnap actors of the musical at the Majestic Theatre, but the real Phantom who is 158 years old rescues the leads and takes their place upon stage. Young Andrew is obsessed with The Phantom of the Opera and demands that his girlfriend Chelsea remove his face in "The Unmasking" by Steve Rasnic Tem. In "The Grotto" by Thomas Millstead, archeologists discover a massive, echo-filled cavern that has been the hiding place for many years of the Phantom. One hundred and twenty-eight year-old Christine Daae seeks out the man who now wears Erik's ring in Gary A. Braunbeck's "Comfort the Lonely Light." Variable in quality, the anthology is a must read for Phantom fans.

1989 –Night Magic: An original novel by Charlotte Vale Allen. New York: Atheneum/Macmillan Books, 1989.

Combining elements from Leroux's original novel and the classic children's fable "Beauty and the Beast, " Charlotte Vale Allen's *Night Magic* is a wonderfully imaginative, modern fairy tale for adults. Beautiful, sensitive, youthful Marisa falls in love with the brilliant Erik, who is so profoundly scarred both physically and emotionally that he cannot face the light of day- Putting aside his most fearful apprehensions, he allows her to enter his dark, labyrinthine world, and they begin to communicate their love for one another through music. Gradually, as he nurtures and tutors her, Marisa gains his trust and coaxes him into the light. Romantic, erotic, mysterious, hypnotic, and moving, Allen's novel represents a thoroughly engrossing variation on the classic tales.

1990 –Night of the Phantom An original novel by Anne Stuart. New York: Harlequin American Romance, 1990.

Another variation of the Gaston Leroux tale.

1991 -Phantom An original novel by Susan Kay. New York: Dellacorte Press, 1991.

Long before Gaston Leroux chronicled the tragic tale of a disfigured musical genius and his love of a young opera singer in *Le Fantôme de l'Opera*, a real Erik lived a life of isolation and rejection. That is the premise behind a recent novel, simply titled *Phantom*. According to the Foreward of her book, popular British novelist Susan Kay was inspired by the Andrew Lloyd Webber version to spend several years researching the life of Erik the Phantom in order to write his "true story." What unfolds is a lovingly conceived prequel that details Erik's aristocratic birth, his musical education, and the years that he spent as a freak in a traveling carnival. Ms. Kay also writes about the Phantom's doomed love affair with Christine and the affect that his undying love has had on the singer's marriage to Raoul, the Vicomte de Chagny. Even though some of the passages are extremely brutal (particularly one scene in which Erik is nearly raped by another man), the material maintains a strong connection to that of the original.

1991 –Mask: Tales from the Underground A fanzine anthology of original stories edited by Kathleen Resch, P.O. Box 1766, Temple City, California 91780. Copyright 1991.

Mask: Tales from the Underground, edited by Kathleen Resch, offers five short stories that are far superior to the ones featured in the professional anothology from DAW Books. Clearly inspired by the love of the material (rather than a paycheck), these five authors provide a much deeper understanding of Leroux's Phantom than many of the authors in *Phantoms*. Fanzines, or fan publications, have been around for years, often challenging their readers with variations on a theme more interesting than those in the mainstream. This collection of short, fan fiction is no exception. In "L ' Autre Que Je Prefere" by Cathy Ehlers, Christine has second thoughts about Erik on the eve of her marriage to Raoul. Carol Smith's "Wandering Child" introduces us to Adele, the very gifted child of Christine and Raoul de Chagny. "Beyond the Lake" by Joyce Rebaric reunites Christine and Erik years after their parting and proposes the kind of life they might have lived. In "Let Angels Reign" by Kay Brinkley, Erik recalls his life, from childhood through Christine. And Susan McLeod proposes that, now the Phantom is dead, someone else may be haunting the Paris Opera House in "Sometimes Dreams Can Be Real." Although fanzines are often quite expensive (in this case, $18.00) and can be difficult to locate, they offer some of the best writing and artwork on the subject. They also provide a much needed creative outlet for writers who would ordinarily not have an opportunity to publish a story about the Phantom of the Opera.

Appendix Two
Chronological Listing of Phantom Productions

1911 - *Le Fantôme de l'Opera* By Gaston Leroux

1916 - **Das Gespenst im Opernhaus** (The Phantom of the Opera). German, Silent. Black & White, 76min. Director: Ernst Matray. Writer: Greta Schroder Matray. Cast: Nils Olaf Chrisander and Aud Egede Nissen.

1925 - **The Phantom of the Opera.** Universal Pictures, Silent, B&W with some Technicolor sequences, 94min (101 original release). Directors: Rupert Julian, Edward Sedgwick, and Lon Chaney (uncredited). Producer: Carl Laemmle. Screenwriters: Elliott J. Clawson and Raymond Schrock. Based on *Le Fantôme de l'Opera* by Gaston Leroux. Director of Photography: Charles Van Enger. Film Editor: Edward Curtiss. Art Directors: E.E. Sheeley, Sidney M. Ullman, and Ben Carre. Makeup Artist: Lon Chaney. Cast: Lon Chaney, Mary Philbin, Norman Kerry, Arthur Edmund Carewe, Gibson Gowland, Snitz Edwards, Mary Fabian, Virginia Pearson, and John St. Polis.

1931 - **Cheri-Bibi, The Phantom of Paris**. M-G-M, B&W, 100min. Director: John S. Robertson. Screenwriters: Edwin Justus Mayer, John Meehan, and Bess Meredyth. Based on *Le Fantôme de l'Opera* and *Cheri-Bibi* by Gaston Leroux. Cinematographer: Oliver Marsh. Film Editor: Jack Ogilvie, Art Director: Cedric Gibbons. Cast: John Gilbert, Leila Hyams, Lewis Stone, Jean Hersholt, C. Aubrey Smith, Natalie Moorehead, and Ian Keith.

Phantoms of the Opera

1937 - **Ye Ban Ge Sheng** (Song at Midnight). Chinese, B&W, 113 min. Director and Writer: Weibang Mz-Xu. Producer: Shankun Zhang. Cinematographer: Boqing Xue and Xingsan Yu. Film Editor: Yinqing Chen. Production Designer: Yigan Mou and Yungqiao Zhang. Cast: Menghe Gu, Ping Hu, Shan Jin, and Chao Shi.

1943 - **The Phantom of the Opera**. Universal Pictures, 92 min. Director: Arthur Lubin. Producer: George Waggner. Screenwriters: Eric Taylor and Samuel Hoffenstein. Based on an adaptation of Gaston Leroux's *Le Fantôme de l'Opera* by: John Jacoby. Directors of Photography: Hal Mohr and W. Howard Greene. Art Directors: John Goodman and Alexander Golitzen. Music Composer: Edward Ward. Makeup Artist: Jack Pierce. Starring: Nelson Eddy, Claude Rains, Susanna Foster, Jane Farrar, Edgar Barrier, Leo Carillo, Miles Mander, Hume Cronyn, J. Edward Bromberg, and Fritz Leiber.

1944 - **The Climax**. Universal Pictures, 86min. Director and Producer: George Waggner. Screenwriters: Curt Siodmak and Lynn Starling. Based on a play by: Edward Locke. Directors of Photography: Hal Mohr and W. Howard Greene. Music Composer: Edward Ward. Cast: Boris Karloff, Susanna Foster, Turhan Bey, Gale Sondergaard, June Vincent, Thomas Gomez, and Scotty Beckett.

1945 - **The Phantom of 42nd Street**. PRC Pictures, B&W, 78min. Director: Albert Herman. Producer: Martin Mooney. Screenwriter: Milton Raison. Based on a novel by: Jack Harvey and Martin Raison. Cinematographer: James S Brown. Film Editor: Hugh Winn. Music Composer: Karl Hajos. Starring: Dave O'Brien, Kay Aldridge, Alan Mowbray, Frank Jenks, Edythe Elliott, Jack Mulhall, Vera Marshe, and Stanley Price.

1953 - **House of Wax**. Warner Brothers, 90min. Director: André De Toth. Producer: Bryan Foy. Screenwriters: Charles Belden and Crane Wilbur. Story by Crane Wilbur. Cinematographers: Bert Glennon and J. Peverell Marley. Film Editor: Rudi Fehr. Art Director: Stanley Fleischer. Cast: Vincent Price, Frank Lovejoy, Phyllis Kirk, Carolyn Jones, Paul Picerni, Roy Roberts, Angela Clarke, Paul Cavanaugh, and Charles Bronson.

1954 - **El Fantasma de la Opereta** (The Phantom of the Opera). Argentina, B&W, 63min. Director: Enrique Carreras. Screenwriters: René Marcial, Manuel Rey, Alfredo Ruanova. Based on *Le Fantôme de l'Opera* by Gaston Leroux. Director of Photography: Alfredo Traverso. Film Editor: José Gallego. Musical Composer: Víctor Slister. Production Designer and Art Director: Óscar Lagomarsino. Cast: Gogó Andreu, Tono Andreu, Alfredo Barbieri, Mario Baroffio, Ines Fernández, Alfonso Pisano, and Amelia Vargas.

1959 - **El Fantasma De La Opereta** (The Phantom of the Opera). Alameda Films, Mexico, B&W, 80min. Director: Fernando Cortes. Producers: Cesar Santos Galindo and Alfredo Ripstein Jr. Screenwriters: Jose Maria Fernandez Unsain, Alfredo Varela Jr., German Valdes, and Cortes. Based on *Le Fantôme de l'Opera* by Gaston Leroux. Director of Photography: Jose Ortiz Ramos. Cast: German Valdes (Tin Tan), Sonia Furio, Pedro de Aguillon, and Edmundo Crispino.

1960 - **El Fantasma de la opera** (The Phantom of the Opera)). Argentina, B&W, 60min. Director: Narciso Ibáñez Menta and Marta Reguera. Producer: Diana Alvarez. Screenwriter: Chicho Libanez-Serrador. Based on *Le Fantôme de l'Opera* by Gaston Leroux. Cast: Narciso Ibáñez Menta, Beatriz Día Quiroga, Juan José Edelman, José María Langlais, and Noemí Laserre.

1961 - **The Phantom of the Horse Opera**. Walter Lantz Productions, Animated, 5min. Director: Paul J. Smith. Producer: Walter Lantz. Music Composer: Clarence Wheeler. Cast: Grace Stafford.

1961 - **Ye Bang Ge Sheng** (Mid-Nightmare). Shaw Brothers International/Hong Kong, 97min. Director, Writer: Yuan Quifeng. Producer: Run Run Shaw. Based on *Le Fantôme de l'Opera* by Gaston Leroux. Starring: Le Di (Betty Loh Tih), Zhou Lai, Fang Li, Zhang Chong.

1962 - **The Phantom of the Opera** -Hammer/Great Britain, 84min. Director: Terence Fisher. Producer: Anthony Hinds. Screenwriter: John Elder (aka Anthony Hinds). Based on a "composition" by Gaston Leroux. Photographer: Arthur Grant. Art Directors: Bernard Robinson and Don Mingaye. Makeup Artist: Roy Ashton. Music: Edwin Astley. Cast: Herbert Lom, Heather Sears, Edward de Souza, Michael Gough, Thorley Walters, Miles Malleson, Marne Maitland, Martin Miller, Marian Karlin, Harold Goodwin, John Harvey, Michael Ripper, Liane Aukin, Sonya Cordeau, Leila Forde, Renee Houston, John Maddison, Laurie Main, and Ian Wilson.

1964 - **Il Vampiro Dell Opera** (The Vampire of the Opera, also known as The Monster of the Opera). Italian. B&W, 80min. Director: Renato Polselli. Producer: Bruno Bolognesi. Screenwriters: Renato Polselli, Ernest Gastaldi, and Giuseppe Pellegrini. Based on *Le Fantôme de l'Opera* by Gaston Leroux. Cinematographer: Ugo Brunelli. Film Editor: Otello Colangeli. Production Designer: Demofilo Fidani. Music Composer: Aldo Piga. Cast: John McDouglas (Giuseppe Addobbati), Vittoria Prada, Marc Marian (Marco Mariani), Barbara Howard, and Catla Cavelli.

1971 - **Phantom of What Opera?** on "Rod Serling's Night Gallery." NBC/Jack Laird Production for Universal Television, 3min. Director and Writer: Gene Kearney. Based on characters by Gaston Leroux. Producer: Jack Laird. Creator and Host: Rod Serling. Makeup Artists: Bud Westmore and John Chambers. Music: Gil Melle. Cast: Leslie Nielson and Mary Ann Beck.

1974 - **The Phantom of Hollywood**. M-G-M, 74min. Director and Producer: Gene Levitt. Executive Producer: Burt Nodella. Screenwiter: George Schenck. Story by: Robert Thom and George Schenck. No acknowledgement for M. Gaston Leroux. Director of Photography: Gene Polito. Art Director: Edward Carfagno. Makeup Artist: William Tuttle. Composer: Leonard Rosenman. Starring: Skye Aubrey, Jack Cassidy, Jackie Coogan, Broderick Crawford, Peter Haskell, John Ireland, Peter Lawford, Kent Taylor, Corinne Calvet, Billy Halop, Regis Toomey, and Bill Williams.

1974 - **Phantom of the Paradise**. 20th Century Fox/Harbor Productions, 91min. Director and Writer: Brian De Palma. Producers: Edward R. Pressman and Paul Williams. No acknowledgement for M. Gaston Leroux. Director of Photography: Larry Pizer. Production

Designer: Jack Fisk. Set Decorator: Sissy Spacek. Music: Paul Williams. Makeup: John Chambers. Cast: Paul Williams, William Finley, Jessica Harper, George Memmoli, and Gerrit Graham. Opening Narration: Rod Serling.

1975 - **The Phantom of the Opera**. The Wimbledon Actor's Company, 120min. Director: David Giles. Producer: The Actor's Company in cooperation with the Wimbledon Theatre. Writer: David Giles. Based on the novel *Le Fantôme de l'Opera* by Gaston Leroux. Cast: Edward Petherbridge, Sharon Duce, and Keith Drinkel.

1977 - **The Mystery of the Hollywood Phantom** for "Hardy Boys/Nancy Drew Mysteries." Universal, 2-Part, 60min. Director: Steven Stern. Producer: Joe Boston. Executive Producer: Glen Larson. Writer: Michael Sloan. Cast: Parker Stevenson, Shaun Cassidy, Pamela Sue martin, William Schallert, Susan Buckner, Edith Atwater, Edmund Gilbert. Guest Stars: Robert Wagner, Jaclyn Smith, Dennis Weaver, Ruth Cox, Harry Rhodes, Lou Antonio, Casey Kasem, James Wainwright, J.D. Cannon, and Clive Revill.

1978 - **KISS Meets the Phantom of the Park**. Hanna-Barbara Productions, 96 min. Director: Gordon Hessler. Producer: Terry Morse. Screenwriters: Jan Michael Sherman and Don Buday. Cinematographer: Robert Caramico. Film Editor: Peter Berger. Original Music by Hoyt S. Curtin. Cast: Anthony Zerbe, Peter Criss, Ace Frehley, Gene Simons, Paul Stanley, Carmine Caridi, John Dennis Johnston, John Lisbon Wood, Lisa Jane Persky, John Chappell, Terry Lester, Don Steele, and Deborah Ryan.

1979 - **Phantom of the Bijoux** (Also known as The Meateater and Blood Theatre). 85min. Director and Writer: Derek Savage. Cinematographer: Fred Aronow. Music Composer: Arlon Ober. Cast: Arch Joboulain, Dianne Davis, Peter Spitzer, Emily Spindler, Gary Dean, Joe Marmo, Frank Montiforte, and Richard Nathan.

1983 - **The Phantom of the Opera**. ABC Television, 100min. Director: Robert Markowitz. Producer: Robert Halmi Jr. and Robert Halmi Sr. Screenwriter: Sharman Yellen. No acknowledgement for

M. Gaston Leroux. Music Composer: Ralph Burns. Cinematographer: Larry Pizer. Film Editor: Caroline Biggerstaff. Art Director: TivadarBertalan. Makeup Artist: Stan Winston. Starring: Maximilian Schell, Jane Seymour, Michael York, Jeremy Kemp, Philip Stone, Paul Brooke, Andras Miko, Gllert Raksanyi, Laszlo Soos, Denes Ujlaky, Terez Bod, and Diana Quick.

1984 - **The Phantom of the Opera**. The Theatre Royal. Stratford, 120min. Director and Writer: Ken Hill. Producers: Allen Spivak and Larry Magid. Music Director: Donald Chan. Music Superviser: Alasdair Macneill. Based on the novel by Gaston Leroux. Cast: Robert Ousley, Sylvia Rhyne, Robert Jensen, David Cleveland, Steve Blanchard. Suzanne Grodner, David Thomas Hampson, Wayne Hoffman, and Tony Lawson.

1985 - **Phantom of the Studio** for "Knight Rider." NBC/Glen Larson Productions for Universal Television, 54min. Producer: Glen Larson. Assistant Producer: Bernadette Joyce. Creator: Glen Larson. Cast: David Hasselhoff. Edward Mulhare, and William Daniels. Guest Star: Robert Englund.

1986 - **The Phantom of the Opera.** The Really Useful Group, 153min. Director: Harold Prince. Producers: Andrew Lloyd Webber and Cameron Makintosh. Music by: Andrew Lloyd Webber. Lyrics by: Charles Hart (with additional work by Richard Stilgoe). Inspired by the Gaston Leroux novel. Production Designer: Maria Bjornson. Musical Director: Michael Reed (with orchestrations by David Cullen and Andrew Lloyd Webber). Makeup Artist: Tiffany Hicks. Original Cast: Michael Crawford. Sarah Brightman. Steve Barton. John Savident. David Firth. Rosemary Ashe. Mary Millar. Janet Devenish, and John Aron.

1987 - **The Phantom of the Opera.** Baltimore Actors Theatre, 120min. Director: Helen Grigal. Producer: Oregon Ridge Dinner Theatre. Music Composer: Eugene Anderson. Lyrics and Book By: Helen Grigal. Based on the novel by Gaston Leroux. Choreographer: Helen Grigal. Cast: Ricardo Chiapetta, Meg Genevese, James Katchko, and Linda Inauzzi.

1987 - **The Phantom of the Opera** (Animated). HBO Cable Television in association with Emerald City Productions. No additional information is available. [55 minutes.]

1988 - **Dario Argento's Opera** (aka Terror at the Opera). Orion/ADC Cecchi Group, 90min. Director and Producer: Dario Argento. Executive Producer: Ferdinando Caputo. Director of Photography: Billy Williams. Screenwriters: Dario Argento and Franco Ferinni. Based on an original story by: Argento. Cast: Cristina Marsillach, Ian Charleson, Daria Nicolodi, Urbano Barbarini, and Vanessa Redgrave.

1989 - **Gaston Leroux's Phantom of the Opera**. 21st Century Productions, 95min. Director: Dwight H. Little. Producers: Harry Alan Towers. Executive Producer: Menahem Golan. Screenwriters: Duke Sandefur and Gerry O'Hara. Based on the novel by Gaston Leroux. Music Composer: Misha Segal. Cinematographer: Elemer Ragalyi. Film Editor: Charles Bornstein. Art Director: Tivadar Bertalan. Makeup Artist: Kevin Yagher Cast: Robert Englund, Jill Schoelen, Alex Hyde-White, Bill Nighy, Terence Harvey, Molly Shannon, Emma Rawson, Terence Besley, Yehuda Efroni, Peter Clapham, and Stephanie Lawrence.

1989 - **The Phantom of the Mall: Eric's Revenge.** Fries Entertainment, 90min. Director: Richard Friedman. Producer: Tom Fries. Screenwriters: Scott J. Schneid, Tony Michelman, and Robert King. Based on an original story by: Schneid and Frederick Ulrich. No acknowledgement for M. Gaston Leroux. Music Composer: Stacy Widelitz. Cast: Derek Rydall, Jonathan Goldsmith, Rob Estes, Pavly Shore, Kari Whitman, and Morgan Fairchild.

1990 - **Gremlins II: The New Batch**. Warner Brothers, 96min. Director: Joe Dante. Producer: Mike Finnell. Executive Producers: Steven Spielberg, Kathleen Kennedy, and Frank Marshall. Screenwriter: Charlie Haas. Based on characters created by Chris Columbus. Cinematographer: John Hora. Film Editor: Kent Beyda. Music Composer: Jerry Goldsmith. Makeup Artist: Rick Baker. Cast: Zach Galligan, Phoebe Cates. John Glover, Dick Miller, Kenneth Tobey, and Christopher Lee.

1990 - **The Phantom of the Opera**. NBC in association with Saban-Scherick Productions, 168min. Director: Tony Richardson. Producers: Ross Milloy, Mitch Engel, Gary Hoffman, Haim Saban, Edgar J. Scherick, and William Wilson. Screenwriter: Arthur Kopit. Based on his play and the novel by Gaston Leroux. Director of Photography: Steve Yaconelli. Music Composer: John Addison. Film Editor: Robert K. Lambert. Production Designer: Timian Alsaker. Art Directors: Jacques Bufnoir and Gary Constable. Cast: Burt Lancaster, Teri Polo, Adam Storke, Ian Richardson, Andrea Ferreol, Jean-Pierre Cassel, Jean Rougerie, Andre Chaumeau, Marie-Theresa Orain, Marie-Christine Robert, Marie Lenoir, Anne Roumanoff, and Charles Dance.

1990 - **Phantom of the Opera.** PBS, 93min. Director and Choreographer: Darwin Knight. Producer: Abe Hirschfeld, Samantha Klein, Linda Bryant, and Karen Poindexter. Screenwriter: Bruce Falstein. Music Composers: Lawrence Rosen and Paul Schierhorn. Director of Photography: Angel Hernandez. Cast: David Staller, Elizabeth Walsh, Darin De Paul, Beth McVey, and Christopher Rath.

1991 - **Dance Macabre** (aka The Phantom of the Opera). Phillipines, 97min. Director and Writer: Greydon Clark. Producer: Menahem Golan. Music Composer: Dan Slider. Film Editor: Earl Watson. Cast: Robert Englund, Michelle Zeitlin, Marianna Moen, Julene Renee, Nina Goldman, Irina Davidoff, Alexander Segeyev, Nastash Fesson, Vadim Zajtsev, and Greydon Clark.

1991 - **O Fantasma da Opera** (The Phantom of the Opera). Brazil, Rede Manchete Productions, 100min. Directors: Del Rangel, Atillio Ricco, and Alvaro Fugulin. Screenwriters: Jael Coaracy and Paul Afonso de Lima. Based upon *Le Fantôme de l'Opera* by Gaston Leroux and an adaptation written by Geraldo Vietri. Cast: Daniela Aguiar, Gesio Amadeu, Isaac Bardavid, Sergio Britto, Rebeca Bueno, Olivia Byington, Mario Cardoso, Marcos Caruso, Ariel Coelho, Cuilherme Correa, Carolina Ferraz.

1991 - **Phantom: A New Musical**. Drury Lane Theatre in Oakbrook Terrace, Illinois, 120min. Director and Choreographer: David H. Bell. Producer: Travis L. Stockley. Music Composer: Tom Sivak. Adaptation and Book Written By: David Bell. Lyrics Written by: Cheri Coons and Bell. Based on the novel by: Gaston Leroux, and the melodies of Peter Ilyich Tchaikovsky. Cast: Larry Adams, Jamie Dawn Gangi, Stephen R. Buntrock, Carol-Ann Edwards, Ronald Keaton, and Thaddesu Valdez.

1991 - **Phantom of the Court House** for "Night Court." Television, 2-30min. Creator: Reinhold Weege. Director: Jim Drake. Writers: Chris Cluess and Stuart Kreisman. Cast: Harry Anderson, Markie Post, John Larroquette, Richard Moll. Guest Star: Gilbert Gottfried.

1991 - **Popcorn**. Movie Partners/Studio Three/Columbia, 90min. Directors: Alan Ormsby, Mark Herrier, and Bob Clark (uncredited). Producers: Bob Clark, Gary Goch, and Torben Johnke. Executive Producers: Karl Hendrickson and Howard Hurst. Screenwriter: Alan Ormsby. Based on an original story by Mitchell Smith. Cinematographer: Ronnie Taylor. Film Editor: Stan Cole. Music Composer: Paul Zaza. Makeup Artist: Bob Clark. Starring: Tom Villard, Jill Schoelen, Tony Roberts, Dee Wallace Stone, and Ray Walston.

1992 - **Phantom of the Ritz**. Prism, 88min. Director: Allen Plone. Producer: Carol Marcus Plone. Screenwriters: Allen Plone and Tom Dempsey. Based on *Le Fantôme de l'Opera* by Gaston Leroux. Cinematographer: Ron Diamond. Music Composers: Wendy Frazier and John Madara. Cast: Peter Bergman, Russell Curry, Joshua Sussman, and Deborah Van Valkenburgh.

1995 - **Ye Bang Ge Sheng** (The Phantom Lover). Chinese, Mandarin Films Co. Ltd. 100min. Director: Ronny Yu. Producers: Leslie Cheung, Michael Ng, and Raymong Wong. Screenwriters: Roy Szeto, Raymond Wong, and Ronny Yu. Based on *Le Fantôme de l'Opera* by Gaston Leroux. Cinematographer: Peter Pau. Film Editor: David Wu. Production Designers: Eddie Ma and Sin Ling Yeung. Music Composer: Chris Babida. Cast: Leslie Cheung, Lei Huang, Philip Kwok, Fong Pao, Roy Szeto, and Chien-lien Wu.

1998 - **Il Fantasma dell'opera** (Dario Argento's The Phantom of the Opera). Italy, 106 min, Director: Dario Argento. Producers: Giuseppe

Colombo and Aron Sipos. Screenwriters: Gerard Brach and Dario Argento. Based upon *Le Fantôme de l'Opera* by Gaston Leroux. Music Composers: Maurizio Guarini and Ennio Morricone. Cinematographer: Ronnie Taylor. Editor: Anna Rosa Napoli. Production Designers: Massimo Antonello Geleng and Csaba Stork. Cast: Julian Sands, Asia Argento, Andrea Di Stefano, Nadia Rinaldi, Coraline Cataldi Tassoni, Istvan Bubik, Zoltan Barabas, Lucia Guzzardi..

2000 - **Phantom of the Megaplex.** Disney, 88min. Director: Blair Treu. Producer: Christopher Morgan. Screenwriter: Stu Krieger. No mention of Gaston Leroux. Cinematographer: Derek Rogers. Film Editor: Martin Nicholson. Music Composer: Bill Elliott. Cast: Taylor Handley, Corinne Bohrer, Caitlin Wachs, Jacob Smith, Rich Hutchman, John Novak, Colin Fox, Richy Mabe, Julia Cantrey, Joanne Boland, J.J. Stocker, Lisa Ng, and Mickey Rooney.

2001 - **Belphégor - Le fantôme du Louvre** (Belphégor – The Phantom of the Louvre). France, Le Studio Canal+, 97min. Director: Jean-Paul Salome. Producer: Alain Sarde. Screenwriters: Jean-Paul Salome, Daniele Thompson, and Jerome Tonnerre. From the novel by Arthur Bernede. Cinematographer: Jean-Francois Robin. Film Editor: Sylvie Landra. Music: Bruno Coulais. Cast: Sophie Marceau, Michel Serrault, Julie Christie, Frederic Diefenthal, and Jean-Francois Balmer.

2004 – **The Phantom of the Opera**. The Really Useful Group, 153min. Director: Joel Schumacher. Producers: Andrew Lloyd Webber. Screenwriters: Lloyd Webber and Schumacher. Inspired by the Gaston Leroux novel. Music by: Andrew Lloyd Webber. Lyrics by Charles Hart (with additional work by Richard Stilgoe). Film Editor: Terry Rawlings. Production Designer: Anthony Pratt. Art Directors: John Fenner and Paul Kirby. Cast: Gerard Butler, Emmy Rossum, Patrick Wilson, Miranda Richardson, Minnie Driver, Ciaran Hinds, Simon Callow, Victor McGuire, Jennifer Ellison, and Kevin McNally.

2006 - **Le Fantôme De L'Opéra** (The Phantom of the Opera). French TV Mini-series. Director-Volker Schlöndorff. Producers: Nora Melhli and Jerome Minet. Based on the novel by Gaston Leroux. Cast: Jeremy Irons, Marie Gillain, August Diehl, and Klaus Maria Brandauer.

Selected Bibliography

Ackerman, Forrest J., editor. *Famous Monsters of Filmland* Magazine. Philadelphia: Warren Publishing, 1958.

_____. *Monsterland* Magazine, nos. 1-6. Los Angeles, California: New Media Publishing, 1986.

Andrews, Nigel. *Horror Films.* New York: Gallery Books, 1985.

Ashley, Mike. *Who's Who in Horror and Fantasy Fiction.* New York: Taplinger, 1978.

Aylesworth, Thomas G. *Monsters from the Movies.* New York: Bantam Skylark Books, 1972.

Butler, Ivan. *Horror in the Cinema.* New York: Paperback Library, 1971.

Clarens, Carlos. *Horror Movies.* London: Secker and Warburg, 1968.

Cohen, Daniel. *Horror in the Movies.* New York: Houghton Mifflin Company, Inc., 1982.

Edelson, Edward. *Great Monsters of the Movies.* New York: Doubleday and Company, 1973.

Everson, William Keith. *Classics of the Horror Film.* New York: Citadel Press, 1974.

Flynn, John L. *Cinematic Vampires: The Living Dead on Film and Television.* North Carolina: McFarland Books, 1991.

Franklin, Joe. *Classics of the Silent Screen.* New York: Citadel Press, 1959.

Halliwell, Leslie. *Halliwell's Film Guide.* New York: Scribner's, 1984.

Huss, Roy Gerard. *Focus on the Horror Film.* New York: Prentice-Hall, 1972.

Kyrou, Ado. *Le Surrealisme Au Cinema.* Paris: 1964.

Laclos, Michael. *Le Fantasique Au Cinema*. Paris: 1958.

Lee, Walt. *Reference Guide to Horror Films*. Los Angeles: Chelsea-Lee Books' 1978.

Perry, George. *The Complete Phantom of the Opera*. New York: Henry Holt and Company, 1988.

Settel, Irving. *A Pictorial History of Television*. New York: Frederick Ungar Publishing, 1983.

Stanley, John. *The Creature Features Movie Guide*. New York: Warner Books, 1981.

Terrace, Vincent. *Complete Encyclopedia of Television Programs*. New York: A.S. Barnes, 1979.

About the Author

Dr. John L. Flynn is a three-time Hugo-nominated author and long-time science fiction fan and critic who has written six books, countless short stories, articles, reviews, and one screenplay. He is a professor a t Towson University in Towson, Maryland, and teaches both graduate and undergraduate writing courses. Born in Chicago, Illinois, on September 6, 1954, he has a Bachelor's and Master's Degree from the University of South Florida and a Ph.D. from Southern California University. He is a member of the Science Fiction Writers of America, and has been a regular contributor and columnist to dozens of science fiction magazines, including *Starlog*, *Not of This Earth*, *Sci-Fi Universe*, *Cinescape*, *Retrovision*, *Media History Digest*, *SFTV*, *SF Movieland*, *Monsterland*, *Enterprise*, *Nexxus*, *The Annapolis Review*, and *Collector's Corner*. In 1977, he received the M. Carolyn Parker award for outstanding journalism for his freelance work on several Florida daily newspapers, and in 1987, he was listed in *Who's Who Men of Achievement*. He sold his first book, *Future Threads*, in 1985. He has subsequently published four other books related to film, including *Cinematic Vampires*, *The Films of Arnold Schwarzenegger*, *Dissecting Aliens*,

and *War of the Worlds: From Wells to Spielberg*. Brickhouse Books published *Visions in Light and Shadow* (2001), a collection of his literary short stories. For the past three years, John has been nominated for the prestigious Hugo Award, which is the Science Fiction Achievement Award, for his science fiction writing, which includes film reviews and cinematic retrospectives. He has appeared on television (including the Sci-Fi Channel), spoken on the radio, and been a guest at national conferences because of his advocacy work in bringing the science fiction film into the mainstream. With Dr. Robert Blackwood, Flynn formed "the Film Doctors," a team of credentiated academics which studied science fiction films and rendered a scholastic view of the genre. Their first project was *The Top Ten Science Fiction Films of the Twentieth Century*. In 1997, John switched gears to study Psychology, and earned a degree as a Clinical Psychologist. His study, "The Etiology of Sexual Addiction: Childhood Trauma as a Primary Determinant," has broken new ground in the diagnosis and treatment of sexual addiction. For the last several years, he has also worked with Bridge Publications, Galaxy Press, and Author Services on behalf of the Writers of the Future contest, in an effort to promote the work of new and emerging science fiction writers.

www.ingramcontent.com/pod-product-compliance
Lightning Source LLC
Chambersburg PA
CBHW061639040426
42446CB00010B/1495